Life Sentence

ALSO BY CHRISTIE BLATCHFORD

Fifteen Days
Helpless

Life Sentence

Stories from Four Decades of
Court Reporting – or, How I Fell
Out of Love with the Canadian
Justice System

CHRISTIE BLATCHFORD

DOUBLEDAY CANADA

Doubleday Canada and colophon are registered trademarks of
Penguin Random House Canada Limited

The epigraph that appears on page 271 is taken from *The Crucible* by Arthur Miller,
copyright 1952, 1953, 1954, renewed © 1980, 1981, 1982 by Arthur Miller.
Used by permission of Viking Books, an imprint of Penguin Publishing Group,
a division of Penguin Random House LLC.

The epigraph that appears on page 52 is taken from *Uncommon Law* by A. P. Herbert
used by permission of United Agents LLP on behalf of The Executors of the Estate
of Jocelyn Herbert, MT Perkins and Polly MVR Perkins.

Library and Archives Canada Cataloguing in Publication

Blatchford, Christie, author
Life sentence / Christie Blatchford.

Includes bibliographical references and index.
Issued in print and electronic formats.

ISBN 978-0-385-66797-5 (hardback).—ISBN 978-0-307-36787-7 (epub)

1. Justice, Administration of—Corrupt practices—Canada.
2. Judicial power—Canada. 3. Judges—Canada. 4. Courts—Canada.

5. Trials—Canada—Cases. I. Title.

HV9960.C2B63 2016   347.71'014   C2016-900650-6
                                                C2016-900651-4

Cover image: Thomas J Peterson/Getty Images
Cover design: Andrew Roberts
Text design: Colin Jaworski

Printed and bound in the USA

Published in Canada by Doubleday Canada,
a division of Penguin Random House Canada Limited

www.penguinrandomhouse.ca

10 9 8 7 6 5 4 3 2 1

With thanks to the Mamas & the Papas,
whose version of the song I knew,
this is dedicated to the ones I love.

CONTENTS

ON A BREAK one recent day in coroner's court, while covering an inquest, I asked the coroner's counsel (these are Ontario prosecutors on loan to the coroner's office) for the third or fourth time about getting a copy of an exhibit.

It was only a transcript of the most significant piece of evidence in the entire inquest, a haunting 911 call made by three teenagers who were trapped in a raging house fire and whose desperate last words were caught on the recording.

The coroner by now had already made it pretty clear, though he'd not yet issued a ruling, that journalists weren't going to get copies of the actual call, and the lawyer for the families of the dead teenagers was already marshalling her arguments against the release of the tape (and indeed, several parents later testified in a brief proceeding held in the absence of the jury, with one agonized father saying, correctly, that the kids were "dying on the phone").

If that weren't enough, there was the fact that even in this spanking-new, one-billion-dollar Forensic Services and Coroner's Complex building, it was SNAFU, or situation normal all fucked up.

The microphones either worked badly or no one knew properly how to speak into them, and witnesses mumbled, with the result that at a proceeding whose singular purpose was to focus public attention and scrutiny onto the death of a community member, the public was neither welcomed nor, often, able to hear what was being said.

But by now, the inquest was into its sixth day, and though I wasn't there for the first week, I figured the powers that be might have managed to at least rouse themselves to get the transcript ready.

There's a whole series of cases, from the Supreme Court of Canada decision in *Dagenais v Canadian Broadcasting Corporation* in 1994 on down, which hold that the rights of the press aren't trifling and are protected as a paramount value by the Canadian Charter of Rights and Freedoms. These decisions apply not just to courts but to quasi-judicial proceedings such as inquests.

In my growing rage at not having a decision on the transcript, let alone the transcript, I dared remind coroner's counsel of the public nature of the proceeding and the rights of the press.

In my fury, I threw the wrong case at him—*Regina v Stinchcombe*, which was about evidence disclosure.

A smile of truly exquisite smugness crossed the lawyer's face.

He whispered to someone beside him; I heard the word "Dagenais" and immediately knew I'd grabbed the wrong case from the recesses of my cluttered head.

Indeed, he turned around to correct me, with unsettling serenity. "It's not Stinchcombe," he said. "It's Dagenais."

In those few minutes was illustrated so much that is enraging about the broader justice system: Its collective overweening self-satisfaction; its increasing deference to the victim and the daily broadening of who qualifies for that status (one of the first responders to the fire wept on the stand, a dispatcher was refusing to testify because of her post-traumatic stress disorder, which nonetheless hadn't precluded her from working overtime on a recent holiday weekend, and another lawyer asked for an early break because of her vertigo); and its disdain for anyone not legally trained—that is, the general public and the public's profoundly flawed representative, the press.

At some points, writing this reporter's-eye-view of the justice system, I was tempted to call it "Contempt of Court"—theirs for the likes of me and mine for the likes of them.

But while I suspect theirs may be a permanent condition, mine is not. My contempt waxes and wanes, depending on the merits of the case, the judge, the lawyers and the state of my own knowledge.

At their very best, what the criminal courts and the justice system's main players care most about is fairness, the presumption of innocence, and reason, not heat.

Despite glorious years spent as a tabloid journalist, and despite a plea from a friend who at my request read a chapter and then begged me for a nice clean beheading, by which he meant a harsh but simple critique of the system, I am, after thirty-eight years, incapable of seeing it in black and white.

I don't want to be a lawyer.

I don't want to sound like a lawyer.

But I wouldn't mind being as fair as one. That's what I've aimed for in this book.

R v BETESH to R v DUFFY

"We are all so darn afraid of saying anything about the judiciary, as though judges were some kind of god. They may be gods in their own mind, but they are human."

—FORMER LIBERAL MP JOHN BRYDEN

WHEN ON MONDAY, January 16, 1978, I first wandered into a Toronto courtroom for the start of jury selection in the first criminal trial I had ever covered, I had no idea I was beginning to serve a self-imposed life sentence.

I was working then for the *Toronto Star*. I was twenty-six and had all of five years in the news business, much of it writing sports for *The Globe and Mail*. As a measure of my youthful arrogance, I had quit the *Globe* in a snit when a fellow hired to be a writing coach for the sports department began messing with my copy. In my defence, his help consisted of inserting errors of fact or grammar into my column. I could manage that nicely all on my own (and still do).

I was hired as a columnist by the *Star*, but no one there knew what to do with me, including me: Then as now, the paper had columnists coming out every available orifice. After a couple of weeks of sitting on my ass, I begged the legendary city editor, the great Newfoundlander Mary Deane Shears, to put me to work as a general assignment reporter.

Now I was in my second year at the paper, and assigned to my first criminal trial, and what I knew was the sum total of sweet fuck all.

It was a huge case, or at least in my memory it was huge. In fact, compared to the way modern media cover criminal trials, even before the arrival of live-tweeting from the courtroom, this one got scant, even genteel, coverage.

My stories, old microfiche clippings show, were played inside and often in the "metro" section, not on the national pages. The only time the story made the front page was the day of the verdict, crisply reached by the jury in two hours.

These days, most judges giving legal instructions to jurors before they head off to deliberate are only getting warmed up after two hours—they can rattle on for bloody days—and any twenty-first-century jury returning so fast would be looked upon with naked suspicion.

But back in 1978, as Eugene Ewaschuk, a trial judge who retired from the Ontario Superior Court in June 2015, points out, the Canadian system was in transition from an oral tradition—what he calls the "Who-do-you-believe?" process—to the more unwieldy modern one of documents, expert witnesses and what were then inconceivable amounts and kinds of real evidence—DNA, wiretaps, cellphone records, cell tower technology that can pinpoint mobile locations, text and email messages, and iPhone and surveillance video footage—not to mention social media in all its ever-changing permutations.

The year before, in the summer of 1977, a twelve-year-old boy named Emanuel Jaques disappeared from the corner shoeshine stand where he worked downtown. On August 1, his body was discovered wrapped in garbage bags on the roof above a seedy Yonge Street body-rub parlour, which is what rub 'n' tug joints were called back then.

The boy had been lured to a tiny apartment above the Charlie's Angels parlour, photographed in decreasing amounts of clothing until he was naked, tied up, raped, almost strangled to death and finally drowned.

Four men were each charged with first-degree murder in the so-called Shoeshine Boy case. Robert Wayne Kribs, twenty-nine, also known as "Stretcher"; Josef Woods, a twenty-six-year-old whose nickname was "Crazy Joe"; Werner Gruener, twenty-nine, a quiet fellow who usually carried a Bible in his back pocket; and Saul Betesh, the twenty-seven-year-old adopted son of a wealthy Toronto couple and in essence the driving force behind the crime, were all pleading not guilty.

It was a wildly unusual trial, I realize now.

For one thing, because of the publicity Emanuel's slaying attracted—that such a measured amount of attention was considered outright dangerous seems touchingly quaint now—the jurors were sequestered every night at a hotel, something I have never seen since in this country. For all the rest of my working life until this moment, the only time I've known jurors to be sequestered is when they retire to begin their deliberations.

Another thing: Despite pleading not guilty when he was first arraigned, three weeks later, on the first day of the trial itself, Kribs changed his plea to guilty, though he remained in the prisoner's box with the others until the jurors were sent out the following week to deliberate his fate alone (obligingly, they promptly convicted him). That, also, hardly ever happens.

Finally, the case was to its era what the story of the hyper-modern Canadian killer Luka Magnotta is to ours—unusually ghastly in the detail. The slaying of Emanuel had many of the same elements that thirty-five years later so revolted yet compelled people the world over to follow the trial of Magnotta, who killed Jun Lin, a thirty-three-year-old international student at Montreal's Concordia University and the only son of hard-working parents in China.

Back then, Betesh, Kribs and Woods (Gruener, who had fallen asleep watching TV as Emanuel was being attacked, was rightly acquitted) had photographed the boy, just as they had other boys all that long summer; pictures of more than a dozen were introduced at trial and a number of the boys testified.

The three men were self-styled "chicken hawks," homosexual adults who preferred sex with very young boys.

They handcuffed and gagged Emanuel and assaulted him as he lay face down on a bed. They tried to inject him with sleeping pills, used a vibrator on him, and then, with Woods making a joke about "the kid wanting a shampoo," they drowned him in the kitchen sink. Then they robbed him of the three one-dollar bills he had in his pocket, wrapped him in garbage bags and dumped him on the roof.

According to Betesh, Woods at one point even suggested putting Emanuel "in a trunk and mailing him to Anita Bryant," the former singer turned Florida oranges pitchwoman turned anti-homosexual crusader who was then much in the news.

Magnotta actually did things like that. He dismembered Lin's body, had pretend-sex with it, videoed the works and posted the results online (to snarky reviews on "gore" sites, where it was almost universally recognized by gore aficionados as a genuine killing, not that most of them worried about that, because they were too busy whingeing about the quality of the accompanying soundtrack). Then, in fancy wrapping and black gift bags, Magnotta mailed off Lin's hands and feet to politicians in Ottawa and two schools in British Columbia.

In retrospect, it's as though the killing of Emanuel Jaques was a very early version, the 0.1 edition as it were, of what happened to Jun Lin.

But the trial of Betesh et al. was unusual in a much more significant way too, though no one knew it then.

The trial itself started about six months after Emanuel's body was found and the men arrested. Prosecutors were easily able to carry into court in a few cardboard bankers' boxes all the evidence in the case. The whole shebang was wrapped and done within eight months of the men's arrests.

That sort of efficiency, in big, high-profile trials particularly, would come to a crashing end just four years later, when the Canadian Charter of Rights and Freedoms was proclaimed and the pace of justice slowed beyond recognition.

The enactment of the Charter isn't the only reason things went to slo-mo, of course—the arrival of all that new kind of real evidence is another—but it's the meaningful one.

Anyway, I had no inkling of any of this back then. I arrived at the courts pretty much fresh from covering sports.

While I immediately liked much about the courtroom—in particular, the collegiality of the smarty-pants lawyers—what I liked most was that this milieu bore a striking resemblance to the arena and the playing field where I'd spent my first years in the business. In other words, it felt familiar and comfortable.

There were two sides (prosecution and defence). There was a referee (the judge) and linesmen equivalents (the registrars, clerks, commissionaires and like officials who carry out the judge's orders and run the courtroom). Usually, there was a clear winner, in that the accused was either acquitted or convicted, unless, and this happens only rarely, the jury couldn't reach a verdict and was hung.

Most gloriously, there were rules for everything, unwritten mostly.

I used to love the rules.

Relatives of the accused and victim might arrive at court together and rumble in through the same door, but by God they invariably divided themselves up as surely as if they were at a wedding and were being grabbed by the elbow and taken to their seats by ushers—family of the victim over there, family of the alleged perp over there.

Everyone had to stand every time the judge entered or left the room, unlike a case I covered many years later in east Texas, where His Honour ambled in and out to no particular notice. (Mind you, also in that case, the prosecutor wore a gun tucked into his cowboy boot, pant leg adjusted so a couple of inches of weapon showed.)

There was no hat-wearing, no gum-chewing, no glasses perched on the top of your head. My great friend and colleague Rosie DiManno of the *Toronto Star* still delights, to this very day, in slapping up her specs on her head and waiting to see how long it takes one of the court officers to show up at her side—never more than minutes, by the way.

Coats couldn't show on the back of the hard wooden pew-type benches and had to be folded out of sight. Newspapers and books were allowed, sort of, but had to be hidden from the judge's view.

In the old days at least, anyone breaching any one of these dicta was smartly rebuked, if not asked to leave, and even now, though things have relaxed a little, there's a funny stern decorum at work.

I've had my cellphone ring in the Pope's private quarters at the Vatican, while his private choir was singing for a special audience of wealthy *Globe and Mail* readers who were on a posh Mediterranean cruise. (I was part of the alleged talent and went for free.) I threw myself upon the phone, barely muffling the noise, and then sat there on the floor in a sweaty pool of relief for a few minutes, too stunned to turn it off.

Naturally, the caller, a reader from Kitchener, phoned back.

Yet not even that horror compares to having your cell ring in court. That's how much of a rules-and-hidebound place it is.

There were other, more important rules too—various publication bans and closed-to-the-jury proceedings, both of which meant some information couldn't be immediately reported and which, at least in the beginning, satisfied my reporter's desire to know things first.

That's how I initially saw it too, as a quirky if benign benefit. It didn't sink in right away that there was much less fun in knowing stuff first if you couldn't also write about it and tell everyone else.

I also liked the edge that print reporters had in court. Television needs "visuals," or at least those running television think it does—thus the perennial stand-up of the reporter outside the courthouse and the walking shot of one poor sucker or another fleeing a pack of cameras with a coat over his head. Courts weren't and aren't visual in this way. And since television generally has the collective staying power of a teenage boy, and trials are a lot about sitting through tons of dullish stuff in order to be able to recognize the sliver of new or interesting, TV poses no competitive threat in the courts.

Even in the late 1970s, when print and newspapers were decades away from the arrival of online and social media and television was still king, the courtroom was one of the few places where ink-stained wretches actually had the advantage. Astonishingly, that's still the case: The thoroughly modern young reporter working in the justice system—live-blogging, live-tweeting, shooting video, doing radio hits (sometimes in two languages) and filing six times a day to a newspaper website—still lives and dies by the power and quality of her observations.

I have a natural affection, absorbed no doubt from my late father, for the institutions of my country—the monarchy, military, police, the bar, the judiciary—so these quirky customs and trappings, found in this artifact from an earlier era, were right up my alley. I loved it unreservedly.

For many years, this bedrock faith in institutional Canada served me usefully as a citizen and as a reporter working in the courts, in that it allowed me to believe in their fundamental goodness and efficacy.

As there was always a point in voting, for instance, so was there a reason to cover trials and the like, and it was the same one—participation and engagement in the democracy. Plus, faith rendered the unendurably dull bearable, because (or so I thought) it was for a greater good.

Later, I would come to loathe parts of the justice system, grow intolerant about others, despise most of the rules and regard many of the key participants with cynicism or distaste.

I still like some things about the courts, but I stick it out for the same reason people stay, sometimes too long, in flawed marriages: It's good more of the time than it is bad.

Barely.

When I read now my stories from the long-ago trial of Saul Betesh, I'm embarrassed. It's more than the sort of morning-after twinge with which most daily journalists live, the recognition you could have done or said it better or that you made dopey mistakes or forgot the single best quote of the day. My Betesh coverage is mortifying in the same way that reading the poetry you wrote in high school is mortifying: Was I really so thick back then?

At the Betesh trial, I was crushing on the judge, the late William Maloney of what was then called the Ontario Supreme Court (now the Ontario Superior Court). I can tell by a couple of the pieces I wrote.

One was about Maloney explaining to Emanuel's brother (then just fourteen) and a young friend what taking an oath meant. Judges often do this with those they deem to be of tender years.

Now, there were some genuinely sweet exchanges, such as one boy, just twelve, being asked what happened to witnesses who didn't tell the truth. "God will punish you," the boy replied.

He looked at the judge and added, "And so will the court, sir."

Maloney chuckled, or as I wrote, giddily, "Maloney laughed. He'd won another friend." Clearly, the judge already had one in me.

Another small story was headlined, "Judge broadens his horizons," and was about how a witness had testified about taking "a toke," to which Maloney responded, "A tote?"

Another day, when the same witness referred to the now-ancient movie *The Island of Dr. Moreau* (the 1977 version), Maloney asked what it was. Defence lawyer Earl Levy, who was representing Gruener, piped up with, "Burt Lancaster was in it, Your Honour."

"'Well, now I might ask you, who's Burt Lancaster?'" the judge asked, seriously, as if being grossly out of touch with the culture was a good thing.

"No one answered," I wrote, "but everyone laughed."

And that's the thing: Even now, because of reactions like mine, there is no one more likely than a judge to imagine that he could do stand-up. Lawyers and reporters and the public routinely howl at the most feeble jokes and positively burst with smiley indulgence at weak judicial witticisms.

No one was guiltier of it than me, though I'd argue it's more offensive in the lawyers who all but slap their knees in anticipation of the judge getting off a bon mot. It must be the sort of premature ejaculation approved of, if not actually encouraged, in law school.

Was I impressed that someone who seemed so old to me then (of course, Maloney was younger then than I am now) could still string together a sentence? Was I relieved at some slight evidence of his humanity? Was I just being my father's daughter, naturally deferential to authority? It was all of that, I expect.

And so dutifully, for too many years, did I faithfully report on Judge David Watt's hockey references (now on the Court of Appeal, Watt was an active hockey official for a long time and while a trial judge in the Ontario Superior Court, regularly peppered his comments with hockey-isms, such as telling a lawyer he was "ragging the puck") and on his Superior Court colleague

Eugene Ewaschuk's flagrant delight in working French phrases, for no particular reason other than he loved them, into the record.

They remain two of my favourite guys on the bench, though Ewaschuk, having turned seventy-five last year, is sadly no longer a judge. They are big brains both, and I think two of the best. It's my own abject reaction to and reporting of their pretty lame lines that's cringe-worthy.

I tell the story to illustrate the sort of clout that comes with judicial robes, and because it shows how constitutionally predisposed I was to genuflecting to power.

My loss of faith was incremental, and came over years, so there's no one case that turned the tide, and it would be dishonest to pretend otherwise.

If I search my memory now, the best I can do is pinpoint a few instances where a particular penny or two may have dropped.

For instance, in 1993, when I was working for the *Toronto Sun*, I got a taste of how ferociously judges and lawyers can turn on one another, and over which subjects, and what astonishing creatures of convention many of them are and what prisoners—despite all the high-minded protestations to the contrary—of the dominant political orthodoxy.

Walter (Wally) Hryciuk was an Ontario Court judge, a very good one apparently but a bit of an old-school guy, even then. He was the kind of man whose wife gave him a joke light switch plate such that when you flicked the light on or off, you were flicking a little penis, and he was the sort who thought it would be a laugh to hang the thing in his chambers at the Old City Hall courts.

Hryciuk was the subject of a complaint with the Ontario Judicial Council, the body in that province that probes allegations against provincially appointed judges.

A young female Crown attorney named Kelly Smith claimed

that in a back hall of the Old City Hall courts, Hryciuk had grabbed her and French-kissed her.

Eventually, the earlier complaint of another female prosecutor, Susan Lawson, was also brought forward. She was the victim—I use the word here in the loosest and broadest imaginable way—of the penis light switch.

The judicial council investigated and eventually, in the fall of that year, Jean MacFarland, then a judge one court up from Hryciuk (what's now called the Ontario Superior Court) and later still elevated to the Court of Appeal, presided over a public inquiry.

This was Bob Rae's Ontario—before he became a federal Liberal member of Parliament, then sage-at-large, and was still the earnest leader of the provincial New Democrats. His party won an unexpected majority in 1990, and as the government, set upon a course that enthusiastically embraced racial diversity and gender equity as core principles. It was Rae who, in February 1993, named London Centre MPP Marion Boyd attorney-general—the first female and the first non-lawyer to hold the post.

Now, these were grand times for a reporter, particularly for a *Sun* reporter as I was then, in that you could wake up mid-morning, do nothing more than scratch your ass and stumble upon one great story after another: the cabinet minister (Peter North) who resigned in a sex scandal that saw him tragically never get any actual sex; the provincial Special Investigations Unit in charge of probing police shootings that hired a hotshot homicide detective (Fred Winston) from Florida only to learn from the newspaper that he'd never investigated a murder in his life and had been dismissed from his last job; the health minister (Shelley Martel) who took a lie detector test to prove once and for all that when at a party she'd seemingly breached a doctor's confidentiality by blurting out how much he'd overbilled she had lied; and the race relations advisor (Arnold Minors) hired by the government to teach its Crown attorneys about racism who unfortunately told a group of them that the Holocaust wasn't a racist act because it wasn't aimed at blacks.

Glory days; I still get verklempt.

But that was the dominant culture of those times, and it was in that context that Hryciuk found himself accused of one count of sexual assault (the alleged French kiss with Smith) and one of making remarks of a sexual nature (for flicking the penis switch in his chambers and allegedly saying to Lawson, "You can flick my switch anytime").

Ultimately, three more complaints were added on.

In a sixty-page document filled with feminist sanctimony and dogma years ahead of its time, MacFarland found Hryciuk guilty and recommended his removal.

Smith and Lawson, the judge wrote, weren't overreacting in their tearful testimony. Why, she said, when Smith testified she fell into a round of hysterical toothbrushing and was afraid of catching a "disease" from the alleged French kiss, she wasn't being irrational, because after all, "It is no secret that in this day and age, one of the ways certain diseases are thought to be transmitted is by bodily fluids including saliva," and when Lawson said she was "terrified" by the one-two punch of the penis switch in Hryciuk's chambers and his remark about it (which he denied making), she wasn't being overwrought.

As for another Crown, Malka Goldenberg, who complained that Hryciuk's overly warm two-handed handshake made her uncomfortable, MacFarland disagreed with Hryciuk's lawyer, who called the allegation patent nonsense.

"I cannot agree," MacFarland said. "A handshake is a normal social physical response most of us engage in daily, whether it be a single- or double-handed handshake.

"It is normal acceptable social conduct, at which no reasonable person would take offence. When that conduct goes beyond what might be considered a normal or usual handshake, it may, depending on the circumstances, become objectionable."

Are you freaking kidding me is what I thought then and think now.

Remember, these were Crown attorneys, tasked with prosecuting, among others, rapists, diddlers, pimps, flashers, fathers and uncles who forced sex upon their young daughters or nieces, the purveyors of up-skirt cameras, pornographers and the whole crazy cornucopia of criminal human sexual conduct.

Could they really be this delicate, this ill-informed (no one with half a wit, even in the very early days of AIDS fears—and this was not that time—believed the virus or any other sexually transmitted disease could be spread by a single French kiss) and this incapable of distinguishing misconduct from serious wrongdoing?

The answer was more than two decades in the coming.

In the spring of 2015, a prosecutor friend asked me to take part in a panel discussion at one of those conferences lawyers often have, this one for Crown attorneys. I agreed, and then promptly forgot about it: I didn't have to give a speech, just take part in a conversation about a couple of recent high-profile trials I'd covered and already knew well, so I knew I didn't have to do much to prepare.

At the time, the FHRITP phenomenon—the initials stand for "Fuck her right in the pussy," which morons the planet over, usually in their cups, had taken to yelling at TV reporters—was much in the news, and CBC's *The National* had just convened "a solemn panel," as a friend called it, to discuss this terrible business.

The discussion had kicked off with anchor Peter Mansbridge, sighing with the pain of it all, asking, "What does that [FHRITP] say about us as a society?"

Now, I'm not saying it isn't appallingly rude and thuggish to yell something like that at anyone, least of all at someone doing live television. But FHRITP was never aimed only at female reporters (men got it too, though I'm sure it was more hurtful to those who actually had the parts in question), and seemed to me to be less a function of chronic misogyny in the culture than it was of the more troubling hunger of idiots to get their mugs on the tube.

Anyway, as I was ruminating on all this, wondering when we had become so fragile, what popped into my head, not surprisingly, was the Wally Hryciuk inquiry, because it was then that I distinctly remembered feeling the planet shift a bit on its axis.

And that, the day before the Crowns' conference, is pretty much what I wrote as my column.

I mentioned Kelly Smith by name, and the bottom line of her testimony, but she wasn't the focus of the piece. What was, as I wrote both about Hryciuk's alleged offences and the FHRITP craze, was that "there's an ocean between sexual assault and a kiss, however unwanted, between harmful actions and hurtful words, however mean, and between rape and a tone of voice, however leering."

It never occurred to me that because I was speaking the next day to a bunch of Crowns, I shouldn't be writing critically about one of them. I simply didn't make the connection. Even had I done so, I can't imagine I would have thought to censor myself or, for instance, not name Smith.

For one thing, if I'd thought about it, I would never have imagined she was still working as a prosecutor, as indeed she is; after all, she'd nearly been undone, as she herself testified under oath, by a single unsolicited kiss.

The conference was early on May 22. The column was in the paper that day, online the night before. As I was heading up to join the rest of the panel on stage at one of those airport-hangar-like convention centres, a furious woman approached me, shrieked that she couldn't believe I'd written what I had on the day I was speaking to hundreds of Crowns, berated me up and down, and marched off.

Later, I learned she was Smith's sister, and a fine prosecutor herself apparently, so good for her, I suppose, for standing up for her sib.

It was a little unnerving, but I made way up to the dais, and the panel discussion unfolded in the usual way.

I was just walking off the stage—behind me, I could see the people I assumed were on the next panel moving up to take their places—when a female Crown, whose name I forget, stopped me and said with alarming seriousness, "Christie, I think you should stay for this."

The room was noisy, as conferences get between events. I didn't understand and said, "Pardon me?"

"I think you should hear this," the woman replied, with a grave nod to the stage.

By then I was almost at the door. I couldn't stay anyway. But I looked back over my shoulder to see a slim bespectacled little fellow, in a bow tie, standing with several others on the stage. He was James Cornish, Ontario's assistant deputy attorney general for criminal law, and he was having a kumbaya moment with some of his Crowns.

A few minutes later, outside the room, I introduced myself to him and asked if it were true, as I'd just been told, that his remarks about himself and the government standing with all victims of sexual assault had been inspired by my column.

He hadn't mentioned me by name, apparently, but the reference to me or the column was sufficiently unmistakable that I got several notes the next day, asking what on earth had happened.

Anyway, with Mansbridge-ian sorrow, Cornish allowed that this was so.

"You might have had the courtesy to tell me beforehand you were going to do that," I said. After all, as I saw it, I was effectively a guest in his house.

His reply was astonishing: Well, he said, I hadn't told anyone in the ministry about my column beforehand.

"I don't submit my columns to the government," I snarled.

In any case, I had my answer, twenty-two years later: Crown attorneys and judges could indeed be as fragile as Kelly Smith and Jean MacFarland, and that delicacy is now sufficiently embedded in the bureaucracy that a deputy AG felt it appropriate to make a public display of it.

Back to the Hryciuk inquiry, where the best bit, by which I mean the most ludicrous, wasn't even the absurd handshake analysis by MacFarland. It came in the person of Ontario Court judge Joe Bovard, who with his then new wife, court reporter Kelly James, was one of the add-on complainants.

Bovard told the inquiry that shortly after he was appointed to the bench, he once saw Hryciuk grab the buttocks of a female judge (who later took the stand herself and absolutely denied it, as did Hryciuk) in the Old City Hall common room.

Bovard, who still sits on the Ontario Court, pronounced himself shocked and appalled by what he'd seen. But, as it turned out, he was ill-positioned as a white knight riding in the name of judicial propriety to the rescue of Hryciuk victims everywhere.

Not long after the inquiry ended, the *Sun* was contacted by a woman who was a bookkeeper at the school Bovard's kids attended—and who said she'd once had sex with him on a couch in his chambers at the Scarborough courts in east-end Toronto.

At the same time, she said, he was having it off with his French tutor. My friend Tracy Nesdoly and I (we shared a byline on the story as fellow *Sun* reporters) confirmed this with the other other woman.

Statements from both bookkeeper and tutor had been given to inquiry counsel, but both had been deemed inadmissible by MacFarland, and neither woman ever testified.

Ergo, sex in chambers good; too-long double handshake and penis light switch bad.

Three years later, a unanimous Ontario Court of Appeal

panel found that MacFarland had "exceeded her jurisdiction" by hearing the three add-on complaints and quashed her recommendation that Wally Hryciuk be dumped. But he never sat as a judge again, while MacFarland was promoted to the appeal court.

It was my first front-row seat at my first old-fashioned witch hunt, though not my last. And it offered more than a hint of what was yet to come in the culture—the spectacular rise of female victimhood, for example.

And in the testimony of Mary Hall—even then a veteran Crown attorney and such a hard-nosed one she was called Maximum Mary until her latter-day conversion at the inquiry where she belatedly testified in support of the young Crowns— the root of the problem with judges was briefly laid bare.

Asked what was the relationship between young lawyers and the bench, Hall said, in part, "I speak not only from personal experience but now as a supervisor of 25 assistant Crown attorneys. You think that a judge is right up there next to God."

How interesting; that's exactly what some judges appear to think too.

A case lodged in my memory—child killings tend to do that—is the story of baby Sara Cao.

I first wrote about her about a month after her death on October 20, 2001, and I was too quick to bang a familiar drum— blaming a child-welfare agency for failing to do its job.

I wasn't entirely wrong, mind you, but I was also undoubtedly spoiling for a fight.

Just six months earlier, I'd covered the entire coroner's inquest into the 1997 death of another baby, Jordan Heikamp, who had starved to death—in the midst of the plenty that is Canada—at a shelter just a couple of blocks from my house in downtown

Toronto, all while under the ostensible supervision of another child-welfare agency.

I was very much still in a state of rage at what happened to Jordan. He died, yes, because his mother, Renee, then a homeless teenager, had got bored and stopped trying to breastfeed him. But he also died because of the incredibly sloppy and inept monitoring given by the Catholic Children's Aid Society of Toronto.

It was the CCAS that placed mother and child in an Aboriginal women's shelter where, under the sleepy eyes of a bunch of paid caregivers, his mother got "supportive" hugs while in her arms, disappearing under his blankets, Jordan slowly wasted away.

He wasn't my first dead-by-institution child.

Her I remember too.

In April 1994, Sara Podniewicz was killed by her vicious father, Mike Podniewicz, and her crack-addled mother, Lisa Olsen.

Mike Podniewicz had already been convicted in 1988 of aggravated assault upon the couple's infant son, Mikey Jr.—such a terrible assault that the little boy was left severely brain-damaged, paralyzed, deaf and blind and with the permanent mental age of two months.

Podniewicz was sentenced to five years and actually served two, and when he got out on parole in February of 1993, among his conditions was that he couldn't be alone with his own kids "without the presence of an adult approved by [his] supervisor." Naturally, the adult cheerfully approved—by both Corrections Canada and the CCAS—was none other than Lisa Olsen, by then about a month pregnant with Sara.

In brisk order, these two then killed the little girl, were duly convicted of second-degree murder (I covered their joint trial) and went off to the slammer.

As my friend, the aforementioned Nesdoly, says, always in such dreadful matters we must try to remember who to be mad at, and in what order, and by that sensible standard, Sara's parents were chiefly to blame.

But complicit in her death was the CCAS, the same agency under whose auspices Jordan later starved and whose workers had watched over Sara Podniewicz with the same breathtaking lack of vigilance.

Two aspects of the case remain seared in my head.

One is the day Martha McKay, a worker from Mothercraft, an agency ordered by the court to monitor the family as part of Podniewicz's parole, testified at trial. She was a perky young woman who had visited the family ten days before Sara died.

At that time, the jury learned, Sara had twenty-three or twenty-four broken bones (including most of her ribs and the thigh bones in both legs) and was actually wearing a tiny cast on one arm.

McKay found Sara pale and stressed, and was inspired to lay a blanket on the floor and put toe jingles on the baby's feet. And that dear little girl, broken bones and tiny cast notwithstanding, tried to play because the baby's first instincts—to be joyous, to trust, to please—were not yet utterly extinguished in her.

McKay was highly pleased by that, if fundamentally oblivious: A good description, actually, of the dopiest of these social workers.

As for Sara's actual dying, it happened as she was in her baby seat in her parents' squalid Parkdale apartment, gasping for air because she had untreated pneumonia and was unable to clear her lungs because of the multiple broken ribs.

She sat there for so long, alone and suffering, that as she died, and the blood pooled in the low places of the body as gravity ensures it does, the pattern of the seat was imprinted on her tiny back. We could see it in the autopsy pictures.

All of this is to say, by the time Sara Cao died, I was well conditioned by hard experience to suspect the worst of child-welfare agencies. These were the first institutions in which I lost trust, as year after year, case after case, many of them continued to make the same fundamental mistake—that is, forget that their clients were the children, not the parents.

But this time, I was wrong.

As the then head of the Toronto CCAS, a very decent man named Bruce Rivers, acknowledged, the agency ultimately had failed their Sara, but it was not for lack of trying. In fact, the agency had tried damn hard, as a closer read of the case showed.

Its nurse and social worker had made six visits to Sara's home within less than two weeks; they warned her mother, Elizabeth Cao, about the dangers of shaking an infant and ensured she understood; they followed up when Cao missed doctor's appointments, and their case notes weren't filled with the usual meaningless drivel about "mother presents well."

My nose is particularly attuned to that smell of smarmy, rear-covering, social-work-ese, and there really wasn't any of that here. (I wrote this too, about a month after the first piece, and admitted I'd been too harsh on the CCAS.)

So in February 2004, when I read in a couple of Toronto papers that Elizabeth Cao's lawyer, Cindy Wasser, was now demanding an investigation of the Toronto CCAS role in the case, I was intrigued.

As it turned out, Wasser was suggesting that the agency, and not Cao, was responsible for Sara's death. But by then, of course, Wasser and the prosecutors had reached a happy plea bargain: Cao, though originally charged with second-degree murder, would plead guilty to the lesser offence of manslaughter, and in exchange, Crown attorneys Anna Tenhouse and Rebecca Edwards signed off on a non-custodial or conditional sentence.

Now, Elizabeth Cao wasn't, it was agreed, the sharpest knife in the drawer. But despite her intellectual limits, she managed to get through grade twelve, and there was an inherent acknowledgement of capacity in her guilty plea; you don't get to plead if you haven't the intelligence to form the *mens rea* (which means "guilty mind" or intent) of an offence.

So there we all were, on February 24, 2004, in courtroom M-1 at the Old City Hall courts—Wasser and her colleague Catherine Rhinelander hovering protectively at Cao's side, the prosecutors, and Ontario Court judge David Fairgrieve.

The entire proceeding took eight minutes.

Fairgrieve waved off the "usual house arrest and community service provisions," deciding Cao had been punished enough by the twenty-two days she was cruelly forced to serve between her arrest and release on bail.

The judge read aloud selected passages of his reasons for sentence. One of them was this: "Given the nature of her loss, it hardly seems necessary to provide explicit or further acknowledgement of the harm she caused."

Fed up with Sara's crying, Cao had shaken her eight-pound, five-week-old daughter into unconsciousness and ultimately, after three days on life support, unto death.

As I raged in the *Globe* the day after the sentencing, "She caused the death of Sara; Sara is dead, dead, dead; ergo, Cao has no baby daughter: That's the nature of her loss."

At autopsy, the little girl was discovered to have at least ten rib fractures, some of them in the early stages of healing, which suggested she'd been hurt not only on the night in question but also on some prior occasion or two. And Cao had three times tried to dissuade her then husband from calling 911—this after he arrived home from work and noticed Sara was bleeding from her nose and mouth.

Judges don't have to accept joint recommendations of the lawyers who stand before them, but they most often do, and I understand that: The courts hardly whiz along tickety-boo, but such that they move at all is in real measure thanks to guilty pleas and plea bargains.

What was galling to me was how Fairgrieve went out of his way to soft-pedal what had gone on. He did the little bit about "the nature of your loss." He told Cao, who was then twenty-five, that the point of the exercise was "not to add to your misery" (she didn't look remotely unhappy). He praised the prosecutors for their "reasonable and enlightened assessment" of what was in the public interest.

And as Cao was about to take her leave from his courtroom, Fairgrieve offered, "I hope things go well."

You know who really understood the public interest there? It was the two investigating Toronto Police officers, Detective Constables Andy Gibson and Shawna Coxon, who were also in court, and near tears. Gibson told me afterwards, "I feel like there's no justice for this five-week-old baby. This is the last day of two and a half years. No one will remember her now."

They were obviously part of the less-enlightened segment of the population who believe that if the death of a helpless infant doesn't call for at least a little jail time, at the very least the sentencing judge ought to be able to stop himself from wishing luck to the person who committed the homicide.

It was a good reminder that it's always the cops—not the child-welfare workers, not the lawyers or judges and certainly not the reporters—who unfailingly remember the dead kids, their birthdays and the number of broken bones they had.

If a single judge were to be held responsible for my radicalization, I realize now, it would be Eleanor Schnall, appointed to the Ontario Court under Bob Rae's NDP government in 1991.

In the early summer of 2002 I covered a long and complicated case before Judge Schnall. Never before had I seen a judge behave quite as rudely and high-handedly. Schnall was consistently markedly late getting to court and coming back after recesses and lunch, and yet she was snarly and uber-critical of lawyers—especially the one representing the media who were fighting her publication bans—for "sacrificing court time."

Now, there is something called "judge time," which everyone but the poor civilians involved in cases understands, whereby fifteen-minute breaks are routinely doubled and the normal lunch, whether an hour or ninety minutes, usually gets an extra fifteen minutes added on. Rarely is any of it—the chronic lateness, the delayed starts, the jiving and shucking that goes on—even tacitly acknowledged. (In Montreal, as the Magnotta trial taught me, you should assume the lunch break will be a minimum of two hours, whatever the judge says. Montrealers simply will not be rushed through a meal, any meal.)

Canadian courthouses are like far-flung island colonies of Las Vegas, where clocks are discouraged lest the guy in front of the slot machine or at the poker table look up and realize how long he's been there, losing money. In Vegas, I can't remember seeing any public clocks. In Canada, virtually every courtroom has one, but they all tell a different time, presumably so the players, if challenged, always have a defence handy for being late, and can blame the faulty clock down the hall, in an office or in the courtroom next door.

By 2002, I'd been in enough courts to know these things as facts of life. But it took Schnall to teach me that it's best to look at my own watch to time everything, and to write down in my notebook precisely when the judge enters and leaves, how long the breaks are supposed to be and how long they actually last.

But chronic tardiness and a dubious work ethic were the least of Schnall's problems.

This was a strange case that had been in the news, on and off, for about a year.

In July 2001, the Child and Family Services of St. Thomas and Elgin County in southwestern Ontario had swooped in and seized seven children from their fundamentalist Christian parents, who were then living in a two-hundred-member fundamentalist Christian sect, the Church of God Restoration, just outside Aylmer.

This couple, and most of the church members, were so-called Mexican Mennonites, some of whom spoke only a language called "low German," a mix of Dutch, German and Russian-Prussian. With their incomprehensible language, modest garb (ankle-length skirts for the women), strict religious doctrine that prohibited them from using vehicles with rubber tires and allowed them to discipline their kids (thus the shorthand for the whole shooting match—"the spanking case"), and their cloistered lives, they were a curious group in secular modern Canada.

It was the parents' spanking of the children that led the child-welfare agency to move in and, without a warrant, apprehend the youngsters, kicking and crying; they remained in the agency's temporary care for less than a month before being returned to their parents under a supervision order that allowed social workers to monitor the family.

Now, a year later, the agency was seeking "a protection order" that would remove them permanently from the family home.

Ultimately, Schnall ruled in favour of the agency and found the parents' Charter rights had not been violated by the warrant-less search, and in the end, the family and child-welfare officials worked out an arrangement whereby the family was monitored.

But worthy of mention is that these children—unlike the recognizably sick and in-danger kids whose homicides I cover and who child-welfare collectively seems so well able to ignore—were ridiculously hale-and-hearty, gorgeous youngsters who were spirited enough to defend their faith and their mom and dad to grown-ups they'd never met before.

If they appeared weirdly devout to most Canadians—one boy was terrified at being exposed to television in the foster home, though in fairness what he may have feared for was his intellect—they were also full of piss and vinegar.

What was extraordinary was how Schnall ran her courtroom—like a tyrant who, given half a chance, would have spanked everyone in it. Despite a regular statutory publication ban to protect the youngsters' identities, mandatory in all child-protection proceedings and never challenged by the media, she imposed an additional series of sweeping gag orders (one even precluded reporters from describing the demeanour of witnesses whose names and testimony were already verboten) that shrouded the case in secrecy.

She banned courtroom sketches. She protected the name of the young social worker who made the critical decision to seize the youngsters. And she berated anyone who dared object to any of it, once threatening to bar Jonathan Sher, a terrific reporter for the *London Free Press*, and yelling at him, "You've just lost your place in the courtroom!"

Later, it took another justice, Tom Granger of the Superior Court, mere minutes to briskly set aside Schnall's various bans and allow the press to tell the country what was happening in the case.

But like several of my colleagues, by then I'd already had a run-in with Schnall.

One day, as she enlarged one of her bans again and told the media lawyer that she would not "sacrifice any more court time on the media issue," I did the unthinkable: got to my feet and addressed her.

"Our lawyer is willing to be here at 9 a.m., Madam Justice," is all I said, meaning, if we started an hour earlier the next day, we wouldn't lose any court time.

"I don't recognize anybody speaking from the body of the court!" she shrilled, staring right at me.

If what I'd done was the equivalent of farting in the presence of royalty, what Schnall did was akin to putting her fingers in her ears and humming while saying, "I can't hear you!"

The message was unmistakable: She had all the power in the room, and I, like other reporters and members of the public, should listen in silence, preferably adulatory.

I started working on this book in 2012, but quit it about a year later, after writing almost fifty thousand words: The subject was just too huge and amorphous for me to get my arms around it, let alone my head.

By the time I started to cover the fraud, breach-of-trust and bribery trial of Prince Edward Island senator Mike Duffy, in Ottawa in April 2015, my friends knew enough not to even ask me about it anymore. On the infrequent occasions I mentioned it, I called it my "alleged" book.

The Duffy trial was dragging its arse along, in the usual stately fashion, and by mid-May, I'd had just about enough of the judge's Schnall-like conception of time.

At this point, Ontario Court judge Charles Vaillancourt had made it to court—whether first thing or after breaks or lunch—on time on only one day, and I'd taken to tapping my watch, or pointing to the clock and shrieking like a crazy person, "Tick-tock! Tick-tock!"

Many of my colleagues there were members of the parliamentary press gallery—they are a great crew too, welcoming and friendly yet ferociously competent and competitive—and perhaps they were more inured than I am to the pace of officialdom. I think they were amused, and later maybe alarmed, by the lunatic clock-watching diatribe with which I began every morning.

Vaillancourt was a judge from Toronto, and when his appointment was announced that April, it was to the usual approbation in the press—glowing stories about his purported experience and wisdom.

"His temperament is ideally suited for a high-profile case like this," defence lawyer Julian Roy told the *Star*.

Vaillancourt, said defence lawyer Howard Rubel, is known for his ability to ensure that trials proceed in a "respectful, fair and orderly manner."

Why, it was "no accident" this judge was chosen for the job, given his background in complex litigation, lawyer Andrew Furgiuele told the paper.

Vaillancourt is "very patient, a good listener, pleasant to appear before, balanced and with no shortage of common sense," lawyer Bill Trudell, chair of the Canadian Council of Criminal Defence Lawyers, told the *Globe*.

And in the same story, Steve Skurka, another veteran lawyer, said Vaillancourt "makes bold decisions . . . will not be affected by public sentiment . . . plays no favourites in the courtroom."

Etc., etc.

Curiously, none of the lawyers mentioned his inability to tell time.

Now, I know most of those lawyers who were quoted, a couple pretty well, and I know they would spout precisely the same sort of horseshit about whichever judge they were being asked to comment on. Lawyers rarely utter a critical word for public consumption about one of their own, least of all about a judge in front of whom they may one day appear (or a judge whose friends on the bench they may appear before), not to mention if they themselves aspire to land the job—and a good many of them, as it happens, do.

(By way of illustration, as of December 31, 2013, in the twenty-three years the Ontario Judicial Appointments Advisory Committee has been keeping track of such things, a total of

3,369 lawyers have applied for Ontario Court judgeships. So it's not exactly an unpopular gig, shall we say.)

Plus, most of the reporters who quoted the lawyers merrily fellating the judge had no way of knowing if Vaillancourt was really a gifted and notable fellow, or completely unremarkable, or a boob.

The truth is, there are about seven hundred judges and justices of the peace working in the Ontario Court, the biggest and busiest in the country. Only a handful of the 200,000-odd criminal cases the court hears every year across the province are even covered by the press, and within that group there are only a few reporters who cover any level of court with any regularity, and thus there is only a tiny crew of journalists who actually know any of the judges or JPs first-hand. So going to a lawyer for anything other than circum-spect, if not adoring, comment about a judge is like asking parents for a reference for their kid: You ain't going to get a bad one.

Vaillancourt had had perhaps three well-known cases in his twenty-five years on the bench (each of which was duly trotted out for mention in most of the stories about his appointment to the Duffy matter, always in the approved-of approving manner).

Most Canadians, like most reporters, wouldn't know him from Adam.

Duffy, everyone knows.

In April of 2016, Vaillancourt acquitted Duffy of all thirty-one charges, but there remains no doubt the veteran CTV and CBC broadcaster had latched on to the public teat like a champ, if not in a fashion that was criminal.

There's no doubt he did the latter. That wasn't even an issue at trial, where all that was really up for grabs was how Vaillancourt would chose to characterize the conduct—sloppy bookkeeping, administrative error made justifiable by the chaos created by the carefully ambiguous Senate rules, something criminal as was alleged or some combination of all of the above.

Anyway, the trial was already way behind schedule—the original estimate of six weeks was rendered laugh-out-loud funny early on—and no one but me seemed to notice or much give a damn.

Adding to my crabbiness, I was sick of living in a hotel room, and weary of Ottawa.

I'd tripped one morning while out for a run and buggered up my left hand in the fall, and the next day while out for another, was bitten by a dog for the first time in my life and ended up with a more seriously wrecked right hand too.

The dog was a white standard poodle named Dennis, and when I spotted him, I trilled to his owner, who had him on a leash, "Can I say hi to your dog?"

Sure, said the man, adding that he might jump on me.

No worries, I said, I can handle an enthusiastic hound.

As advertised, Dennis jumped up, but then, without warning or provocation, also began to savage my hand, tearing the fleshy inside part of my thumb and index finger so deep you could see the muscle. As I stood there spurting blood, the owner said helpfully, "That's why he usually wears a muzzle."

All this culminated in my increasingly foul, snappish mood—I also needed a muzzle—and one day, it occurred to me that the secret to my alleged book was hiding in plain sight, right there in courtroom No. 33.

There I was, covering the criminal trial of a man who'd been living the good life on the public dime, and there, sitting in judgment of him—it was a judge-alone trial, as all at this level are—was none other than another lucky fellow who lives a similar sort of life.

On May 18, I wrote to my book editor, whom I call Bond because he's a luscious Brit with a nice accent and a bit of mystery about him.

"Dearest Bond," I said, "it occurred to me one day that the judiciary is much like the Senate. Like senators, they are unelected, unaccountable, entitled, expensive to maintain and remarkably smug.

"A few of them are excellent; some try; a lot are unworthy."

Duffy, for example, was appointed to the Senate in late 2008; by the time he was suspended, in 2013, he was earning $135,200 a year.

In addition, of course, like his brothers and sisters in the Red Chamber, he had a plethora of other entitlements—an office and research budget of about $150,000 a year to pretty much spend as he liked; sixty-four return flights within Canada, business-class don't you know, and unlimited free train travel if he wanted; ordinary expenses for hospitality and meals and the like; and, the source of so darned much confusion for a number of senators, the ability to claim about $20,000 a year in expenses incurred for living in the National Capital Region (or NCR) if their so-called primary residence was more than a hundred klicks from Ottawa.

The purported senator for Prince Edward Island, who had lived by any reckoning most of his adult life in the Ottawa area and still did, nonetheless claimed his P.E.I. cottage as his primary residence, as he was constitutionally required to do, but also immediately began to file for those living-in-the-NCR expenses, which contrary to his professed view, he wasn't required by any law or rule to claim.

Thus did he avail himself heartily of every available dish on offer at this particular public buffet.

By comparison, Vaillancourt earned $287,938 in 2014, or more than double what Duffy would have pulled in as salary alone in his best Senate year. And while the judge enjoys fewer perquisites—as far as it is possible to tell, and suffice to say it is much harder to tell—than senators do, his are far less scrutinized.

And that's the rub, as it were, about "judicial independence," the two words used to erect the necessary and proper barriers between the judiciary and the legislative and executive branches.

You can't have, and no one who values the democracy would want, judges at the mercy of politicians. But judicial independence has come to serve as a shield for the judiciary, not only insulating it from critical analysis (not that there's so much of that going around) but also making it virtually opaque and thus bulletproof—not to mention furthering the notion that judges are somehow *sui generis*, sprung fully formed onto the bench and cut from nobler cloth.

Consider:

Judges, and only judges, hear complaints about judges, via the Canadian Judicial Council, the CJC, which is composed entirely of judges.

Judges control their courtrooms and all their administrative processes.

For the Supreme Court, it's done via their registrar and deputy registrar and a staff of about 210, all of whom are members of the federal public service, and for all other federal judges it's via the Office of the Commissioner for Federal Judicial Affairs Canada (the FJA) through its commissioner, deputy commissioner and a staff of about 70.

(Much the same holds true for provincial judges, with the only fiscal oversight, such as it is, provided by the respective provincial justice ministries, where claims are approved either by the chief justice or ministry staff. Certainly, nowhere in the country are judges' expenses exposed to the harsh public light.)

The FJA also manages the federal judicial appointments secretariat, which in turn administers the seventeen advisory committees across the country that evaluate judge candidates.

It's these judicial advisory committees, or JACs, that put the artificial sheen of impartiality on the judge-picking process. (More about judge-picking later.)

With the CJC, the FJA, the National Judicial Institute— an independent non-profit with a staff of about fifty, the NJI, responsible for judicial education, gets its money from government but its budget is secret—and the Supreme Court Registrar's office, there are at minimum 330 full-time people kept busy with the care and feeding of the federal judiciary.

(Speaking of feeding, the nine Supreme Court justices also have their own chef, at least during the ten months a year the court sits; even senators don't have that. While the chef's salary is confidential, and the judges must pay for the meals, the net cost of the dining room for 2014–2015 was $121,580.)

And while judges' salaries are set by Parliament, there's an independent Judicial Compensation and Benefits Commission, composed of three lawyers (one recommended by the judiciary and one by the justice minister, with the two of them appointing a chair), which at least every four years reviews the salaries and makes recommendations to the government of the day.

The last commission wrote its final report in May 2012; the new one was appointed in December 2015.

The chair of the old one was Brian Levitt, corporate counsel at Osler, Hoskin & Harcourt and chair of the board of the Toronto-Dominion Bank; the other members included Paul Tellier, former president of Bombardier Inc. and before that head honcho at CN and former clerk of the Privy Council, and Mark Siegel, a partner in Gowlings' Ottawa office.

The members of the new one are similarly distinguished; given their accomplishments and probable pay packets, none of them seems likely to be mean-spirited about awarding generous raises.

The Canadian Superior Courts Judges Association, the CJC, the Canadian Bar Association and the Barreau du Québec, of course, all made submissions to the old commission. (Most of the cost of these commissions is borne by the public, with taxpayers picking up all government costs and two thirds of the costs for the lawyers who fight for pay hikes for the judiciary. The three commissioners earn a per diem.)

And where the government may occasionally dare to try to cap judges' salaries in tough times—as lawyers for the Stephen Harper government did in the last round—the commission and the unofficial advocates for judges, which is to say lawyers and their professional associations and law professors, aren't shy about making their displeasure known.

Basically, citing the economic downturn, the government wanted to limit the annual indexing of judicial salaries from a net increase of 7 percent over the four-year period to an increase of 6.1 percent.

The commission, in its final report, went quite mad in its lawyerly way; you would have thought the government was recommending judges eat cat food. Why, it said, such index adjustments were a key part of setting judicial remuneration "without affecting judicial independence" and "as such are not to be lightly tampered with."

It noted, sounding positively Senate-like, that after all, judges' salaries and benefits "constitute a relatively small outlay in the context of total federal government expenditures, being less than $452-million in the 2010–2011 fiscal year," or only about 1.4 percent of the federal deficit.

Federally appointed judges get a removal allowance (if they have to move to take the job), a travelling allowance (for meals, lodging, etc. if they have to temporarily uproot to hear a case in another jurisdiction), reimbursement of expenses incurred while attending conferences and meetings, and as a pension a lovely two thirds of their salaries if they meet the usual requirements of minimum service and age, or a pro-rated one if they don't.

The Supreme Court judges each get a so-called representational allowance—meant for travel and expenses incurred by them or their spouses in discharging their judicial responsibilities—of $18,750 (for the chief justice) and $10,000 (for the others). For security reasons, the chief justice is provided transportation by the RCMP. The eight other justices share, for court-related business, a fleet of five cars, which are replaced every five years. All provincial chief justices and senior judges get similar, if smaller, representational allowances. All of these—at the SCC and superior court levels—are tax free.

All federal judges are also encouraged, according to the CJC, to take what's called "study leave," to spend a year at university. Only judges who have been on the bench a minimum of seven years can apply.

According to the 2006 testimony of David Gourdeau, the former commissioner for federal judicial affairs who was appearing before a Senate committee, judges are "entitled to travel business class, but they are encouraged to fly economy class and in fact most do so."

Gourdeau said the guidelines then in play called for a maximum of $150 a night for accommodation and $85 a day for meals. But these amounts, he said, weren't static and were often adjusted.

According to deputy FJA commissioner Marc Giroux, the meal allowance for 2015 was the same, the hotel rate two hundred dollars a night, more in larger cities. "Judges remain entitled to fly business class," Giroux said in a July 2015 email, "and many still choose to fly economy anyway."

But surely the point is, however carefully judges may handle these allowances, or not, Canadians have no way of knowing. The only accountability is indirect—not from the judges themselves, but from the FJA—and incomplete.

As of April 1, 2015, federal judge salaries were as follows: For Supreme Court Justice Beverley McLachlin, $396,700, and for the other eight SCC justices, $367,300 apiece; for the superior court chief justices across the country, $338,400; and for regular judges, $308,600 a year. It makes for a "comfortable living," as former Supreme Court judge Ian Binnie, writing for the court, modestly described it once in a 2011 paper on judicial independence in Canada.

Yet even the creaky old Senate, where a member's honour and thus his word was for so long held to be good enough, has been posting some financial data online since 2010. Much more information is available now, of course, post–Duffy and the widespread expenses scandal that threatens to consume the Red Chamber.

But if senators have only belatedly and at the point of a gun recognized that saying, "Trust me, I'm the Honourable Member" is no substitute for scrutiny, at least there's some acknowledgement on their part of the need for accountability, grudging and bitter though it is.

Ditto cabinet ministers and high-ranking civil servants in the House of Commons, whose expenses first began appearing publicly online almost a decade earlier.

Yet the same can't be said, even now, for either provincially appointed judges like Vaillancourt or their federally appointed counterparts—the 1,139 judges of the superior courts of every province and territory across the country, the various federal courts, and the Tax Court of Canada.

Judges aren't required to disclose travel claims because they're not considered part of the public service, and the reason for that is, again, judicial independence. And the judiciary's independence, which is guaranteed by the Charter, is inextricably linked to what's called "security of tenure," meaning judges are permanently appointed "during good behaviour" until the age of seventy-five (so they can't just be canned if they annoy a government or PM) and must be adequately paid, because that enhances their independence both from the legislative and executive branches.

The three pillars of security of tenure are as follows, according to what Binnie wrote in that paper. First, judges' salaries can be reduced, frozen or increased, but only through the independent commission, which acts as a firewall between the judiciary and the government, and even then the government must justify any proposed freeze or disagreement; second, direct negotiations between the judiciary and the executive or legislature are verboten; and third, judicial salaries shall not fall below a certain, albeit undefined, minimum level.

(Much of this was determined in three cases, heard as one that is now colloquially known as the "provincial judges reference," at the Supreme Court in 1997. Provincial governments in Manitoba, P.E.I. and Alberta had lowered judges' salaries as part of broad deficit-fighting measures. The SCC majority decided the three governments had breached the Charter because they either didn't consult the provincial salary commissions or they didn't have them.)

What it all means, in practical terms, is that judges are virtually unaccountable except to one another and to the organizations they control. And only the three senior civil servants who administer or govern those organizations—at the Supreme Court, for instance, it's the registrar, at the FJA, the commission and deputy—are even subject to the provisions of so-called proactive disclosure first enacted by the then prime minister, Paul Martin, in December 2003.

"Proactive disclosure" simply means that the expenditures of selected senior government officials, such as ministers, must be publicly and routinely disclosed.

It's the opposite of "reactive disclosure," which refers to what happens when someone, often a reporter but sometimes an activist or citizen, requests information and the government flatly denies it or, usually slowly and reluctantly, provides it, or some of it.

Of the only three senior federal justice officials who are even subject to proactive disclosure, only Roger Bilodeau, a Manitoba-born, Duke University–educated lawyer as well as former law professor and former deputy justice minister in New Brunswick, has had much to declare.

The SCC registrar since 2009, Bilodeau has travelled widely abroad for the court, attending international justice group meetings in Gabon in 2015 (total cost $9,274); and in Singapore and Australia (total cost $20,233) and Brussels and Senegal (another $5,313) in 2014; and, for two related francophone justice organizations, in Paris and Monaco in 2013 (totals $6,177, $5,089 and $6,146); and even charging the taxpayer for the occasional attendance at funerals of unnamed, but undoubtedly deeply worthy, individuals.

(That's a page right out of the Duffy playbook: Whenever there were quasi-notable constituents—or relatives—dying, Duffy was in the death house, on the taxpayers' dime.)

Bilodeau's counterparts at the FJA get around markedly less frequently. Commissioner William Brooks and his deputy, Giroux, file for expenses that are downright frugal.

Neither are judges subject to the prying eyes of the federal ethics commissioner or privacy commissioner. Deliciously, only once in recent memory did Parliament ever come close to even broaching the subject of whether judges might be in some way scrutinized. It happened, of course, completely by accident.

This was in 2003, when then Liberal MP John Bryden misread his government's draft bill on creating an ethics commissioner for public office holders and mistakenly thought it would also encompass the judiciary. This was Bill C-34, which died in November 2003, when the session ended.

But on September 22 that year, the former journalist and author could hardly contain his delight at what he thought he'd found. (In fairness, such bills are written in obfuscating legalese. I misread it exactly the same way.)

"I think this is an enormous forward step because we do know that the judiciary has been almost completely exempt from any kind of scrutiny, other than that done in camera essentially by the judicial council," Bryden burbled happily. ". . . the reality is that there has been little movement in a century toward modernizing the judiciary, making it transparent in the same way as other government institutions have been moving forward in that fashion."

A little later, having discovered he'd completely misunderstood the clause, Bryden stood up to correct the record.

"The judges are exempt from this legislation and from the purview of the ethics commissioner," he said, adding that, "I would say the reason I made the mistake is that it made so much logic to have judges under the scrutiny of the ethics commissioner."

Later still, he was on his feet again, now saying he couldn't understand how judges—or lieutenant-governors or officers of the Library, who were also exempted in the proposed bill— "could be adversely affected because they had some sort of oversight from this place by an officer of Parliament on their standards of behaviour.

"And I come back to the judiciary," Bryden said. "We are all so darn afraid of saying anything about the judiciary, as though judges were some kind of gods. They may be gods in their own mind, but they are human. They do make mistakes and they can be in conflicts of interest. And as I said earlier, it is true that we hear in our constituency offices of judges who have problems and those judges are unreachable."

Worth noting, perhaps, is that Bryden seems to have twigged to his goof all on his own, or via a whisper in his ear. (He doesn't now remember which it was. Certainly, no one from the government—and it was then his government, remember—or any party officially corrected him, and in the House of Commons, they don't tend to be shy about this sort of thing.)

And, the Hansard of the day shows, in the purported discussion about the bill that followed Bryden's remarks, there was nothing of substance said about the judiciary or the apparently radical, if not insane, notion of judges being subject to scrutiny.

And that's the weird thing: that as judicial power has grown in post–Charter Canada—and even those who believe it's a good thing grant that it has done so by leaps and bounds—there's been no matching cry for reform, transparency or accountability.

As Philip Slayton, the unusually cheeky lawyer, Rhodes Scholar and former law clerk at the SCC, said in his 2011 book about the Supreme Court, "broad and troubling transparency issues" remain. "Despite routine genuflections to transparency . . . the justices are secretive about what they do. They are sensitive to criticism. They care very much about what people say about them."

Slayton's book was subtitled "How the Supreme Court of Canada Runs Your Life." And in the end, he pronounces it a good thing that it does, and himself a proponent of an activist court.

"The Supreme Court of Canada is the real opposition to the government," he said. "But an interventionist court, doing this essential job, must be staffed and structured differently, to make what it does tolerable in a true democracy."

So often in recent years have laws passed by Parliament been overturned at the Supreme Court—to mention a few, mandatory minimums for gun crimes, assisted suicide, sentencing discounts for time served in pretrial custody, Senate reform, prostitution and even the former prime minister's choice of Marc Nadon for a vacant SCC seat—that newspapers routinely published "score-cards" of the Harper regime's win-and-loss record there.

Ours is an age of increasing demands for scrutiny—from government at every level, from politicians, police, publicly owned companies and even the mainstream press—yet the courts have escaped the collective notice.

And though judges often position themselves as wholly unable to defend themselves from criticism, the poor lambs, nothing is further from the truth.

Consider what happened to Wally Oppal in 2006.

A former B.C. Supreme Court judge, Oppal was then serving as the province's attorney general, and halfway down in a long story in the *Vancouver Sun* about "slow justice" in the provincial courts, he had posed a mild rhetorical question to the reporter: "Why do we still start trials in the Supreme Court at 10 a.m.?

"The judges will tell you that we have pretrial conferences and pre-hearings. They do that. You know, they do them in Seattle Superior Court at 8:15 in the morning and they start their trials at 9 a.m."

That prompted the then Supreme Court chief justice, Donald Brenner, to send off a snippy email to Oppal, demanding an apology if the story quoted him accurately (it did) or a clarification if it didn't. He called the AG's remarks "incomprehensible" and "a deliberate attempt to demean the judges of this court who work hard every day to see that the litigants before them have their cases heard in a timely fashion."

"You owe the judges of this court an apology," Brenner sniffed. He likely sniffed a good deal more when the *Sun* managed to get a copy of the email.

Oppal, perhaps because he was once one of them and thus was unconcerned about the tenderness of judges' feelings, breezily blew off the chief justice's remarks and told the paper he'd said nothing needing an apology.

Then there are the prothonotaries of the Federal Court of Canada, who are judicial officers, sort of super-clerks who do case management work, though they can handle trials where up to fifty thousand dollars is at stake.

There are six of them, and like judges, they enjoy the protections emanating from the famous "provincial judges reference" case, and so their salaries too must be subject to periodic review by an independent commission.

That happened first in 2008, and when the government disagreed with the report of the "special advisor," who had recommended that the prothonotaries be paid 80 percent of a Federal Court judge's salary (they were then getting 69 percent), the prothos took the matter to the Federal Court.

Their motion to set aside the government response was dismissed on February 11, 2009. So the prothonotaries, aggrieved, appealed the ruling at the Federal Court of Appeal, which also dismissed it.

A second "special advisor" was appointed in 2012, made essentially the same recommendations as the first, and the following year the government made some of the suggested improvements—and boosted the prothos' salary if not quite to the 80 percent they wanted, to 76 percent of a Federal Court judge's salary, or about $218,000 a year.

But now the prothonotaries also wanted more money for the legal fight they'd just waged—another $30,000 for their lawyers on top of the $50,000 the government had already handed over in an *ex gratia* payment.

The government declined.

The point is, these folks know very well how to go to war, thanks for asking.

But the best illustration of how judges, despite the alleged constraints about their not speaking out in their own interests, usually manage to do so, is the 2014 cat fight between the then prime minister, Stephen Harper, and Chief Justice McLachlin.

In the spring of 2013, Supreme Court judge Morris Fish (who was, I feel compelled to point out, a former reporter with the long-defunct *Montreal Star*) was then approaching his seventy-fifth birthday. With his mandatory retirement looming, he announced on April 22 that he would retire effective August 31.

McLachlin met with Harper that day to tell him.

About two months later, members of the all-party selection panel—three Tory MPs, one each from the New Democrats and Liberals, all chosen by their party leaders—were announced. Their job was to go over the so-called long list of six potential names from the government (meaning the PM and the then justice minister, Peter MacKay), consult widely with the usual suspects and whittle down the names to three unranked recommended candidates.

The appointment of Supreme Court judges is the prerogative of the PM, but in recent years, the process has been tweaked to make it look more consultative.

On July 29, the chief justice met the panel members at their invitation to have a gander at the long list. According to the *Globe*'s Sean Fine, McLachlin was troubled by the list because four of the six names, including Marc Nadon's, were from the Federal Court. At the time, it was controversial whether judges from that court were eligible to take one of Quebec's three seats.

Two days later, McLachlin called MacKay's office and the PM's chief of staff, Ray Novak, and then spoke to MacKay directly and, as her office later put it, "made preliminary inquiries to set up a call or meeting with the Prime Minister, but ultimately the Chief Justice decided not to pursue a call or meeting."

Harper's spokesman, however, said that McLachlin had indeed tried to speak to the PM, but that on MacKay's advice, he'd declined to take the call.

It's not quite the same thing, is it?

Did McLachlin decide not to pursue the matter only after the PM wouldn't take her call? Is that not a little bit like a woman saying she refused to go out with a guy who didn't actually call and ask her?

Anyway, it wasn't until the following May, after the Supreme Court ruled six to one that Nadon's appointment was unconstitutional, that the matter blew up in the press.

The conflagration was sparked when John Ivison of the *National Post* inquired of the SCC if, as he'd been told, McLachlin had "lobbied against Justice Nadon's appointment."

Ivison then wrote a story quoting unnamed Conservatives unhappy in general about the court, and in particular about what they saw as McLachlin's interference in the appointment process.

The PMO released a statement, making it clear McLachlin's advice wasn't welcome and saying, "Neither the Prime Minister nor the Minister of Justice would ever call a sitting judge on a matter that is or may be before the court." The inference was sharp: McLachlin shouldn't be calling them, either.

That in turn led to the statement from McLachlin's former executive legal officer, Owen Rees, a lawyer on leave from the boutique litigation firm of Stockwoods, in Toronto, where he is a partner. The chief justice, Rees said in a news release on May 2, 2014, wanted only "to flag the potential issue" with Federal Court nominations, not with Nadon's in particular. She certainly "did not express any views on the merit of the issue," he said.

But Rees also told the CBC that "the question concerning the eligibility of a Federal Court judge for appointment to the Supreme Court . . . was well known."

It was also a classic judge-ly move to say she was only flagging an issue, not commenting upon it: When you're the chief justice, the flag *is* the comment, in some real measure.

And the government, whether because of McLachlin's heads-up or not, hired Binnie, the former Supreme Court judge, for an opinion on whether a Federal Court judge was eligible for a Quebec seat, and he replied with a resounding yes, an opinion later shared by another retired SCC judge, Louise Charron, and the renowned constitutional expert Peter Hogg.

The question, in other words, may now be deemed legally settled, but the argument rages on.

In the end, the spot on the Supreme Court remained vacant for a year, until Harper—this time without bothering with a selection panel, a shortlist or a public hearing in Parliament— named Quebec Court of Appeal judge Clement Gascon to the seat in June 2014. He started that October.

But the PM's suggestion that McLachlin had inappropriately called MacKay and sought to speak to him was enough to incite outrage across the land among lawyers.

Fred Headon, then the president of the Canadian Bar Association, spoke out about it at a conference.

The Advocates' Society publicly released a letter it sent the PM, saying, "there is no substance" to the government's allegation. "The comments at issue here," the letter continued, "can only serve to undermine the respect and confidence of ordinary Canadians in the proper administration of justice, and we therefore urge you to make a public statement advising Canadians that the chief justice did not conduct herself inappropriately in any way."

The heads of legal bloggers blew up, some dutifully repeating the mantra that "Chief Justice McLachlin can't publicly respond to Stephen Harper's allegations."

But, in fact, McLachlin *did* respond, if not directly.

Owen Rees may have been her executive legal officer, but he was also perfectly capable of acting as her spokesman, and indeed that's part of the job. The chief justice was hardly muzzled. Her views were made perfectly clear and, as ever with the bar and bench both, with the usual gobsmacking condescension.

As Rees's press release put it, after referencing the media reports—that is, Ivison's story—and prior to laying out McLachlin's view, "The facts are as follows."

It was a classic of the legally trained: They're the ones who will set the record straight. They're the ones who will decide the facts. They must always be the smartest folks in any given room.

What's more, the orthodoxy of Canadian opinion—what Western University law professor Robert Martin calls "the ideology of a small and unrepresentative clique" that he says is so dominant it's essentially a secular state religion—virtually ensures that McLachlin, and most any of her fellows on that bench or any other, will always be slavishly defended.

So here we all are, living in the age of transparency—police forces under pressure to equip every officer with a video camera and citizens with their iPhones at the ready to film any wrong-doing; Edward Snowden leaking classified secrets; the hacktivist group Anonymous threatening to expose ever more sinners; voices everywhere demanding even more openness from corporations, governments, charities, every imaginable institution—and yet, somehow, judges have remained a class apart, exempt, unexamined and, most startling, almost completely unquestioned.

The reason for that, Slayton says in *Mighty Judgment*, is in part what he sees as the widespread Canadian inclination to forelock-tugging. As he put it once, "Canadian deference to authority and excessive respect for judicial mystique must be overcome."

In other words, too many Canadians are too much like I used to be.

It isn't just about reforming the Supreme Court and it certainly isn't just about making judicial expenses publicly available. It's everything about the judiciary and it's all courts—even the six lonely but aggrieved prothonotaries (remember them?).

Financial transparency is the least of it, but it is part of it. A federal prosecutor once told me—and he was quoting a colleague but I think the quote is original—"The justice system is the means by which the upper class pays the middle a good living wage to keep the lower classes in check." By "middle," the prosecutor meant the police.

But I think a more accurate and surely a more Canadian interpretation is that judges and their most senior advocates, those lawyers with the best pedigrees and most impeccable connections, are the upper class, other lawyers are the middle class, and the rest of us—not legally trained and thus without that special jelly—are the bottom rung, sufficiently in their thrall that, much of the time, we don't see them through the glasses with which we view the rest of the world. We just aren't as critical of them.

It's not as though judges return the favour by being equally tolerant of the failings of the citizenry, the police or even the bar.

An accused person who doesn't show up for court may find there's now a bench warrant for his arrest. A police officer or civvy witness who's late will at least be reamed out. A hapless citizen who dares offend the bench by having his cell ring will be glared at, if not asked to leave.

One hot July day four years ago in a Newmarket provincial court north of Toronto, a prosecutor who was about seven minutes late getting back to court after the morning recess—on this one occasion, apparently, time mattered—found that in his brief absence the judge had had a hissy fit and dismissed the remaining thirty-three criminal charges left on the list. That was Howard Chisvin of the Ontario Court.

The poor prosecutor, Brian McCallion, apologized and attempted to explain what had happened—he'd been in his office, reading a report for one of the scheduled cases, and thus missed the page to court because pages aren't heard in Crown attorney offices.

"That might be," Chisvin said haughtily. "Court comes when court is back."

In the end, charges had to be re-laid, one case went to the Court of Appeal, and the Ontario Judicial Council received three complaints about Chisvin's high-handedness.

One of these was from the attorney general's ministry, and another from a member of the public who was also a lawyer. But the third came from the sleeping giant that is the Canadian public, in the form of two ordinary Joes who made a joint complaint.

After a hearing, during which Chisvin admitted misconduct and was remorseful, an OJC panel found that this had been, in effect, a one-off for him, and settled on a reprimand, with a warning that if things were to go south again, Chisvin could be in big trouble.

Then, of course, the judiciary having perfected chutzpah if not invented it, Chisvin and his lawyer, Brian Greenspan, asked for his legal costs—$43,241.99 worth.

The panel, bless its heart, declined to pay, saying that while the judge was to be commended for facing up to his misconduct, the fact was, it was misconduct, and "it is our view that the public purse should not be required to bear the cost of his legal representation."

A day of reckoning is coming, though not in the way you might expect, and judges and lawyers have only themselves to blame for not changing with the times—and by times, I mean of course the last century.

They work for us, after all, not the other way around.

R v ABREHA

*"Gentlemen of the jury, the facts of this distressing
and important case have already been put before you
some four or five times, twice by prosecuting counsel,
twice by counsel for the defence, and once at least by
each of the various witnesses who have been heard.*

*"But so low is my opinion of your understanding that
I think it necessary, in the simplest language, to tell
you the facts again."*

—THE FICTITIOUS JUSTICE SWALLOW ADDRESSES
THE JURY IN A.P. HERBERT'S *UNCOMMON LAW*

THERE'S SOMETHING ABOUT the formal arraignment of an accused person in Canada that still stirs my blood, cynical and crabby as I am.

By this point, days, weeks or months of pretrial motions—mostly aimed at kicking out contested evidence and keeping it from the jury—are in the rear-view mirror.

The geography of the field of play, the boundaries placed around the evidence by the judge, have been decided: The case is the case.

Twelve jurors have been picked, or as is more common now in long and complex Canadian trials, twelve and two alternates.

The registrar stands and reads aloud the most brilliant paragraph:

"Accused, look upon the jury.

"Jury, look upon the accused and hearken to his charge.

"He stands indicted by the name of Bill Smith, that on May 21, 2011, in the City of Red Deer in the County of Red Deer, did unlawfully murder Mary Smith contrary to the Criminal Code of Canada.

"Upon this indictment, he hath been arraigned, upon his arraignment, he hath pleaded not guilty, and for his trial he has put himself upon his country, which country you are.

"Your charge is to inquire whether he is guilty or not guilty, and to hearken to the evidence."

Not once upon hearing this have my eyes failed to well up.

For pure excitement, it can't compare to the moments much later on, such as when we in the press first get word there's a verdict and tear off to the courtroom, hearts pounding, or when the jurors file in and we try to read them—*Are they looking at the accused? Do they seem wrung out or serene? Do we still think Nos. 2 and 7 are shagging?*—or when the judge asks the accused to stand and the jury foreperson gets to his or her feet and reads aloud the verdict.

But for me the arraignment is electric.

It isn't just the archaic language I love, but the noble idea underlying it: Whoever he is, the poor S.O.B. who is the accused now officially has put his fate in the hands of this disparate group of strangers, this unknowable mixed bag of his fellow citizens.

They are his country, and he has entrusted them with nothing less than his liberty.

The thing is, they rarely let him down.

For all the passing irritation I've felt over the years about particular juries—chiefly, why are they taking so bloody long?—it's clear that the great majority of people approach the job seriously, which is also, of course, sometimes why they take so long to make a decision.

As a former *Globe and Mail* colleague, Kirk Makin, once remarked, you can actually see jurors growing into the gravity of the job.

They noticeably up the quality of the going-to-court wardrobe; they adopt the inscrutable mien of the impartial observer, even as they hear or watch terrible evidence; they begin looking down their noses at members of the media—the TV folks—they were, on day one, pleased as punch to recognize.

And despite old and enduring concerns about juries—not least, that because their deliberations are by law secret, so is their reasoning or lack of it—the system is still held in remarkably high regard.

As an aside, I have to say I think not having a clue about the jury's reasoning may be a blessing.

After the very long and intense trial of serial killer Paul Bernardo ended, in a move that was in my experience unprecedented, some of the jurors invited some of the regular reporters out for an off-the-record dinner.

We honoured their ground rules of course, and they honoured the sanctity of what had gone on in their jury room. But I was a little shaken nonetheless by the glimpses we got into their thought processes, and in particular by how wholly some had bought into the vision of Bernardo's wife, Karla Homolka, as a helpless victim.

All in all, I'd rather have remained blissfully ignorant and let them continue to live large in my imagination, as the bright and fair-minded repositories of all that is good and wise they once had been. What many Canadians may not realize is how close the jury system came in the past few years to being changed beyond recognition, if not ruined, and how vulnerable, for very different reasons, it remains.

About seven years ago, a new multi-headed issue came to the fore—the composition of juries and whether they are sufficiently representative of their communities, particularly in parts of Ontario with large Aboriginal populations; just what "representative" ought to look like anyway, and whether the authorities, notably Crown attorneys and police in a few jurisdictions, were improperly "vetting" jurors beforehand.

The vetting consisted of background checks about prospective jurors, sometimes with prosecutors even informally asking around of local cops to determine if any candidates, for instance, were considered "disreputable," an alarmingly broad description that would certainly capture many of us, depending on who was doing the defining.

If it's doubtful whether such canvassing ought to have been done in the first place, it's not debatable that the results of it, whatever they were, ought to have been formally disclosed to defence counsel. And they weren't.

As a result of a brouhaha about this in the press in 2009, the practice of vetting itself was pretty quickly stopped in its tracks.

A number of convictions were appealed, mostly unsuccessfully; the provincial information and privacy commissioner investigated the breach of the potential jurors' privacy rights and the extent of the problem (it was confined to a handful of jurisdictions) and ordered Crown prosecutors to cease and desist, and the Juries Act was amended.

But that's not where it ended, not by a long shot. As is so often the case in this country, root causes, and their root causes, had to be explored and fully aired.

In August 2011, the Ontario government appointed Frank Iacobucci, a retired Supreme Court judge, to review the broader, bigger question of First Nations' representation on Ontario juries.

He reported back in February 2013. It's too lengthy a report to summarize here, but suffice to say that unsurprisingly, given his mandate and those he consulted, Iacobucci concluded the justice system was failing Aboriginal Ontarians in every imaginable way, and his report arrived just in time for it to be deemed "fresh evidence" in a case then being considered at the Ontario Court of Appeal.

That case involved an Aboriginal man named Clifford Kokopenace from the Grassy Narrows First Nation, near Kenora in northwestern Ontario.

He was convicted of manslaughter in 2008 in the stabbing death of a friend. At the appeal court, his lawyer alleged that Kokopenace's Charter rights—two of them in particular: the one, to a trial by a fair and impartial tribunal, the other, where the potential jail sentence is more than five years, to a jury trial—had been violated because his jury came from a jury roll that didn't guarantee Aboriginal representation.

Though Aboriginal people then made up about 32 percent of the adult population in the Kenora area, only 29 of 699 potential jurors were from local First Nation reserves, and none of them made it onto the actual jury itself.

Two members of the three-judge panel, Harry LaForme, who was the first Aboriginal to be appointed to a Canadian appellate court, and the now-retired Stephen Goudge, tossed the conviction and ordered a new trial, with LaForme even hinting that perhaps the Crown in its wisdom might decline to proceed with one.

Fortunately, the Crown in its wisdom appealed to the Supreme Court, and a good thing too, because had the Kokopenace decision been left alone, it would have meant sweeping change, so nothing less than the future of the jury system hung in the balance.

Only in May 2015 at the Supreme Court was the question of what constitutes fair representation finally determined. There, led by Justice Michael Moldaver, the majority found that while the state must make reasonable efforts to ensure a representative jury, no one is entitled to a perfect jury or even one that exactly reflects the makeup of the accused's particular community.

In other words, accused people—whether gay, black, of Maltese or Irish origin, transgendered, born-again Christians, Orthodox Jews, Muslims, disabled, etc.—aren't owed a jury that perfectly represents them, in their exact proportions, in their city or town.

What an accused is entitled to, what we're all entitled to, is a jury fairly chosen, period; the view from the prisoner's box to the jury box isn't supposed to be just like looking in the mirror.

The LaForme decision had imposed an enormously high standard that would have required Ontario to "actively encourage" responses from reserve residents by investigating and addressing other causes of their marked lack of interest (disengagement with the justice system, cynicism, racism, the effects of residential schools, etc.) and to engage band leaders on a government-to-government basis.

Jury rolls are prepared by provincial officials, and in Ontario, it's done using Municipal Property Assessment Corporation lists.

It works much the same in other parts of the country: In Manitoba, officials use Manitoba Health numbers; in British Columbia, rolls are prepared using voters' lists; in Nova Scotia, names are randomly picked from Health Registration lists; in Saskatchewan, they use computerized hospitalization records, etc.

In Ontario, where property assessment lists don't cover reserves, the Juries Act developed a separate process—putting the responsibility for gathering names on the local sheriff (or a designate) and telling him or her to treat the reserves as if they were municipalities.

Questionnaires are sent out to the number of people—their names drawn from either the property assessment list or from lists of band members—that officials estimate will be required for the following year's trials. From the completed forms that are returned—and the Juries Act purports to require citizens to do this—the names of potential jurors are randomly selected for the various jury pools, or arrays. And from these pools, both petit juries and trial juries are selected.

It's this representativeness that gives the jury its legitimacy as the "conscience of the community."

But by 2008, the rate of return of completed questionnaires for reserves in the Kenora district, never as high as for non-Aboriginal communities, was only 10 percent.

The de facto sheriff at the time, a trial coordinator named Laura Loohuizen, made what the SCC called "repeated and escalating efforts over the years" to get updated lists from the reserves—doubling the number of questionnaires sent out, consulting local First Nation leaders, sending follow-up letters and visiting fifteen remote reserves herself to make clear to band leaders that the province was serious about including more Aboriginal people on jury lists.

In one instance, Loohuizen wrote to forty-two local chiefs, seeking updated lists of residents; all of four responded. The lack of cooperation was staggering.

Moldaver said the two appeal judges—and his own colleague on the Supreme Court, Thomas Cromwell, who wrote the dissenting opinion there, supported by Chief Justice McLachlin—used the wrong definition of "representativeness."

They defined it in relation to the ultimate makeup of the jury roll, as opposed to the method used to compile it.

Nonsense, said Moldaver, it's the fairness and good-faith effort of the process that is guaranteed by the Charter, not the result.

He explained that he was not suggesting for a minute "that the state should not take action on this pressing social problem" of Aboriginal estrangement from the justice system, only that a jury trial wasn't the appropriate vehicle for the job.

The right to a representative jury, he said, "is not a mechanism for repairing the damaged relationship between particular societal groups and our criminal justice system more generally—and it should not be tasked with that responsibility."

And just how would the state go about discovering a prospective juror's race, ethnicity, sexual identity, religion and the like, anyway? Moldaver asked.

He predicted disaster.

Presumably, he said, defence counsel would be "permitted to access the source lists and the jury roll at the outset of every trial. He or she could then argue that the roll is unrepresentative if any group's rate of inclusion does not approximate its percentage of the broader population—assuming we could somehow solve the impenetrable problem of what groups we are talking about.

"The effect of this is two-fold," Moldaver said. "First, it would create a procedural quagmire at the outset of jury trials. Second, if a jury roll is found to be unrepresentative, it cannot be used for any trial—and each judicial district has only a single jury roll for a calendar year."

And any requirement for proportionate representation, he said, "would also do away with well-established principles, such as juror privacy and random selection."

Adopting the "expanded view of representativeness risks compromising, if not crippling, the ability to proceed with jury trials throughout the country."

A former defence lawyer himself, Moldaver could see clearly down a road that surely would become well travelled.

He said that before long "the jury selection process would become a public inquiry into the historical and cultural wrongs and damaged relationships between particular societal groups and our criminal justice system and the failings of the state to take adequate steps to address them.

"In turn, this would make it virtually impossible to have a jury trial anywhere in this country—and the administration of criminal justice would suffer a devastating blow."

It's a brilliant decision that got remarkably little attention—beyond sorrowful regret from the usual quarters—given its ramifications. For my dough, Moldaver ought to be known as the judge who saved juries.

The best evidence that they're worth saving is the fact that the jury trial remains mandatory for those who are charged with murder. For its biggest and most important criminal cases, in other words, the state insists that trial be by judge and jury.

While the right to a jury trial can be waived by the accused person in most cases—it's an option only for those charged with indictable offences that carry a potential prison sentence of five years or more—murder is the exception.

If it seems counter-intuitive that the state can insist it knows what's best for someone charged with murder and force upon someone a jury trial, it reflects the public interest in justice and aligns with the traditional view that trial by jury provides the purest justice.

For less serious indictable offences, and what are called summary conviction offences, the accused has no choice at all and is tried by judge alone.

This is hardly to say juries are perfect; how could they be?

In fact, there are some spectacular examples of juror dopiness, where cases have gone off the rails or almost done so because of a single juror.

Many of these cases are recent, and at first blush, most have to do with social media and jurors' inability to recognize that for however long a given trial lasts, they must stay off the web and refrain from commenting upon the proceedings or acting like a private detective.

In truth, the responsibility for these train-wreck trials has at least as much to do with the judiciary's failure to spell out the rules and the rationale for them in plain English, a dialect with which some judges have only passing familiarity.

It used to be that judges would several times during a trial remind jurors, in a pro forma sort of way, that they weren't to read or watch media coverage of the case or discuss it with their family and friends. Now, if they're on the ball, judges will explicitly tell them not to produce their *own* coverage—that is, no blogging, no Facebook, no Instagram or Twitter, etc.—and no discussing the case with the world at large.

As of 2012, the Canadian Judicial Council's model jury instructions—these are guidelines for judges written by their peers—tell judges to specifically warn jurors not to tweet or text, not to do Internet research about the case and not to blog or post anything online about the trial.

And yet, for the fully modern being, not being able to tweet or otherwise "share"—feelings, opinions, thoughts, jokes, links to cat videos or pictures of dinner—for even an hour is akin to eternal exile in the desert, and hence in part the rising tide of juror-caused mistrials across the planet.

As retired Florida circuit judge Ralph Artigliere wrote in a 2011 paper published in the *Drake Law Review*, "There is a landslide of juror misconduct nationwide in spite of admonitions from judges."

He gave plenty of examples—the juror in a capital murder trial in Pennsylvania who looked up and shared information about retinal detachment on the web and caused a mistrial; the Florida foreman who searched the meaning of "prudent" on his phone and showed his fellows during deliberations, which saw a first-degree murder conviction overturned on appeal; the jurors in another Florida case who made phone calls and texted during their deliberations and caused a mistrial.

As Argliere wrote, ". . . judges and lawyers nationwide are struggling to catch up with a culture that is more independent, more plugged in and less deferential to authority than traditional jurors."

A Reuters Legal analysis done in 2010 found that jurors' adventures on the Internet have "resulted in dozens of mistrials, appeals and overturned verdicts in the last two years" in the United States.

Over a three-week period during that November and December, Reuters monitored Twitter, reading tweets that showed up when "jury duty" was typed into the site's search engine. Tweets from people describing themselves as sitting or potential jurors "popped up at the astounding rate of one nearly every three minutes," Reuters's Brian Grow reported.

And while many were simple complaints about being bored— we collectively appear to have turned into large toddlers, with attention spans to match—"a significant number included blunt statements about defendants' guilt or innocence."

"Looking forward to a not guilty verdict regardless of evidence," read one message Grow quoted. Another juror tweeted: "Jury duty is a blow. I've already made up my mind. He's guilty. LOL."

In a case in Maryland, the corruption trial of a former Baltimore mayor (she eventually resigned as part of a plea deal), the sixty-five-year-old judge found that five jurors had become Facebook friends.

He brought them in for a hearing.

Afterwards, a young male juror posted on his Facebook page, "Fuck the judge."

When the judge then called him on that, the young man told him, "Hey judge, that's just Facebook stuff."

It isn't happening just in the United States. There are some stellar made-in-Canada examples, too.

In the case of *R v Dowholis*, it was Juror No. 12, a Toronto radio producer and sometime on-air personality named Derek Welsman.

Joshua Dowholis was accused of aggravated sexual assault and forcible confinement against four men. The assaults followed encounters at a gay bathhouse downtown; Dowholis would ply the men with crystal meth and then invite them back to his flat.

Because the trial necessarily would touch upon sexual activity between gay men, potential jurors were "challenged for cause," which means they were questioned about any potential bias against homosexuals. Welsman didn't indicate any.

Superior Court judge Faye McWatt gave the standard cautions—the basic don't-discuss-the-case-outside-the-jury-room.

On September 27, 2013, the jurors—many apparently visibly upset—returned with a verdict and convicted Dowholis on three counts of aggravated sexual assault and two of unlawful confinement.

Standing to deliver the guilty verdict was Welsman, who had been chosen as the jury foreman.

Only about two weeks later did Dowholis's lawyer, Kathryn Wells, hear from his client's mother, who told him people had told her they'd heard a jury member on the radio "bashing" about the case.

By October 11, Wells and the prosecutor had tracked down and listened to a radio podcast from September 20, while the trial was going on, wherein Welsman was featured live as a guest on the Dean Blundell show, which Welsman also produced, on 102.1 FM, or "The Edge" as the station bills itself.

Welsman didn't name the accused or specify the trial, but talked all around it: He expressed distaste at having to "sniff" evidence and referred to "butt love" and "disease." At one point, Welsman even asked "psychic Nikki," another guest, what the jury's verdict would be, and they all had a good laugh about the jury being "hung."

Then the Crown discovered there had been a second segment on the show about the trial, on September 30, the Monday after the verdict.

That time, Welsman had told Blundell that where a big Friday night for him might be going out for dinner with his wife and kids before hitting the sack, "a certain segment of our population that will do similar things . . . but instead of going to bed, they say, 'You know, I should go to a gay bathhouse and have sex with six hundred people.' . . . And that was the world that I had to delve into for three weeks."

It wasn't quite as outlandish as the behaviour of one Kasim Davey, a twenty-one-year-old juror on a child sex assault case in London, England, who in 2013 wrote on Facebook, "Wooow I wasn't expecting to be in a jury Deciding on a paedophile's fate, I've always wanted to F★★★ up a paedophile & now I'm within the law."

Davey, who admitted he'd just been seeking attention, was booted off the jury; it was a little late to do that with Welsman.

Welsman's on-air comments didn't lead to a mistrial—McWatt declined to hold an inquiry into his conduct or call him in for questioning since the verdict was long done by the time his transgressions came to light and there was no evidence he'd influenced the other jurors—but Dowholis's lawyer plans to appeal the conviction.

Regardless, running his mouth off cost Welsman dearly.

In the wake of critical press stories (including a couple by me) and the predictable online backlash, Dean Blundell ended up apologizing on air for them both. Some short time later, Corus Radio axed the show, and Welsman and Blundell were out of a job.

Then there was the Jennifer Pan trial, held in Newmarket, Ontario, just a little north of Toronto, and spread out over almost a year.

On November 8, 2010, in the nearby suburb of Markham, there appeared to have been a horrific home invasion: A woman was killed, her husband left for dead, and weeping, almost incoherent on a 911 call, was a purported survivor, the couple's twenty-four-year-old daughter, who said she'd been tied up on the second floor and listened as armed intruders shot her parents.

This was Jennifer Pan.

With four men, the so-called robbers, she was accused of first-degree murder in the slayings of her mother, Bich Ha Pan, and attempted murder in the wounding of her father, Huei Hann Pan. Pan and three of her co-accused were subsequently convicted; the fourth will be tried separately.

But during the Pan trial, the wife of one of the jurors regularly came to court and was texting her husband, juror No. 4.

While most of her comments were innocuous—she gave him a thoughtful heads-up, for instance, that an upcoming witness had big breasts—a couple weren't.

On July 11, 2014, as the Crown case was drawing to a close, the jury sent Ontario Superior Court judge Cary Boswell a note, telling him what had been going on.

Boswell immediately questioned each juror—including No. 4, who said it was his flat refusal to discuss the case with his wife that prompted her to show up in the first place—and satisfied himself that the fairness of the trial hadn't been damaged.

"This texting incident aside," Boswell said in a written decision, juror "conduct has been exemplary."

And over such a long trial—it was then already three months behind schedule—Boswell said it would be naive to imagine jurors were wholly insulated either from media coverage or the prying questions of family and friends.

What the court must rely upon, he concluded, was not the complete severance of jurors from the world at large, but rather "their sworn oaths to be impartial. . . . This is about recognizing that they—all twelve—remain committed to justice and fairness."

The judge dismissed the applications for a mistrial, and banned the wife—who also had begun acting as a self-appointed cheerleader for the police and Crown until a detective reported her—from the courtroom.

Still, all these instances pale in comparison to two notorious English cases, one of which ended with a juror being jailed for her online conduct.

Joanne Fraill was a juror in a multi-million-dollar drugs trial in Manchester in 2010. It was a big deal involving multiple defendants, an allegedly corrupt police officer, one high-profile gangster, and charges of conspiracy to supply heroin and amphetamines.

Among those charged was a woman named Jamie Sewart.

When the prosecution opened on May 26, Judge Peter Lakin gave the jury explicit instructions on staying away from the web, saying in part, "Most of us these days have access to the internet; it contains lots of fascinating information, some about the criminal justice system and some about specific criminal offences. . . .

"Please do not go on the 'net during this trial to explore any issues which may arise. That would be wrong."

And he explained why: Jurors must base their decision solely on what they hear in the courtroom.

The jury retired on July 28 to consider its verdicts, and over the ensuing days, delivered some, mostly acquittals, on a number of charges.

By August 2, Sewart had been cleared of all three charges against her, though the jurors were still deliberating the fates of others.

That's when Fraill, who'd set up a Facebook account in the name of Jo Smilie, sent an email message to Sewart's Facebook, saying, "You should know me, I cried with you enough," and submitted a friend request.

Sewart recognized a picture of Fraill as one of Smilie's purported friends, knew she was dealing with one of the jurors who had acquitted her, and responded.

The two then had a nice juicy chat in the pig English of the web, with Sewart at one point asking "what's happenin with the other charge?" and Fraill replying, "cant get anywanone to go either no one budging pleeeeese don't say anthing cause Jamie they could call mmistrial and I will get 4cked toO."

At another point, Fraill said, "don't worry about that chge no way it can stay hung for me lol."

After the conversation, Sewart had second thoughts and wisely told her lawyer what had happened, who notified trial counsel, who told Judge Lakin, who promptly called in the jurors one by one for questioning.

When Fraill's turn came—she was Juror No. 8—she confessed all, was charged with contempt of court and released on bail.

Judge Lakin dismissed the remaining jurors.

The extent of Fraill's contact with Sewart and her Internet forays were investigated—she'd also searched out information on the central accused gangster as well as other defendants—and while a diary she handed over to police detailed her conduct and offered an explanation (she said she'd felt badly for Sewart and wanted her to know she wished her well), she denied trying to pervert the course of justice.

The matter was heard in London on June 14, 2011, in the High Court of Justice before a three-member panel composed of the lord chief justice and justices Duncan Ouseley and Timothy Holroyde.

Fraill was sentenced to eight months—she gasped in shock and wept of course—and was expected actually to serve half of that behind bars. (Sewart, who was also charged, received a two-month sentence, but it was suspended for two years and, as the court said, "if nothing further is heard," it would lapse.)

Fraill was the first juror in the U.K. to be prosecuted for contempt of court for using the web.

Still, for sheer gall, nothing beats the November 2008 case of an unidentified woman who was a juror in a child abduction and sex assault case in Burnley, a town in Lancashire, north of Manchester.

Three local men were on trial for various offences, including child abduction, sexual activity with a girl of fourteen and sexual assault.

When the jury retired to deliberate, the woman posted the following on her Facebook page: "I don't know which way to go, so I'm holding a poll."

Some of her Facebook pals, unsurprisingly, came back with guilty verdicts.

(This squares with my own experience of online comments during a trial, in that the less informed about a case people are, the surer they are that the accused is guilty and should hang, at least figuratively.)

Anyway, the woman was given the heave-ho, leaving eleven jurors to soldier on. They acquitted the three men.

Though she was investigated for possible contempt of court, a spokesman for Burnley Crown Court said no action would be taken against her.

Three years later, Joanne Fraill wasn't as lucky.

The High Court judges began their eight-page decision by saying, "This is a troublesome case and, we must do our best to ensure, an exceptional case."

They pointed out that "there is nothing new about the proposition that a juror may be in contempt of court" and noted that "as long ago as the reign of Henry VII, jurors were fined both for disobedience to the orders of the judges and also for discussions by one of them about the case they were trying with an external party."

The basic problem is ancient as well as international, in other words.

Defence and prosecution must know the case they face, and the use by jurors of extra-judicial material not in evidence— however it arrives, online or in the morning papers—"offends our long-held belief that justice requires that both sides in a criminal trial should know and be able to address or answer any material which may influence the verdict. . . .

"We are aware that reference to the Internet is inculcated as a matter of habit into many members of the community, and no doubt that habit will grow.

"We must however be entirely unequivocal.

"We emphasize . . . that if jurors make their own inquiries into aspects of the trials with which they are concerned, the jury system as we know it, so precious to the administration of criminal justice in this country, will be seriously undermined and what is more, the public confidence on which it depends will be shaken . . .

"The revolution in methods of communication cannot change these essential principles.

"The problem therefore is not the Internet: the potential problems arise from the activities of jurors who disregard the long established principles which underpin the right of every citizen to a fair trial."

The retired Florida judge Ralph Artigliere came to much the same conclusion in *The Florida Bar Journal* of January 2010: With connectedness no longer a convenience but "a way of life or an ingrained lifestyle" if not actually an addiction, courts had better figure out how to deal with it, and fast.

And sanctions against wayward jurors, as with Fraill's contempt of court prosecution, aren't a cure-all, though they're probably part of the fix for the most outrageous offenders.

In America, courts have tried banning smartphones (at least while court is sitting and during deliberations); sequestering jurors for the whole kit and caboodle (but that's a gross inconvenience for citizens already giving their time, and expensive to the system too); and in a few jurisdictions, using pre-recorded videotaped trials, or PRVTTs, in a bid to shorten trials and thus minimize temptation.

In a PRVTT, witness testimony is pre-recorded and edited by the judge before jurors see it. Things move along more quickly, but the worry is that too much is lost in the translation from live to recorded testimony.

But the real and better fix, Robbie Manhas, then a law student at the University of Michigan, wrote in 2014 in the *Michigan Law Review*, is recognizing that juror "ignorance and passivity" does not equal "impartiality."

He examined a 2012 U.S. case where a juror had researched the word "sponsor"; it was a cockfighting case where the statute in question prohibited "sponsoring" an animal in a fighting venture.

The jury convicted the defendants, but when it was discovered later that the juror had done his own research and shared the fruits of his labour with his fellows, the convictions were vacated and a new trial ordered.

Imagine, Manhas wrote, how much trouble and expense could have been avoided if the juror "had simply been allowed to ask the parties or the court for clarification on the definition of 'sponsor.'"

And why not allow jurors to ask questions themselves—of witnesses, and, Manhas suggested, of the lawyers and judge? Why not build a court-maintained online electronic record of the trial and allow jurors access to it?

"Both examples channel juror activity in a way that quells the desire to go outside the system to get information," he said.

It might also tend to make jurors more active and engaged decision makers.

But it's unusual, in both the U.S. and Canada, for jurors to ask questions during a trial. In most jurisdictions in both countries, it's theoretically permitted, but hardly encouraged, and in this country is rendered as cumbersome as possible.

A curious juror must raise his or her hand (as elementary school kids do when they have to go to the loo), put the question on paper and submit it in an envelope to a court constable, who gives it to the judge, who then opens it and discusses it with counsel in the absence of the jury and decides if it will be answered and how.

Contrast this to the coroner's inquest system in several provinces, where jurors ask questions throughout the hearing and have done so for years, without either the sky falling or the system getting hopelessly bogged down.

Yet the courts, as ever, are uber-cautious.

For instance, Ontario Court of Appeal judge David Watt in his unofficial judicial bible, *Watt's Manual of Criminal Jury Instructions*, suggests judges tell jurors they can ask questions if they follow the proper procedure.

But Watt also urges them to say such things as, "In most cases, however, it is not necessary for jurors to ask questions . . ." and "You don't have to ask questions" and "It is best to leave the presentation of the evidence to Crown and defence counsel . . ."

Ditto the Canadian Judicial Council's model jury instructions, where the message is much the same: "It's not the role of jurors to conduct the trial. It is your duty to consider the evidence that is presented, not to decide which questions the witnesses should be asked or how to ask them."

From memory, I've seen jurors ask questions—outside of deliberations, when they're much more free to do so, and usually, thanks to a judge's obfuscating charge, have a far greater need—only once, at the 2014 trial of Luka Magnotta, when they were allowed three questions of an expert witness, a forensic psychiatrist.

In truth, a good chunk of the responsibility for both juror bewilderment and juror web excursions properly belongs with the rules and practices that infantilize jurors, and with judges, whose instructions tend to the wordy and condescending.

I covered a terrorism trial in 2015 where the judge took three days to "charge" the jury. In the 2016 trial of a Toronto Police constable, the judge took two whole days to instruct jurors, then, after hearing complaints from the lawyers, devoted another morning to re-instructing them. He said *reasonable* so many times—"reasonable belief," "reasonable grounds," "reasonable doubt," "reasonable police officer"—that my ears nearly bled, and not unreasonably.

Such instructions now routinely run to several hundred pages, such that if jurors weren't confused when the judge begins talking, they certainly will be by the time he or she stops—if they've managed to stay awake.

Coincidentally, in a different 2015 case, where the judge took a full day and two hundred pages to give jurors their marching orders, Moldaver at the Supreme Court availed himself of the chance to bemoan such lengthy and complicated charges.

"I feel obliged to comment on the detrimental impact that increasingly long and complex jury charges are having on our criminal justice system," he wrote for the majority in *R v Rodgerson*.

"Rote, repetitive and generic charges are of little value, and are often harmful to the jury's comprehension," Moldaver said. "Indeed, they can and do lead to instruction that is all but meaningless."

A judge's job, Moldaver said baldly, is to "decant and simplify," not cloud and complicate the works or shovel truckloads of legal jargon at jurors.

As a Prairie lawyer once told me, having just finished a date-rape trial, "I swear, the charge to the jury took longer to deliver than the time it took the jury to deliberate." In less than two hours they came back with an acquittal.

"Interestingly," he said, "I got the impression the jury was not wanting all of the coddling, super-simplification, decision trees, etc."

A friend of mine was a juror on a high-profile case in Toronto. She said that despite having grown fond of the trial judge, she wanted to smack him when he swept around in his chair and turned to the jury to explain, in pigeon-English terms, a phrase she and her fellows already understood.

As Manhas wrote, "Pronouncements from on high are not nearly as powerful as conscientious explanations that treat jurors with respect as intelligent individuals."

Artigliere—who was a judge, remember—agreed, pointing out that "The court system can ill afford to antagonize jurors, especially if the genesis of the problem is based in whole or in part on the failure of the bench, bar or system to effectively adapt to changing times in order to connect with jurors and provide them with information they need to do their job."

It's not good enough, now, just to tell jurors to stay off the web; they want to know *why* they should abstain, and they're much more likely to follow the rules if they understand what it is they're protecting—the right of someone whose actual liberty is at stake to know every iota of the case against him.

As Artigliere says, quoting a former juror interviewed in *The New York Times*, jurors still want to do the right thing, but many feel that includes doing their own research and communicating with others about the case.

He quoted what one state court judge used to tell his jurors:

"I have two ways I can do this.

"I can lock you up—that's called sequestering, it's a fancy word for locking you up—during the course of the trial, or I can have you promise me that you will strictly abide by my instructions during the trial and not do any investigations, not have any communications about the case. . . . Will each of you promise me you will follow those instructions?"

That was former chief judge Donald E. Shelton of Washtenaw County, Michigan. He retired in 2014 after twenty-four years on the bench.

As Shelton explained to his juries, "We go to great lengths to make sure that the information you get is from people who come in and swear to tell the truth. Because that's the fair way. It's not fair for you to get information that [the parties] can't see and hear."

Or consider what Georgia State assistant law professor Caren Myers Morrison wrote for the American Bar Association in a paper published in the Winter 2011 issue of *Criminal Justice*.

If an instruction "comes across as nothing more than another admonition," she said, "jurors may well shrug it off."

But if the rationale for it is explained, as Shelton used to do, they're more likely to pay attention.

Morrison's paper was based on a longer article published in July 2011 in the *Hastings Law Journal*, a six-times-yearly publication of the Hastings College of the Law at the University of California.

Titled "Jury 2.0," this was the first scholarly look at the impact of the web on the functioning of the jury in the United States.

What permeates the piece is something completely foreign to Canadian courts, and American ones, too, apparently—respect for the seriousness jurors bring to their task and for the magnitude of their desire to do the right thing.

Referring to what she aptly called the "gleeful horror" of the media toward the recent plethora of jurors-behaving-badly stories (in fairness, we in my business react to almost everything with gleeful horror), Morrison suggested that Internet searches and the like "may not reflect misconduct so much as a misplaced sense of responsibility to render the 'right' decision."

As one juror wrote to *The New York Times*, in response to the original "Jurors Turn to Web" story the paper published in April 2009, "The legal system is not designed to discover the truth, but rather to reward whichever party presents the most convincing argument and evidence.

"Jurors, on the other hand, feel the weight of their responsibility and would prefer to know the truth. As someone who has sat on several juries, I can tell you that in each case the other jurors and I felt frustrated by the lack of key information that would help us feel comfortable that we made the right decision; we also felt deeply frustrated at our inability to fill those gaps in our knowledge."

Morrison found there appeared to be four ways jurors use the Internet: factual research, such as checking out a defendant's background or the history of the case; legal research, such as looking up legal terms or studying sentencing information; publicizing their experiences online, thus imperilling the secrecy of deliberations; and private communications with third parties such as witnesses or investigating police officers.

All of this behaviour is verboten in most Western justice systems, including those of the U.S. and Canada, but Morrison questions whether the risks posed are to the actual fairness of a trial (and thus to a defendant) or to the revered status quo, and asks how they can be mitigated.

Factual research, so much easier to do now than ever before, is dangerous mostly because there's no system of fact-checking on the web, and so much of what purports to be hard factual information is inaccurate, incomplete, misleading or even maliciously false.

A juror curious about a defendant's background, for instance, can easily find out if he's been criminally convicted before through news stories about past offences or even, in the U.S., via free criminal records databases.

The rules of evidence in both America and Canada strictly limit the use of a criminal record—Canadian prosecutors aren't allowed to introduce evidence of an accused's criminal past unless he testifies in his own defence, and sometimes, as you'll see, not always even then. Jurors are even given what courts call "sanitized," or fictitious, records.

The fear is that jurors will use criminal records improperly as "propensity" evidence, in other words that they will reason, "Well, this guy has a long history of committing assaults, so he's probably guilty of this one too."

Mock juror studies, Morrison said, suggest that the danger is real, that juries are more likely to convict someone with a prior record.

And as what used to be information known only to a few (police, lawyers and judges) becomes ever more available to anyone with a mobile, it leaves the defendant with a prior record, especially a serious one, in what's potentially a no-win situation.

Dare he testify, knowing the jury may convict him because of his egregious record? Worse, does he avoid a trial and a harsh punishment by pleading guilty even if he isn't in order to receive a lighter sentence?

And does that mean trials may one day be left to the rich and powerful who can wage, or afford to have waged on their behalf, Internet propaganda campaigns, as Martha Stewart did, albeit in vain, with a defence website during her 2004 prosecution?

It is, if nothing else, a powerful illustration that in a web-permeated world, as Morrison said, "the rules of evidence are losing their ability to preserve the legal fiction that the defendant stands before the jury unencumbered by his past misdeeds."

More amenable to the simple fix, she said, are jurors who go online to do legal research. For the most part, this doesn't introduce new facts to the jury and so is mostly "ultimately deemed harmless" by the courts. Most American reported cases involve jurors who looked up definitions of legal terms and the like.

The exception is information about punishment, which most courts in most jurisdictions warn jurors not to worry their pretty heads about. Canadian judges, like their American counterparts, routinely tell jurors that sentencing is just not in their wheelhouse.

Morrison cited a North Carolina cocaine case where the jury foreman researched the state statute setting out penalties and asked the judge if he could show it to his fellow jurors, explaining that, "he felt the judge had not answered his questions clearly and he simply wanted to tell the others what the law was."

The judge declared a mistrial.

But forbidding jurors from caring about punishment may be less about the traditional division of labour in the courts (jurors decide the facts, judges dictate the law and handle sentencing) than about the codified condescension that is now the norm.

"To say that jurors should not be concerned with the consequences of their verdict because it is not their place to be concerned with the consequences of their verdict is no more than circular," Morrison wrote.

And why shouldn't they be concerned? If juries are the conscience of the community, doesn't the community have a vested interest in what constitutes a fair penalty and what doesn't? What could be more important?

While courts in the States have been quick to grant mistrials in cases where jurors researched sentencing information—on the theory that that will somehow prejudice the defence—Morrison cited an exception.

In 2008 in the Eastern District of New York, a jury convicted Peter Polizzi, then fifty-four, of multiple counts of "receiving" and possessing child pornography.

Though Polizzi was a sympathetic defendant—he'd been raped multiple times as a child in his native Sicily and gone on by dint of hard work to build a successful life and family in America and there was no suggestion he'd ever directly harmed anyone, least of all a child—the jury convicted him.

But before he let them go, the unorthodox Judge Jack B. Weinstein told the jurors that the offence carried a minimum of five years in jail, and then polled them, asking whether, if they'd had that information beforehand, it would have affected their verdict.

Several said it would have, that they wouldn't have convicted Polizzi if they'd known, and that they believed treatment, not prison, was what he needed.

Weinstein, a brave voice on the federal district court who has long railed against the harshness of mandatory minimums in both child pornography and certain drug offences, then declared that he himself had erred by not telling the jurors about the minimum, and ordered a new trial on the "receipt" counts.

Weinstein wrote in part, "The American petit [trial] jury is not a mere fact-finder.

"From the time the right to trial by jury was embedded in the Constitution as a guarantee to criminal defendants . . . it has been expected to bring to court much of the wisdom and consensus of the local community. . . . It has, when jurors deemed it necessary, stood as a guardian of the individual against the sometimes cruel overreaching of government and its menials."

And in an era when mandatory minimum sentences proliferate, in Canada as in the U.S., a jury informed about sentencing is better armed to express what Morrison called "the community's judgment of what constitutes just punishment."

She concluded that given how easy it is for juries to find out sentencing regimes, perhaps it's time for courts themselves to give the information to them.

That's the theme of her whole paper, in fact—that modern jurors are increasingly chafing under old restrictions on what they're allowed to know and that "the time seems ripe to re-evaluate both the functioning of the jury and the symbolic role it plays in our justice system."

One aspect of the jury that would be affected by a move to more transparency is the air of mystery that has traditionally attached to its workings.

Even in the U.S., where jurors are often named and interviewed and occasionally even become celebrities after a trial, jury verdicts themselves remain largely immune to review.

In Canada, where jurors come and go in perfect and complete anonymity, it's even more true.

But as Morrison says, "when the nameless, faceless jurors burst into the public consciousness with inane tweets, their mystique is jeopardized."

Dispatches from what she calls the "black box" of the jury room "subvert the gravity of the process"—particularly if they're riddled with LOLs, bad grammar and inanities—and thus may be less benign than they appear.

"If the linchpin of the jury's legitimacy is that its verdicts are opaque," Morrison said, "so all mistakes are hidden from sight, the fact that increasing numbers of jurors are blogging, revealing the petty rivalries, potential misapprehension of evidence and irrelevant matter they actually considered may change the calculus that keeps jury decision-making hidden.

"Whether we are really ready to see what is behind the curtain is open to question," she wrote.

Jurors' improper contact with third parties—whether witnesses or involved cops, and even if only as Facebook friends—is strictly forbidden and for good reason.

"Any such communication will invalidate the verdict," Morrison says, "unless their harmlessness is demonstrated."

But technology has made all these impermissible contacts easier and, as with so many other sorts of online encounters, lowered inhibitions about them in the process.

Morrison's conclusion is that because most online transgressions happen by stealth and may stay private if one party doesn't out the other, the size and pervasiveness of the problem is hard to measure.

Nonetheless, she said, the trend of jurors to research cases and go online is "not just a passing fad. . . . Regardless of the exact number of jurors involved, the issue nevertheless needs to be addressed.

"One clear cost of inaction is the risk of unfairness to individual defendants, who may be defending not only against criminal charges brought by the prosecutor, but against the unseen enemy of Internet gossip and innuendo."

If the tipping point is that defendants begin to believe it's "sufficiently likely that their jurors will be digging into their backgrounds, scouring the web for evidence of their criminal past, sending friend requests to attractive witnesses and blogging about the experience," Morrison says, they may give up on jury trials, or trials altogether.

Still, she asks, "Why is this happening?" and then offers an answer: "One plausible explanation is that jurors are frustrated with the fact that they are barred from considering all available evidence."

And there's the bloody rub.

In the United States, federal rules of evidence and their state equivalents "operate to exclude even relevant, probative evidence, if that evidence poses a substantial risk of unfair prejudice."

The situation and the rules of evidence are essentially the same in Canada, and for the same reason Morrison suggested— judicial mistrust, or at least limited judicial trust, in juries.

She quoted one former juror, Ladislav Nemec, saying furiously that jury research "is not a corruption of the jury process.

"The arrogance of the judicial system doling out just enough information to keep us 'pure' is intolerable."

Judges go to great lengths to deny that this is what they're doing, or that collectively, they hold jurors in low regard.

I can't count or remember the number of times I've heard a judge sing the praises of the jury and the jury system. They laud jurors' common sense and real-life experience. They tell them that trial by jury is a shining jewel of the democracy and that this is probably the most significant act of public service— "transcendent," the revered eighteenth-century English jurist Lord Blackstone called it—that as citizens they will be asked to perform.

And—coming from them, of course, this is the highest praise of all—they even tell jurors that they too are judges, of the facts, if not the law.

They lay it on thick and in their instructions to jurors they lay it on at sometimes numbing length.

Yet you can make a good case that they mean hardly a word of it.

Every day, in courts across Canada, in high-profile cases crowded with press and public and trials attended by no one but the defendant and his family, lawyers and judges do what, if you or I were doing it, we'd describe as screwing with the truth.

They do it by making pretrial rulings that keep evidence from jurors, by editing or "sanitizing" defendants' criminal records and sometimes even by falsifying those records—actually replacing serious criminal convictions with minor ones, with the result that jurors are presented with fraudulent information.

Consider:

At the end of Daniel Nathaniel Abreha's trial on charges of second-degree murder and attempted murder in Toronto in the fall of 2008, Ontario Superior Court judge Brian Trafford began his charge to the jury.

Among the first words out of his mouth were these: "Your task, as judges of this court, is to determine whether the Crown has proven its case beyond a reasonable doubt.

"You have now heard all of the evidence in this case . . ."

In fact, they'd heard nothing of the sort.

What they'd heard was all the evidence he'd decided they could manage.

It's not the same thing.

Daniel Abreha is, or was then, a drug dealer.

He had what his lawyer, David Maubach, delicately called in his closing address "a life style involving guns and drugs" and on January 11, 2007, he went to a parking lot with three men— Jeffrey Watson, Jeremy Kiriopoulos and Vasilios Pilios—who shared his lifestyle.

They were all drug dealers.

They were doing a cocaine deal for $2,900.

Pilios had arranged it with Abreha.

He got three ounces of coke from Kiriopoulos, who in turn had got it from Watson.

The money Pilios got from Abreha was to be used to pay Kiriopoulos, who was to pay Watson, and the three were in a car, Watson at the wheel, waiting for Abreha.

Abreha brought a gun to the party, as did Watson—for guys like them, it's part of getting dressed. Watson had handed his to Kiriopoulos, who'd tucked it under his seat before Abreha arrived.

Pilios sat behind Watson, in the rear passenger seat, with the coke and a scale. He asked Abreha, who was beside him in the back, for the money, but, both Pilios and Kiriopoulos said, Abreha produced his handgun instead and demanded the cocaine.

Kiriopoulos reached under his seat for the gun Watson had given him, and cocked it, to even things up.

He was turning toward Abreha, who was in the process of opening the back door, when he was shot by him. Watson then got out of the car to confront Abreha, and as they met at the rear of the vehicle, Abreha shot Watson twice and killed him.

At trial, where Abreha admitted using the gun, his position was that he shot in self-defence: He said that Kiriopoulos had pulled out a gun first and pointed it at him and demanded the money.

In fear and outnumbered, he said, he reached for his own weapon, shot at Kiriopoulos and then, in a struggle with Watson, fatally shot him too.

Now, it's impossible to know which, if any, of these mooks was telling the truth. And certainly one version of what happened is as possible as the other.

But the problem was, only one of the mooks had a proven track record of robbing people. Only one was a demonstrated robber, as opposed to a robbee.

That was Abreha, who had a long, thirty-eight-conviction sheet with no fewer than eight prior convictions for robbery, which by definition is theft accompanied by threats, violence or assault.

Kiriopoulos also had a criminal record, for selling cocaine, lying under oath, and possession of a loaded firearm.

Pilios didn't have a record, though he admitted he was a coke dealer, and that he and Daniel Apostolov, the friend who'd introduced him to Abreha just the day before the drug deal, were also involved in a fraudulent cheque scheme.

All admitted lying both to Toronto Police when they were questioned and to the court at the preliminary hearing.

Watson, being dead, had nothing to say.

Abreha's lawyer, Maubach, made what's called a Corbett application. It's named after Lawrence Wilburn Corbett, who was charged with first-degree murder in the December 2, 1982, shooting death in Vancouver of Réal Pinsonneault.

They too were drug trade associates. Corbett denied any involvement in the killing and wanted to testify, so his lawyer sought to prevent the prosecutor from cross-examining him on his criminal record, which was considerable.

Under a section of the Canada Evidence Act, all witnesses, including an accused person who decides to testify in his own defence, can be asked about prior convictions. But because of Corbett's record—which included an unfortunate conviction for what was then called non-capital murder—his lawyer said cross-examination on it would be so highly prejudicial it would infringe on his right to a fair trial under Section 11 of the still-spanking-new and untested Charter of Rights.

Up until then, if an accused anywhere in Canada took the witness stand, his entire criminal record was routinely presented to the jury. The caveat was that the presiding judge would tell the jurors how they could use the information—that is, only to gauge the accused's "credibility" and not as any indicator he had a "propensity" to commit that sort of crime or any other.

(That this flies in the face of common ordinary experience—which may tell us that if Mary is a notable liar, she may be lying now, or that if Bill has two priors for rape, it may indeed mean he's prone to raping, and so on—is precisely why propensity reasoning is deemed so dangerous by lawyers.)

In the Corbett case, the judge rejected the argument from defence counsel, who then himself led the record in examination-in-chief of his client (a pre-emptive strike aimed at softening the impact) and the jurors heard that Corbett had convictions for armed robbery, escaping custody, theft, and breaking and entering—and, oh yes, the non-capital murder.

For about fifteen years ending in 1976, when Canada abolished capital punishment, there was capital murder, reserved for premeditated murder and the slaying of police, guards and wardens, and punishable by a mandatory death sentence, and non-capital murder.

Corbett was convicted, and the British Columbia Court of Appeal dismissed his appeal.

Slow forward to 1988 and the Supreme Court, where the majority also dismissed the appeal and found that Section 12 of the Canada Evidence Act didn't violate the Charter, all in fairly ringing terms.

In general, the SCC judges said, "to conceal the prior criminal record of an accused who testifies would deprive the jury of information relevant to credibility and create a much more serious risk that the jury will be presented with a misleading picture."

And about the Corbett case in particular, the majority said, "Had the accused's criminal record not been revealed, the jury would have been left with the quite incorrect impression that . . . the accused had an unblemished past."

The then chief justice, Brian Dickson, writing for the majority, said that while there was a risk a jury might misuse a criminal record, "the best way to balance and alleviate these risks is to give the jury all the information, but at the same time give a clear direction as to the limited use they are to make of such information."

And he said, "Rules which put blinders over the eyes of the trier of fact [i.e., the jury] should be avoided except as a last resort." And he further said, "It is preferable to trust the good sense of the jury and to give the jury all relevant information. . . ."

What's more, Dickson wrote, while "juries are capable of egregious mistakes and they may at times seem to be ill-adapted to the exigencies of an increasingly complicated and refined criminal law," until Parliament changes the law, "the court should not be heard to call into question the capacity of juries to do the job assigned to them. The ramifications of any such statement could be enormous."

Justice Gérard LaForest disagreed, concluding that the trial judge goofed and shouldn't have let the jurors hear about Corbett's previous murder conviction, and that the fact that they did hear it rendered the trial unfair.

However, the lot of them agreed on a few things: that the Canada Evidence Act didn't breach the Charter and that trial judges have the discretion to kick out evidence in "unusual circumstances" but that, as even LaForest acknowledged, "the better approach would be to err in favour of inclusion."

All in all, for judges, the language and message were pretty clear.

Yet in the intervening years, the decision has been absolutely turned on its head.

Instead of being restricted to "unusual circumstances" where letting in the record might undermine the fairness of a trial, judges now routinely sanitize defendants' criminal records— especially of offences involving violence—leaving in only those for fraud and dishonesty because they purportedly have more to do with credibility than other offences.

Corbett applications are a dime a dozen in Canadian courts.

A search of the CanLII (Canadian Legal Information Institute) database, for all courts, looking for cases that cited *R v Corbett* and included the search terms "prejudicial effect" and "criminal record," reveals 393 from 1988, the time of Corbett, to July 2015.

Many are instances where judges have denied the application and allowed jurors to hear the full record.

But given that the verdicts of jury trials aren't reported unless they are appealed, this makes the 393 likely a gross underestimate of the number of Corbett cases.

So when Judge Trafford ruled on the one in Abreha's case, deciding not only to edit his significant criminal record but also to replace his most recent robbery convictions with convictions for theft—to fictionalize his record—he wasn't the first judge to do it, nor the last.

Wiped from the record jurors were told about were six robbery convictions, with the two most recent, one of which got Abreha a penitentiary term, changed to theft.

Convictions for carrying a concealed weapon, uttering threats and sexual assault were also removed, but with the agreement of prosecutor Michael Callaghan.

Coupled with the judge's two-hundred-page-long charge to the jury, which was replete with the usual warnings about wrongful convictions based on testimony from unsavoury characters like Pilious and Kiriopoulos and Apostolov, Trafford also explicitly gave jurors what's called a Vetrovec warning and told them "it is dangerous to rely" upon the evidence of witnesses such as these three without corroboration.

(The name comes from a B.C. case decided at the Supreme Court in 1982. It involved a heroin trafficker, and unsavoury witness, named Joseph Vetrovec.)

"It would be entirely appropriate for you, looking at the evidence as a whole, to decline to regard any of them as confirming the testimony of any of the others of them," Trafford said, adding, "Be careful, extremely careful, in this aspect of your deliberations."

Ironically, given that he'd not let the jurors hear that Abreha was the specialist in robbery, Trafford reminded them of what he called "the pivotal factual issue in this case"—"who robbed whom of what."

The jurors retired to begin their deliberations at 2:33 p.m. on October 24, 2008.

Once they were out the door, prosecutor Callaghan was on his feet, objecting to the charge, practically sputtering.

"The Crown has grave concerns that the charge, in combination with the Corbett ruling, provides the jury a skewed lens in which to assess credibility . . ."

He said Trafford's summary of the defence position—judges usually summarize the theories or arguments of each side—"is making light of the criminal record, or downplaying the criminal record, given the number of offences that were expunged from the record, serious offences, given the fact that those offences were, many of the serious ones, a sexual assault and two robberies, were in his adult life, where he received significant sentences, it really, in the Crown's submission, gives a totally inappropriate take on what the nature of the record is."

He got nowhere with the judge, who wryly noted that the prosecutor himself had agreed to some of the editing, but not before Callaghan got off a stinging line that nicely sets out the Canadian legal landscape on this subject:

". . . the Court of Appeal and the Supreme Court of Canada have allowed putting fictitious records to the jury, and I'm not saying that in a facetious way, that's something that's accepted in this country and that's the state of the law."

The jurors acquitted Abreha on both counts, just in time for him to celebrate his twenty-seventh birthday.

It appears he didn't mend his ways, at least not immediately, because his name came up yet again less than a year later, when a twenty-two-year-old named Zabiullah (Zabi) Mojaddedi was shot to death on August 5, 2009, near a basketball court in Scarborough in east-end Toronto.

Two men were found guilty of manslaughter in the death, but as part of an agreed statement of fact entered into evidence, the lawyers agreed the shooting was part of a drug deal gone wrong, that multiple firearms were fired that day, and that the leader of one of the quarrelling groups was Daniel Abreha.

Almost three years before he shot Jeffrey Watson, Abreha testified as a witness in someone else's trial, and the judge gave those jurors a Vetrovec warning about *him*, telling them his record made Abreha an "unsavoury witness."

Abreha was one of three men who robbed a 7-Eleven store in Toronto about 3 a.m. one morning in January 2003.

The robbery was caught on videotape, and Abreha pleaded guilty, even helpfully telling Toronto Police that a fellow named Ahmed Gelle was one of his accomplices.

But, when he was called as a witness at Gelle's trial in the fall of 2004, Abreha, shockingly, couldn't identify Gelle and said he'd never clamped eyes on him before.

Gelle's conviction was appealed, and in dismissing it, the Court of Appeal described Abreha's record as "lengthy and serious."

That robbery, of course, was one of those that Trafford changed to "theft" at Abreha's own murder trial.

Probative value versus prejudicial effect: It's one of the mantras I've heard hundreds of times in court.

These are the five words judges most often use as the reason for sanitizing a defendant's criminal record, altering convictions or keeping from the jury other information that is relevant and therefore ordinarily admissible: How valuable is a given piece of evidence and how potentially inflammatory would it be for the jury to hear it?

The words come right from the Corbett decision, where the trial judge allowed the jurors to know that Corbett previously had been convicted of murder, but told them sternly that this knowledge "must not be used by you . . . as evidence to prove the accused person committed the murder of which he stands charged," and that they couldn't conclude, in other words, once a murderer always a murderer.

A prosecutor once described it like this: "Corbett enshrines in our law a strong faith in jurors' ability to understand and obey instructions."

And yet what Corbett has come to stand for is not the proposition that the record should usually go in, but oddly, that the judge has the discretion to bar it.

Gérard LaForest in his dissent came up with a now oft-repeated list of "factors to be considered" by a judge faced with a Corbett application.

These are the nature of the previous conviction and how similar it is to the current charge (and the more similar it is, the more dangerous or potentially prejudicial it's considered to be); when the previous conviction occurred (if it's far in a defendant's past, it's deemed less probative); and how vigorous the defence lawyer's attack was upon Crown witnesses (the more serious the attack in cross-examination, the more it may be a factor in favour of admission) who may be in a credibility contest with the defendant.

LaForest's own view was that while there may be cases where "the interests of not presenting a distorted picture to the jury might require permitting cross-examination," he didn't think "this factor can override the concern for a fair trial."

But where he really tipped his hand was in paragraph 130 of

his Corbett dissent, where he argued that recognizing "the limitations of the human reasoning process" is not to "discredit the general utility of the jury as an instrument of justice."

Rather, he said, appreciating human limitations only helps the system, because then they can be defended against.

After all, as he said, "We deceive ourselves if we expect the jury to reason in ways that we, as lawyers and judges, know from experience to be often unrealistic, if not impossible."

You see? They're special. You're not.

Perhaps no one in the justice system has been madder about how LaForest's one-man dissent has come to be interpreted than lawyer David Lepofsky, who once snarled at the Ontario Court of Appeal that "some courts erroneously treat Corbett's dissent criteria as if Corbett's majority adopted them per se."

Lepofsky is a blind, Harvard-educated lawyer who spent more than three decades in Ontario's Ministry of the Attorney General, the last twenty of those years as an appellate Crown. He's also been a fearless advocate for the disabled in various capacities, most recently as the chair of the Accessibility for Ontarians with Disabilities Act Alliance.

When he appeared for the AG at the appeal court on the Tyson Talbot case in late 2006, seeking a new trial for Talbot, it was on the grounds that the trial judge, Gloria Epstein, then of the Superior Court, had made multiple errors that led to Talbot's acquittal.

But an enormous factum of more than three hundred pages makes it clear that Lepofsky was animated not only by Epstein's suppression and sanitizing of Talbot's criminal record but also by the fact the same thing is happening all across the country.

"Corbett case law, especially in trial courts, is all over the map," Lepofsky told the appeal court. "Some judges allow criminal records involving violence even when the offence charge involves violence. Others don't. Some admit an accused's record for the same or similar offence as that being tried; others don't.

"Some state or strongly suggest that an accused sufficiently opens the door to admission of his entire record when he attacks the credibility of Crown witnesses.

"Some don't even require this as a precondition.

"Others require more, such as an attack on character.

"Justice isn't served by random roll-of-the-dice rulings and jurisprudential incoherence," he thundered.

"This cries out for this court to fix jurisprudential chaos."

Lest anyone doubt the law was in a mess, Lepofsky provided the court with a schedule of 102 cases, broken down by Corbett rulings yea and nay, and concluded: "Yet, increasingly, exclusion of all or part of an accused's record is being permitted. Corbett's exception is tending towards becoming the rule.

"Corbett's rule is becoming the exception."

The appeal court, in a February 8, 2007, decision written by David Doherty, tossed the appeal and was so dismissive of Lepofsky's Corbett arguments it noted the court hadn't even asked Talbot's lawyer to respond to them.

"Crown counsel's assertion that the Corbett application jurisprudence is in a chaotic state misunderstands the nature of judicial discretion," Doherty sniffed.

Well, what Epstein in her discretion either had kicked out or sanitized was a good chunk, or about a third, of Talbot's extensive criminal record, including every single conviction that involved violence, among them a recent 2002 one for assault with a weapon.

In fact Talbot, who was then thirty, was out on bail for attempted murder and aggravated assault in an attack with a knife on a forty-four-year-old man who was leaving a bar, when he sucker-punched Christopher Shelton in the early morning hours of November 29, 2002, and killed him.

Shelton had been out earlier that night with two pals, Trevor Mitchell and Darryl Sharpe, all of them big strong young men,

Shelton the oldest, at 23, and the heaviest, at 228 pounds. They started off playing hacky sack at Sharpe's place, then went to a couple of bars, where they had a few drinks and danced with each other.

Then, hungry, they drove up to a now-defunct joint called the Golden Embassy on Broadview Avenue in the east end.

Curiously, it was just a few blocks from where the old CBC series *The Kids of Degrassi Street* had filmed for its seven-year run.

And Tyson Talbot, who played a character named Billy Martin in the show, and briefly later another character in a spin-off series, arrived in a cab at the restaurant about the same time with two young women, one of them his girlfriend.

All he had in common with Shelton and his friends was that he and his had also been out clubbing and drinking.

Whereas Talbot's life may have peaked with Degrassi and his fame as a child actor—after leaving the spinoff series in 1986, he only ever came to public attention for getting in trouble—the best of Shelton's appeared to be on the horizon: He was a pre-law student in his first year at the University of Toronto.

Their paths crossed at the Chinese restaurant.

As the women got out of the taxi, according to Mitchell and Sharpe, Shelton made an innocuous remark, something silly like "Hey ladies!" or "Hey, what's up girls?" Talbot allegedly objected and the two exchanged words, though in his testimony, Talbot denied that.

In any case, the two groups went on in, were seated separately, ordered their food and had no further interaction at all.

But shortly after 3 a.m., Talbot left the restaurant to go to a bank machine, came back, then left again; while he was outside the second time, Shelton and his friends settled their tab and were out the door.

Talbot said that as the three emerged, they began yapping at him, Mitchell especially aggressive, saying, "What the fuck's your problem?" and "We'll kick your fucking ass" and that he felt threatened, as though he was going to be jumped.

He acted, he said, only to protect himself, in self-defence.

That's when, out of the blue and purportedly as a distraction, he punched Shelton, who by the accounts of his friends and an independent witness-cum-Good Samaritan, wasn't expecting it and "fell like a tree," arms at his sides, smashing his head on the pavement.

Shelton never regained consciousness, but, as he lay there motionless, Talbot either kicked or stomped on his head, leaving a footprint on his forehead.

Then he hailed a cab. His girlfriend and the other young woman he left at the restaurant.

Shelton died at St. Michael's Hospital later that day from complications of a skull fracture—suffered when he fell to the sidewalk—and bleeding within the brain. Pathologist Dr. David Chiasson testified at trial that the footprint would have required considerable force, and though it didn't result in any direct brain injury, it could have worsened the bleeding.

Sent to their black box of a jury room without a clue about Talbot's capacity for violence, the jurors acquitted him of second-degree murder on June 4, 2004. (Six months after that, he was also acquitted of attempted murder and aggravated assault in the stabbing for which he'd been out on bail when he punched Shelton.)

Five days later, a letter from Shelton's mother, Theresa, was published in *The Globe and Mail*.

"If the justice system entrusts 12 individuals selected at random to perform the weighty task of jury duty," she began, "then it should extend that trust to allow them to weigh all relevant facts."

She then correctly described Talbot's violent past and the judge's whitewashing of it, pointing out that in the courtroom, everyone but the jurors knew all about it.

"Members of the jury who delivered the final verdict likely felt duped when they learned of Mr. Talbot's violent history, as have countless other jury members who have served under similar circumstances. If I had been a member of this jury, I would feel as though a cheap trick had been played on me. . . ."

I met Theresa Shelton at her home in Guelph, Ontario, in August 2015. Eleven years after her oldest child's death, she'd had lots of time to come to grips with it, and was graceful and welcoming.

She still worried about Christopher's friends, Trevor and Darryl, saying, "I feel so sorry for those boys. I'm sure they feel responsible, being up there on the stand, not being able to help Christopher, you know? They did help." And she misses her son, of course, as do his little brother and sister, Jesse and Nicki, who was then about the age Chris was when he died. He was "so sweet with them," she said.

But her view of the jury system had hardened. Prosecutor John Scutt, she said, had explained the Corbett application to her and her former husband, David, and they felt involved and informed all the way through the process.

But, knowing all they did—and that Talbot's defence lawyer had wanted to plead him to manslaughter but that Scutt "felt strongly it was a second-degree for sure"—she said, "I just thought it was so obvious [what the verdict should have been]."

She wants to believe in the jury trial, she said, but can't quite make the leap.

"[Jurors are] just not given the tools, the tools of information but also the tools of the process of the law, because it can be very tricky. I'd like to think people are equipped," she said, "but I'm not very confident of that . . . I like the democratic idea of a jury, but does it work?"

The one sure thing she knows is that it would have a better chance of working if judges didn't persist in treating jurors as though giving them all the information in a case was like "giving a match to a baby."

It's the rare murder trial I cover now where the jury actually gets to hear all the evidence that my colleagues and I know about.

So common are the cases where jurors are kept in ignorance that newspapers have developed an entire shorthand for it—the "what the jury didn't hear" story.

It's only after a jury has retired to begin deliberations, when jurors are actually sequestered—accompanied every time they leave their jury room by court officers; their cellphones confiscated; phone calls home monitored; and hotel rooms, if they end up deliberating over several days, stripped of working televisions and radios and access to news—that the automatic publication ban under Section 648 of the Criminal Code expires and media can publish the content of pretrial motions and what went on in the jury's absence and the like.

A search on Infomart.com, a media monitoring website, shows that from January 2000 to January 2016, there were 407 results for "what the jury didn't hear." That number includes many duplicates and smaller, related stories.

But while most stories originated in Ontario—a function probably of media concentration but also of the fact that Ontario courts are the most censorious—it's clear that the phenomenon of keeping information from jurors isn't confined to one province. There are stories from most of the others in the bunch.

Editing or cleansing of the criminal record is but the tip of the iceberg.

Since Sir William Blackstone first wrote in his famous *Commentaries on the Laws of England*—and having read them, I can report he wrote at the usual tedious length and with the usual self-regard—"All presumptive evidence should be admitted cautiously, for the law holds it better that ten guilty persons escape than one innocent suffer," it has been a sacred canon of the profession.

And probably, few would seriously argue it's not better that a whack of guilty fellows go free than that a single innocent be wrongly convicted; nor, for that matter, would they disagree that just as the tie goes to the runner, so should the break always go to the accused person.

This is the single overriding concern of the courts, and the main driving force, once you cut through the mumbo jumbo, for keeping things from jurors.

No one wants to see another wrongful conviction.

No one ever wants to see a wrongful conviction caused by a jury being given information it shouldn't have had or being inflamed by prejudicial evidence.

Still, I can't remember a modern case that has more severely put that maxim to the test—does the system, and the public to which it owes its legitimacy, really have the stomach to watch an obviously guilty man walk free because a jury was kept in the dark?—than the high-profile murder trial of Francis Carl Roy in 1999.

Roy was eventually convicted of first-degree murder in the 1986 abduction, rape and strangulation death of an eleven-year-old Toronto girl named Alison Parrott.

A suspect in the original, less-than-stellar Toronto Police investigation—Roy's alibi was checked out only in a knee-jerk way and he was cleared—he got lucky for a decade until science, in the form of DNA technology, caught up with him, thanks to a prescient scientist named Norm Erickson, who kept seven swabs from Alison's vagina safely in a freezer even before the technology existed.

Roy's DNA profile was matched with the profile of semen on those swabs only in the summer of 1996, whereupon he was arrested and charged. He went on trial three years later.

The case is memorable for a lot of reasons, but chief among them Roy's preposterous gobsmacker of an explanation for how his DNA came to be in the dead little girl.

Why, he testified, he woke up early that Saturday in the summer of 1986, went to the loo, and back to bed. Then he masturbated—after all, he explained, his then girlfriend was out of town—and when he got up for good, he put on his running gear and headed to Kingsmill Park in the west end of the city.

All pretty normal so far, if in the modern jargon, entirely TMI. Then it got insane.

He ran about thirty-six minutes, he said, then had to relieve himself, and was doing so in some bushes when he saw a flash of "something white," walked over and realized it was "a body, a young girl." He moved closer, saw "she was dead."

He looked around, bent down, and stuck a finger—the right index—into her vagina, pulled it out, purportedly heard a car door slam, panicked, and resumed his run.

And that, said Roy, was how his semen got into Alison's body—it was transferred from his uncircumcised member during the earlier masturbation, after which those cunning sperm sat in the weeds on his finger.

(I confess to having had entirely too much fun with this whopper of a tale at the time, and wrote that now we knew that everything teenage girls had been told about sperm in the 1950s really was true—the buggers really did live forever and could scale tall buildings.)

But the important thing was the pile of evidence against Roy that was kicked out in pretrial motions by one of my favourites, Ontario Superior Court judge David Watt, as he then was.

As prosecutor Ken Campbell, who handled the appeal of Roy's conviction—astonishingly, given the enormous breaks Roy got at trial, he appealed anyway, unsuccessfully—wrote in his factum for the appeal court, there was only one "seriously contested piece of significant evidence" that Watt ruled admissible and allowed the jurors to hear.

This was a severely edited video of a lengthy post-arrest interview between Roy and former Toronto Police detective sergeant Vic Matanovic, and of which Watt allowed only the good parts—the good-to-Roy parts, that is—to be shown to the jury.

Roy's appeal lawyer, Anil Kapoor, then a frequent co-counsel with Roy's trial lawyer, Todd Ducharme, who is now a judge on the Ontario Superior Court, argued that by failing to exclude the whole kit and caboodle of the video, Roy's Section 7 rights to remain silent had been violated.

"As if," the appeal court might have said. Roy had been advised of his rights to counsel, had consulted with duty counsel once and with his own lawyer on the phone and in person, and had multiple times during the interview been reminded of his right to remain silent. He didn't say much that was damaging, but he sure banged on.

Plus, most of the video that the judge allowed was exculpatory of Roy—for instance, him protesting his innocence about four hundred times.

But the list of what Watt didn't let the jury know about was staggering.

He excluded "similar fact" evidence of two young women whom Roy had also abducted and violently raped.

Both women, who were respectively nineteen and fourteen when they had the misfortune of meeting Roy, testified in a pretrial voir dire.

Both had been taken to remote areas, both had been physically assaulted (one was punched in the face and kicked in the ribs, while the other was grabbed by the hair and had her face smashed against a car window), both were bound at the wrists, both were raped vaginally and anally, and both were threatened with death.

Alison's body showed she had been bound at the wrists and ankles and gagged; she had two areas of bruising to her head, which suggested she'd been hit or punched; and her vagina was torn and bleeding, though insect damage made it impossible to determine whether she'd also been anally raped.

But that wasn't where the similarity ended.

All three girls had been lured, one way or another, away from a busy part of Toronto. All encountered Roy inno-cently—one through a boyfriend, one via a friend and Alison through the sport she loved. She was lured to Varsity Stadium, and her eventual death, when Roy, posing as a photographer, pretended he wanted to take her picture there for a track publication.

Both she and Roy were serious runners, specialists in the three thousand metres. Though there was no evidence they'd ever met, it was possible Roy had spotted her before at one of the parks or clubs they had in common.

My favourite trial prosecutor in all the world, Paul McDermott, argued strenuously that the jurors should hear from Roy's two previous victims—one was attacked on October 30, 1979, the other on August 26, 1980, and Roy was convicted at trial in the first case and pleaded guilty in the second.

For the defence, Ducharme said the women's testimony would be "alarmingly prejudicial" and would "profoundly inflame" the jury.

Watt simply said the evidence was out, and never issued writ-ten reasons why.

But that's not where it ended.

Roy was in prison for the first two rapes long enough to receive phallometric testing, which measures the penis's response to various sexual stimuli. He showed "high levels of arousal to episodes of sexual violence" and a special affinity for bondage and "sexual activity with an unconscious female." Documents

I had at the time of my "what the jury didn't hear" story also cited his high sex drive and history of cruelty to animals, and noted that before he took up long-distance running, his previous hobby was boxing.

"He assesses various people he works with . . . in terms of how many punches it would take him to knock these people unconscious," the documents revealed.

While in the pen, Roy also worked as the inmate photographer, taking pictures at prisoner graduations and family days and the like with a 35-mm camera.

Now, none of this information was ever in the mix even for the judge's consideration, let alone the jury's. It was information only my newspaper had.

But what was up for grabs for the judge was that photography interest, which Roy apparently kept up, because when he was paroled to the Keele Centre halfway house in west-end Toronto in April 1985, he was often seen carrying a camera.

And this was relevant because, found in a police search of the apartment he shared with his girlfriend at the time of his arrest nine years later, was a 35-mm camera, a book on photography and a brown leather wallet.

In the wallet, which was hidden above a hot-air duct in the basement of the house, was a complete set of identification for one Philip Pendry, an Aboriginal man who then worked for the CTV network. And pasted over one of Pendry's pictures on one of the network ID cards was a photo of Roy.

Pendry had reported his wallet stolen in the early 1990s.

It was a critical link between Roy and the modus operandi of the mysterious man who had tricked Alison—who had just qualified to represent Ontario in an international meet—into going to the stadium in central Toronto.

Judge Watt ruled that the probative value of the evidence was outweighed by its possible prejudice.

That ruling allowed Ducharme, in his closing address to the jury, to point out that there was no evidence that Roy had ever had a camera, heaven's no, and to suggest he didn't have the wherewithal to "have successfully posed" as a photographer.

Well, there was just such evidence, but the jurors weren't allowed to know it.

Neither, perhaps most critically, did they learn that in the middle of his preliminary hearing (which serves for the defence as a preview of the evidence), when it became evident that his Plan A explanation for how his DNA ended up in a dead little girl might not fly—and he'd come up with that only after his post-arrest interview—Roy dreamed up a Plan B.

It was an identical twin brother—the only other possible explanation for his DNA being found where it was, for only identical twins share the same genetic profile.

Roy, sitting in a cell, wrote two letters to a mysterious friend named Walter Stadnick, whose name he spelled two different ways. He sent them care of an Aboriginal centre where he'd once worked or volunteered, and where, shockingly, no Mr. Stadnick of either spelling ever picked them up.

In the letters, Roy referred to his "Bro," and wrote, ". . . the homicide detectives have no idea that I have an identical twin brother . . . tell him that I said I'm sorry for the inconvenience, but he must remain in Venezuela. . . . The police still have no idea I have a twin brother. Are they in for a loop."

As an experienced inmate, he surely would have known that jail authorities monitor prisoners' mail, and that the police would get the letters before the ink on them was dry.

In fact, Roy's birth certificate of September 18, 1957, records his birth as a single one.

But the jurors, of course, were never told about the letters, which almost certainly would have wrecked Roy's claim of the magical semen transfer, not to mention revealed his talent for changing his story to suit the facts as he learned about them.

The picture of Roy that was left with the jurors as they trotted off to their jury room—their hands effectively tied behind their backs just as firmly as Alison's had been—was that he was this dignified Aboriginal fellow who swore his oath on a grey and white eagle feather; that he had but a minor criminal record, mostly for theft and fraud offences; and that while he may have done a morally repugnant thing he was, as Ducharme put it in his closing, "not that bright a guy," certainly not bright enough to have stalked Alison, posed as a track photographer, and convinced that child to leave Varsity Stadium with him.

The jurors were there in their black box for almost a week, during which Canadians learned far more about Roy than they ever did and the halls of the University Avenue courthouse thrummed with a single burning question: Would this be the case where jurors were given so little to work with that a blindingly, irredeemably guilty man who had snuffed out a young life would go free?

It was on everyone's lips—lawyers, those involved in the case and those who weren't; clerks and registrars and constables; court rats, both the paid ones like me and the citizens who attended the trial on their own time and dime; and Alison's parents.

"It's absolutely shocking," Alison's mother, Lesley, said after the jurors retired. "[The excluded evidence] is part and parcel of who Mr. Roy is. How it can be kept from [the jurors] is totally beyond me."

Normally, I wouldn't look to a grieving parent for comment, any more than I'd ask a lawyer about another lawyer: The natural vested interest is too great.

But Lesley and Peter Parrott are generous and lovely people. They didn't seek or expect vengeance, only justice, and the legal system, as Lesley said after the verdict, "almost betrayed" them.

In the end, though it took six days, the jurors muddled their way to the truth, and the right verdict. But it was a close bloody thing, and as I wrote that day, there wasn't much room in the prisoner's box, crowded as it was with the invisible faces of all the judges who can't bring themselves to trust the people whose glories they sing and who, in courtrooms across the land every day, perpetrate a fraud.

Nobody much cared if the drug dealer Daniel Abreha really was guilty. Nobody but the people who loved Christopher Shelton really cared if his killer improperly walked free.

But a lot of people would have cared very much if Frank Roy had been wrongly acquitted, because he was indisputably so very guilty.

That it hasn't happened yet, at least to my knowledge, is only because juries can usually find their way through the mountain of bullshit they are fed and the lies they are told to see if not the whole truth, just enough of it.

They just seem to have a nose for that sort of thing, thank God.

I'm not sure how we ended up with the notion that the correct twenty-first-century juror is but a lumpen receptacle to receive judicial wisdom and instruction, but it sure hasn't always been that way.

The criminal jury in England, the mother ship in which Canadian and American juries are rooted, dates back to 1166, when King Henry II ordained in the Assize of Clarendon that twelve lawful men should identify for the royal justices and sheriffs all the locals suspected of serious wrongdoing; they in turn were to make proof by ordeal.

Only in 1215 did the medieval Roman church abolish the ordeal, which saw the accused people subjected to trial by fire or water or some equally ghastly life-or-death experience whereby the guilty perished and the innocent survived, presumably by the grace of God.

The ordeal's happy death, as Roger D. Groot writes in his essay on the early-thirteenth-century criminal jury in *Twelve Good Men and True (The Criminal Trial Jury in England 1200–1800)*, "necessitated a search for its successor," and the trial jury was born.

For the next three hundred years or so, jurors were largely "self-informing," as it's called: They were drawn from the neighbourhood, locals who were expected to be well acquainted with the allegations and perhaps the accused and alleged victim both, and who were as much witnesses as triers of the facts.

For instance, in 1403, after the theft of fines from the Treasury of Receipt at Westminster, it was a jury of clerks and officials from that very department who "tried" the accused man, one John Freeman.

"Clearly," Edward Powell writes in his essay on jury trials in the early fifteenth century in *Twelve Good Men and True*, "such jurors were summoned because of their first-hand knowledge and professional expertise."

It's an accepted maxim of English legal history that, as Professor J.H. Langbein, author of *Prosecuting Crime in the Renaissance*, put it, "Medieval jurors came to court more to speak than to listen." And these juries were famously reluctant to convict.

But at least by the early fifteenth century, the system had evolved—cases were brought to court both by private appeal (usually from the victim, or as Powell calls him, "the victim-prosecutor") and by indictment, which likely saw court officials providing at least some information or evidence to the jury.

In the sixteenth and seventeenth centuries, juries were more passive than they first had been, but they fought judges sufficiently often—to be free of judicial coercion and free also of the fear that they might be tossed in the joint by a judge who disagreed with them—that University of Michigan law professor Thomas A. Green, co-editor of *Twelve Good Men and True*, says the jury's history in that time "is the history of a struggle for control of an institution that stood in the front lines of many kinds of political struggle."

Despite the highfalutin rhetoric that apparently has always surrounded the role of the jury, in practice juries have long had feet of clay.

Obviously, at various times in history they have excluded or underrepresented large swaths of the population—everywhere, those who didn't own property and women; in the United States, African-Americans; in Canada, Aboriginal people.

But even when a jury was solely composed of white male members of the governing class, Green says, "at the moment of trial, and especially at the moment of judgment—that is, of rendering verdict—its perspective may often have been shaped by other inclinations and concerns as well.

"The courtroom," he writes, "was not a meeting room for an association for the prevention of crime. Its doors may have been open to people and attitudes whose presence caused jurors to see themselves and their role in a more broadly representative fashion."

Green says there were two prevailing views about the eighteenth-century English jury. To some, it was "an unlearned and rustic mob," while to others "an arm of landed elites," and, he says, "Both of these perspectives were, of course, true. That is what made the jury so powerful an institution, one fluid enough in the impressions society had of it to weather all attacks. It was both the cutting edge of reform and the bastion of the status quo, and those who reviled it in one context lauded it in another."

And yet, in both early Canada and America, as the right to a jury trial took hold—in Nova Scotia, it was recognized in the

1850s, and the U.S. Sixth Amendment guaranteed the right to an impartial jury trial for every federal defendant in 1791—the role of juries almost simultaneously began to decline.

This was, in both countries, partly due to an entirely reasonable concern about jury-packing, or stacking the jury with partisans.

In "A Brief History of the Criminal Jury in the United States," a 1994 paper by Albert Alschuler and Andrew Deiss, respectively a University of Chicago Law School professor and a lawyer based in Salt Lake City, the authors cite a murder case in 1800 where the judge stopped the proceedings after learning that jurors were chosen from a list of prospects submitted by the defendant's father.

And, as Saint Mary's University history professor R. Blake Brown writes in *A Trying Question (The Jury in Nineteenth Century Canada)*, "Allegations of packed juries flew furiously in the pre-responsible government period" as political activists, Roman Catholics and Irish immigrants cried that Tories and Protestants dominated juries.

But after 1850, Brown says, the year Robert Baldwin, a Toronto lawyer and politician and advocate of responsible government, got the Upper Canada Jurors' Act passed, which reformed the jury selection process, most of those concerns faded.

And the Fenian prosecutions—Fenians wanted an independent Ireland and hoped to capture British North America to use as a bargaining chip to get Ireland's freedom, and in 1866 made raids in both New Brunswick and Fort Erie—proved the worth of the new jury act.

Despite convictions in the multiple controversial trials that followed in the most charged of atmospheres, not even the Fenians seriously complained that their juries had been packed against them.

Yet as Brown says, despite "the ability of the jury selection machinery . . . to form relatively impartial juries . . . Ontario greatly reduced the use of jury trials in civil and criminal cases after Confederation."

Thereafter, attacks on the use of the jury came mostly from lawyers and even judges, who bemoaned lay jurors' lack of professionalism. Coupled with the challenges of geography and the inconvenience and in some cases hardship of serving, many people were at best ambivalent about the jury's usefulness.

Grand juries, which decided whether alleged criminal activity should go to trial, were replaced by lawyers, and then disappeared completely before the end of the twentieth century. Ontario did away with them in 1974, and Nova Scotia a decade later.

And in the U.S., where once jurors judged both the law and the facts—this at a time when lawyers were in scarce supply—that practice effectively ended in 1895.

Now, as Alschuler and Deiss conclude in their history of the U.S. criminal jury, "overproceduralization has infected the American jury trial.

"Prolonged, privacy-invading jury selection procedures, cumbersome rules of evidence, the repetitive cross-examination of witnesses, courtroom battles of expert witnesses (who sometimes are called 'saxophones' because they play tunes for those who pay them), jury instructions that all the studies tell us jurors do not understand, and more, have made trials inaccessible for all but a small minority of defendants."

Or, as Caren Myers Morrison puts it in "Jury 2.0," "Viewed in the most negative light, the jury's role has been reduced to that of an adding machine, mechanically crunching the carefully screened evidence that is funnelled into it, and producing a verdict."

No wonder jurors chafe so under these constraints, she says, born as they are of the "modern conception of impartiality, which is frequently confused with ignorance and passivity."

Internet access has given jurors a way, an unauthorized one but still a way, around all that, and it's a signal, Morrison says, that should be taken seriously. She envisions a twenty-first-century jury that "may share some characteristics with its more active forbears."

She quotes Jeremy Bentham, the eighteenth-century English lawyer and philosopher who was an early critic of the then-emerging rules of evidence.

Bentham urged that the jury hear all the evidence and decide for themselves.

"If there be one business," he wrote in his *Rationale of Judicial Evidence*, "that belongs to a jury more than another, it is, one should think, the judging of the probability of evidence; if they are not to be trusted with this, not even with the benefit of the judge's assistance and advice, what is it they are fit to be trusted with?

"Better to trust them with nothing at all, and do without them altogether."

He also wrote, in another section of his opus on evidence, "it would be a prodigious benefit to justice if exclusion of evidence were . . . itself, forever and in every instance, excluded."

Now, Bentham was a radical and a reformer. For instance, he believed in the separation of church and state, in freedom of expression and equal rights for women, in decriminalizing homosexuality, and in abolishing slavery and the death penalty. He was clearly light years ahead of his time in many regards, so perhaps he was right about the jury too.

He might have liked Morrison's imagined Jury 2.0—a system where jurors can ask questions, take notes, request clarification; where, at least when there are mandatory minimum sentences, jurors are given sentencing information and have a way of expressing themselves, an outlet, even if it's only anonymously on a court-maintained forum; where judges give instructions in plain language and rid themselves of the desire to conduct themselves as though they are giving, in Theresa Shelton's inimitable words, a match to a baby.

Bentham, my new hero, once wrote, and here he was explaining that it was judges who make the common law:

"Do you know how they make it?" he said. "Just as a man makes laws for his dog. When your dog does anything you want to break him of, you wait till he does it and then beat him. This is the way you make laws for your dog, and this is the way judges make laws for you and me."

R v ELLIOTT

"The first thing we do, let's kill all the lawyers."

—WILLIAM SHAKESPEARE, *HENRY VI*

IT OUGHT TO have been a garden-variety murder trial—if not quite a slam dunk, close enough to count.

Instead, it roared so badly off the rails that more than two dozen police officers, Crown attorneys and senior provincial law officials were wrongly smeared as hapless boobs or corrupt thugs; a guilty woman walked away free, at least for a time; and, thirteen years after the story began, the guy most responsible for the mess, Ontario Superior Court judge Paul Cosgrove, lost his job, if not his $178,133-a-year pension.

It was on August 19, 1995, that two fishermen discovered the severed thighs of sixty-four-year-old Larry Foster floating in the Rideau River near Kemptville, Ontario, a small town about an hour's drive south of Ottawa.

Over the next few days, the Ontario Provincial Police proceeded to recover much of the rest of Foster—his head, arms, hands, lower legs and feet—in and around the same part of the river. His torso was never found.

Six days later, a Barbadian woman named Julia Yvonne Elliott was arrested in connection with Foster's death.

The two first met in the spring of 1993, when Foster, about to embark upon treatment for a blood cancer called multiple myeloma, went on vacation to Barbados. It isn't quite certain exactly where Foster first encountered her—it was likely at the beauty-and-massage parlour she owned in Bridgetown—but it's clear that Elliott, then thirty-three (or about half Foster's age), if not outright trolling for a fellow like him, was at least not blind to the possibilities.

As his son, Steve, says with a grin, "She probably assumed he was rich, though he wasn't rich. I'm sure he was spending like a drunken sailor, living the last spring of his life, right? And he probably put on that impression."

In any case, the two developed a relationship, and when Foster came back to his George Street condo in Kemptville, "He was pretty sparked up," Steve says. "He was talking about her a lot; she was going to be his girlfriend. Yeah, okay Dad."

Steve kept his mouth zipped, pleased to see his old man happy.

Elliott came up for a visit soon after. Though Steve didn't know it at the time, she also quickly got her hooks into Foster for what court documents suggest was five thousand dollars, but which Steve figures may have been twice that figure. In any case, it was money that, as a retired auto mechanic, Foster could ill afford.

Steve actually met Elliott once, at a family cottage on the Rideau River, where his dad proudly brought his new girl. She was a big, solidly built woman, he remembers, with strength that would later serve her well in dismembering and disposing of her victim.

In any case, his dad was pleased as punch as he paraded her around.

That was shortly before Foster went into treatment, and for almost a year, Elliott faded from the scene.

Larry Foster's twin brother, Len, donated bone marrow for a transplant, and it was successful, but Larry had an aneurysm during his recovery and surgeons had to cut a plate into his head to fix him, a procedure that left him for a time with one normal-sized eye and one bigger cockamamie one.

"It took him the better part of a year to heal up and get normal again," Steve says.

By the late summer of '95, though still frail, still only 135 pounds soaking wet and still unnaturally hairless from the chemo, the real Larry Foster was nonetheless back—back on the dancing circuit at area bars, and back, as Steve says, "having fun again."

And then Steve heard him say that Elliot was coming to visit. "It was the week before she killed him that he said that."

Steve didn't hold his tongue this time: "'Dad, that's a year ago. I thought that was past history.' He said, 'Oh no no, she's coming up for a visit, and she's gonna pay me back the money I loaned her.'"

That was the first Steve knew of any loan and it felt hinky to him that someone who was snug as a bug in Barbados would bother to return to Canada to repay money. As he says, "Seems kind of strange she'd come back with a wad of cash in her hand."

He told his father to do what he liked, but said he didn't want to see Elliott again, that "As far as I'm concerned, it's bad news. Life's back on track, there's all kinds of fish in the ocean. . . . Just give me a call whenever she's gone, and I'll talk to you next week kind of thing."

It was on the Monday, August 21, that Steve believes Len, who lives in nearby Nepean, called him. "He was pretty agitated. He said, 'Look, I've been trying to get in touch with your dad, he's not answering his phone.'"

Both of them were worried that maybe Larry had fallen and hit his head; he'd had a few dizzy spells after the surgery.

Steve stopped in at his dad's apartment on his way home from work. His car was there in the parking lot. He let himself in and had a look about, calling out for his dad. His shoes were there, and his wallet, but no sign of his dad.

"Now I was starting to get a little nervous," Steve says.

Yet he saw nothing out of the ordinary until he went into the bathroom, where a chunk of carpeting had been cut out. I immediately would have thought the worst (bloodstain alert!), but Steve Foster is a nice, normal person.

What he thought was, "Something's weird here. . . . Is he getting the carpet changed? Has he got a roll under his arm, downtown, you know what I mean?" So he called Len back and filled him in.

With that closeness twins have, Len had sat up in bed one night that weekend filled with dread. Now he was done messing around; he told Steve to call the cops.

In those days, Kemptville still had its own municipal force, since taken in under the Ontario Provincial Police umbrella. Ron Laderoute answered the call and came right over to Foster's apartment.

Unknown to both Laderoute and Steve, the OPP had already made a positive identification of Foster, matching fingerprints from those taken many years earlier when he'd been arrested on an impaired driving charge.

The body parts discovery was big news in town: it was on the radio, and Steve heard it, but at the time, police were saying the remains appeared to be those of a middle-aged woman, so he made no connection. The gender confusion, short-lived, was because his dad's slim frame was so hairless, a side effect of the chemo.

The OPP were, in fact, staking out Foster's apartment, and were watching as Constable Laderoute, who died in 2011, arrived and Steve let him into the building.

It was as he was showing the officer around the apartment that Steve mentioned his dad had had a visitor that weekend, a black woman from Barbados.

At that, Laderoute "kind of looks up and says, 'Really?'"

It turns out that on that on the Friday night, August 18, Laderoute had been running a RIDE program and stopped a car that he sort of recognized as a local one, but with a black woman he didn't know behind the wheel.

She said it was Foster's vehicle, and that he'd lent it to her. Steve believes now that she likely had his father "in pieces in the trunk" and was on her way to the river.

Laderoute later testified that he had no reasonable grounds to search the car, and that while he'd felt in his bones something might be amiss, absent finding Elliott "with an empty gin bottle in her hand," he couldn't take it further. He did make notes of the stop—incomplete ones, as later became a real issue at trial—in his memo book.

Anyway, Laderoute asked Steve if there was a picture of this woman, and sure enough, he found one in his dad's bedroom.

"So I gave that to him and he goes, 'Oh yeah, that's her. That's the one I saw on Friday night.'"

They headed down to Laderoute's cruiser to fill out a missing person's report, and it was there, as they sat in his car, that an OPP officer tapped on the window and asked for a private word with Laderoute. He filled Laderoute in and told him to bring Steve back to the detachment.

That's when Steve found out that his dad was dead and had been dismembered.

The OPP kept the identification quiet and let the media continue to describe the remains in the river as a woman's. Working out of a little command post on Highway 43, right by the Greyhound bus stop, they were watching for Elliott—who hadn't been found despite the usual alerts going out—and had a big picture of her up on the wall for reference.

Later, the police told Steve that one officer was idly looking out the window when a bus stopped, and as it pulled away, "There she is, standing by the side of the road.

"She came back."

The OPP followed Elliott as she walked through town, heading toward Foster's condo.

"When she turned the corner and went up the street to go there, she saw the yellow tape, the police tape, [and] she turned" right around.

It was Friday, August 25. Elliott was arrested.

As it turned out, she'd been staying with another man in Ottawa, and it was him she first blamed for Foster's death, at one point telling police he was jealous of Foster and had strangled him.

Alas for her, that story quickly fell apart when post-mortem examination of Foster's head and neck inconveniently revealed no evidence of strangulation: The other man was duly released and the charges against Elliott were raised to second-degree murder and interference with a dead body, a dainty-sounding charge given what she'd done to Foster after she stabbed him.

Prosecutors had heaps of evidence against her, of all sorts. They had circumstantial evidence of opportunity, this from various of Foster's neighbours in Kemptville who saw a black woman, wearing clothing that matched what Elliott wore that night, moving boxes out of Foster's apartment and into his car. Suffice to say, in this small white town in eastern Ontario, there weren't a lot of big black women about. Elliott stood out like a neon sign.

They also had forensic evidence linking her to the crime, including Foster's DNA on various items, notably on the knife Elliott used to cut up his body and on her bag and distinctive dress. They had phone records that showed a couple of calls, one the day after Foster's death, made from his apartment to Elliott's place in Barbados. They had evidence of what's called post-offence conduct in the fact that after his death, Elliott used Foster's credit card, shipped some of his worldly goods (his stereo, microwave, camera and hair dryer) in a barrel to herself back home, and then tried to skip out on an early flight.

Even taking into account the lethargic pace of Canadian justice—the typical court purportedly sits for six and a half hours, from 10 a.m. to 4.30 p.m., but with all the breaks and recesses it adds up to much less than that—the trial was originally estimated to last no more than six weeks.

It took two years even to approach a state of readiness, during which time there was a preliminary hearing and the required disclosure of the case to the defence by prosecutors.

All proceeded, as the Ontario Court of Appeal was later to note in a scathing ruling, "relatively uneventfully" to this point. (That such a two-year gap between arrest and the start of trial should be considered unremarkable is telling.)

But shortly before the trial was to begin, Elliott fired her lawyer, Mike Neville, and his junior, Kevin Mark Murphy, took over as lead counsel.

Murphy was then thirty-eight. But he had gone late to law school, this after getting an undergraduate degree at Carleton and then a master's from the London School of Economics, and was called to the bar only in 1993. Still very much wet behind the ears, he had never before done a murder trial.

His taking over the case was significant, and not because it saw the judge grant, and the Crown agree to, a two-week adjournment so Murphy could fully bring himself up to speed. That was a perfectly reasonable request.

It was significant because the request was perhaps the last of its kind. On September 29, 1997, when the trial on paper began—I qualify it that way because this was the day pretrial motions were to begin, which are always argued before the jury actually reports for work—the wind appeared to be gathering under Murphy's wings.

Where once there had been a manageable four pretrial motions to be argued, including the one for a short adjournment, there soon were thirteen more—a Twelve Days of Christmas–like recitation, two of this kind, three of that, one of each of those, an application for this relief, a request for that.

Included in the group, as was almost immediately the norm as soon as the Charter was proclaimed, were two motions alleging breaches of Elliott's constitutional rights and attendant requests that the evidence gleaned be excluded.

In the result, though Murphy lost most of them, the motions that originally were slated to last about two weeks didn't finish until December 17.

The trial itself had been slated to wrap up by then.

It finally did begin, with a jury, before Judge Paul Cosgrove in Brockville, a gorgeous small city on the banks of the St. Lawrence River, on January 27, 1998—almost two and a half years after Elliott's arrest.

After less than nine full days of evidence in front of the jury, the court embarked on a voir dire—a trial within a trial, involving arguments about legal issues, held in the jury's absence. This voir dire lasted in various shapes and forms for almost twenty months.

The trial itself never did resume. Cosgrove declared a mistrial; that jury never came back.

Another jury was empanelled in Ottawa, where the trial was then moved, and twelve fresh faces were selected. But these jurors never sat, as the proceeding was by then in legal quicksand, hopelessly mired in ever more motions from Murphy and ever more latitude for him from the judge.

And on September 7, 1999, Cosgrove stayed the trial as an abuse of process and found that the police, Crown lawyers and senior officials of the Ontario Ministry of the Attorney General had committed more than 150 violations of Elliott's rights under the Charter.

He also assigned all costs to the Crown, noting smarmily that "the legal aid plan should not be required to reduce its budget allocation for other needy persons because of the Crown-generated expense of the accused's legal representation."

By then, two top-notch outside private defence lawyers, David Humphrey and Harvey Strosberg, were in place as contract prosecutors.

The ministry basically had run out of staffers, as, one by one, Cosgrove had either given them the boot or forbade them from discussing the case, or both.

Humphrey and Strosberg had anticipated this very ruling. Given all that had happened before, it hardly required foresight to have figured out where the judge was going to go.

They had arranged for an immigration officer to be present in court with a warrant that would keep Elliott in Canada long enough to be served with the appeal notice they had ready to go.

But the judge quashed that too.

Elliott was able to sashay out of the courtroom, and Canada, and no one could do anything to stop her.

The notice of appeal had to be served on her several days later, by which time she was back in her native Barbados.

Four years later, in 2003, when the Court of Appeal tossed the entire Cosgrove decision, called the trial in plain language the insanity it had been and ordered a new one, Elliott fled to Costa Rica.

She was extradited to Canada in 2004, and in December 2005, more than a decade after she'd stabbed Larry Foster to death in his apartment and taken him apart, Julia Yvonne Elliott pleaded guilty to manslaughter.

The next day, the *Ottawa Citizen* reported that she had been sentenced to seven more years in prison, a sentence the paper described as unusually long, given the then standard two-for-one credit Elliott received for the almost five years she served in total in pretrial custody as a purportedly innocent person.

It worked out, the *Citizen* reported, to "18 years and eight months."

In fact, as Barbados' *NationNews* reported on September 3, 2010, Elliott had returned to the Caribbean island on statutory release two days earlier, having served five years, not seven, and by no one's reckoning anything close to eighteen years.

When she returned my message sent in August 2012 to her Facebook account, where she now calls herself Yves Elliott, she declined an interview and wrote, "I had a horrible experience in the 'injustice' system in Canada, something I would like to forget. . . . I am just trying to get my life back in order."

The appeal court was merciless in overturning Cosgrove. The three judges—Marc Rosenberg, Michael Moldaver (who is now on the Supreme Court of Canada) and Janet Simmons—seemed scarcely to fathom what was before them. A collective sense of outraged disbelief infuses their judgment.

Even to layman's eyes like mine, the Cosgrove decision is starkly unusual, chiefly because while the judge found more than 150 breaches of Elliott's Charter rights, rarely does he say *which* rights were being abused or under which section of the Charter they purportedly were trampled.

That's the way it's supposed to be done. (In fact, you could make a very good case that evidence wasn't ever supposed to be tossed out routinely, and that the intention of the drafters of the Charter, the parliamentarians and the big legal brain who advised them—the retired judge, then a federal justice department lawyer, Eugene Ewaschuk—was rather the opposite.)

But if it's done right, it usually goes something like this.

A judge might find, for instance, that a warrant for a search of an accused person's house or car or computer was flawed, and that the person's Section 8 right against unreasonable search or seizure was thus violated.

And then the judge might rule under Section 24.2 of the Charter that since the evidence found in the search—drugs, weapons, whatever—was illegally obtained, it should be excluded from the trial and, as "fruit of the poisoned tree," not used against the accused.

Or the judge might say that the violation wasn't so serious that the evidence had to be kicked out.

Or he might kick out some of it and allow other parts.

But any way you cut it, the judge identifies which right was violated and how.

Cosgrove didn't do any of that.

Again and again, he just ruled in the broadest language that Elliott's "Charter rights" had been breached, never saying which one(s) or what weighing process he followed.

As the appeal court noted (as but one example), Cosgrove found, preposterously, that Elliott's rights were breached by the then assistant deputy attorney general Murray Segal's merely instructing the Crowns who worked for him on the arguments they might use or the positions they should adopt.

Segal, who has since left the ministry and is in private practice, would have been aware of the Elliott trial even had it gone along tickety-boo. That was his job as Ontario's chief prosecutor. But certainly, once the case turned wonky, he would have been paying close attention.

Yet Cosgrove found that simply by directing one of his few remaining prosecutors who hadn't already been kicked off the case by the judge, Segal had violated Elliott's rights.

"The trial judge never explained how making submissions to a court could constitute a breach of the Charter," the appeal judges wrote. "He did not explain what provision of the Charter was engaged by this conduct or what legal principle was involved."

The judges ruled, as Elliott's appeal lawyers conceded from the get-go, that almost none of the Charter breaches on Cosgrove's long list was sustainable, and those few that were certainly didn't warrant the stay of proceedings he'd granted.

The appeal court was deeply troubled by much else too—Cosgrove's strange penchant during the trial for turning Crown prosecutors into witnesses (thus taking them off the case) on the feeblest of grounds and then ordering them not to speak to the Crowns who replaced them; his astonishing finding that a whole series of police officers had lied through their teeth, again without any evidence that they had; the judge's allowing of defence lawyer Murphy to make wildly irrelevant forays into the immigration system, funding for halfway houses and even the alleged relationship between the Crown and Bell Canada; and last but not least, Cosgrove's blatant abuse of his contempt power.

Contempt of court is a judicial tool for controlling the courtroom and the administration of justice; it exists purely to protect the dignity and processes of the court. Thus, if someone disobeys a court order, such as a publication ban, she can be cited for contempt. Penalties can range from a fine to imprisonment.

But contempt power is to be used sparingly, because to do otherwise will erode the judicial confidence and dignity the sanction is designed to guard.

Cosgrove, in the Elliott trial, used the sanction as a sword that he waved over the heads of witnesses and spectators with obvious relish: He actually cited two witnesses for contempt, threatened to cite thirteen others and even threatened to order the arrest of two civilians.

The appeal court found this behaviour was coercive and outrageous.

One of those he threatened was none other than Steve Foster.

An early witness in Elliott's first trial, Steve was being cross-examined by Murphy about a description of Elliott he'd given Constable Laderoute the night he joined the officer at his father's apartment.

"I'd said she was built like a brick shithouse," he says.

The phrase is a brilliant Anglo-Saxonism, brilliant because anyone with half a wit knows immediately and precisely what it means. When Murphy asked what he'd meant by it, Steve replied, reasonably enough in my books, "What do you mean what does that mean? What kind of brain do you have?"

The lawyer went on to suggest that perhaps "it had to do with [her] being black," Steve says now, adding, because he still can't quite believe it, "Come on!"

Months later—and by now the trial was well into the voir dire and Steve had had it up to here with Murphy's schtick—he was in the courthouse cafeteria with his aunt and uncle, fixing a coffee, when the lawyer showed up right beside him.

"All I could think of was, if I was him would I go and stand beside the guy in the coffee line that I was just a few months ago grilling on the stand, accusing him of being a dink?" he says.

"Have you always been such an asshole?" Steve inquired.

It was, Steve says now, a stupid thing to say, and he certainly wouldn't have gone out of his way to search out and insult the lawyer. But when Murphy sidled up to him, he simply couldn't resist.

The lawyer blew a gasket.

"He starts screaming and yelling, yelling in the cafeteria, 'This man has just assaulted me verbally!'"

Steve took his coffee and sat with his aunt and uncle and kept his mouth shut as Murphy went about the cafeteria, trying to solicit other lawyers to act as witnesses to the monstrous injustice that had been inflicted upon him.

When they all went back into court, the lawyer raised the issue with Cosgrove, who promptly told Steve to get himself a lawyer and come back the next morning when he might be charged with contempt.

Steve was going to do nothing of the sort, but one of the prosecutors warned him, "Don't mess with this guy or you might find yourself in Innes Road," which is how the Ottawa-Carleton Detention Centre, the local jail, is known locally. "He said, 'Don't take it lightly. We think there's nothing to it, but you never know.'"

Steve called the family lawyer, who acquitted himself nicely, and the judge let it lapse, as a sort of boys-will-be-boys sort of thing.

But as angry as he was with Murphy, Steve had figured out by then that the principal behind this disaster was not the defence lawyer but the judge.

The proceeding increasingly reminded him of a scene from *And Justice for All*, a 1979 courtroom drama starring Al Pacino.

"There's a crazy judge in it," Steve says, "who seems perfectly normal, but throughout the movie, you realize more and more this guy is close to the edge. He owns a helicopter, or rents one, and he flies around out of New York City, I think it was, and he takes Pacino for a ride . . . and as they're flying out, talking about different things, Pacino looks down and sees that the thing is almost on empty and he says, 'Look, we're almost out of fuel.'

"The judge goes, 'No no. I go out every day, I go out further just to see how much further I can go.'"

He ends up crashing the thing, runs out of fuel right near the pad and crash-lands on the pad. "It struck me as a good parallel."

But the real point is, Cosgrove—this after sitting on the bench as one of the Superior Court's busiest and hardest-working judges for fifteen years at the time of the Elliott decision—didn't understand what was contempt of court and what wasn't.

He didn't understand the law on calling counsel as witnesses, which is supposed to happen only in the most exceptional circumstances, and not served up as the daily fare he made of it with Crown counsel.

He even seemed to misunderstand the positions of the lawyers appearing in front of him.

He misapprehended the role and function of the provincial attorney general.

He didn't understand the nature of the Crown's disclosure obligations, which are to disclose all relevant material with reasonable dispatch, not to give the defence lawyer every scrap of paper ever generated by a case.

Most astonishing, this veteran judge didn't understand the document that is a fundamental part of the law of Canada, the Charter.

He didn't get the law of the land.

How could this happen?

It wasn't just the Court of Appeal that had a go at Judge Cosgrove.

In April 2004, four months after the three judges carved him a new one, the Ontario attorney general, who was then Michael Bryant, formally complained to the Canadian Judicial Council about the judge.

The CJC is the federal body responsible for investigating complaints about the country's approximately 1,100 federally appointed judges.

The equivalent of an AG's letter in the criminal courts is a preferred indictment, which bypasses a preliminary hearing and sends an accused directly to trial. Ditto a letter like Bryant's: It means the CJC has no discretion and is bound to proceed with a full inquiry.

The debate about whether this is fair ball or not is legitimate. Cosgrove's position, rather rich given his own weakness on the Charter, is that the section under which the AG had proceeded is unconstitutional.

His position was supported by the Canadian Superior Court Judges Association and the Criminal Lawyers Association.

Of course it was.

Both groups were concerned that a judge who displeased a provincial attorney general (i.e., the state) could then be disciplined and even removed as a result, without recourse to the CJC's usual procedural safeguards.

Security of tenure, which to the rest of us means a job for life, is key to judicial independence and is the only protection a judge has against removal from office other than for cause.

But what it really means is security against interference by the state: A judge, in other words, is not to be treated as just another civil servant who can be sent packing if he pisses off the government.

And the CJC's normal process—which involves various stages of inquiry and opportunities for a complaint to be dismissed or resolved or for the judge to acknowledge inappropriate conduct in a nice quiet way—is bypassed when an AG complains the way Bryant did, under Section 63 (1) of the Judges Act.

It's a very serious matter indeed. But the legal discussion about whether Section 63 (1) is constitutional did provide some delightful revelations—for instance, the notion that incompetence, in and of itself, is not a sufficient reason to fire a judge.

Quoting Professor Shimon Shetreet of the Hebrew University of Jerusalem, whose 1976 book *Judges on Trial* is apparently still regarded as the last word on such matters, the inquiry committee noted that "the great price" paid for tolerating incompetence on the bench is a necessary one.

"Just as society is prepared to let some guilty go free to protect the innocent," the good professor wrote all those years ago, "so is it necessary to let some incompetent judges stay on the bench to protect the [good, or innocent] judges against abuse."

Had Cosgrove's lawyers succeeded, Canada could have had that rarest of combinations, the one-two punch where both a guilty person walked free (as Elliott did, though just for a time) and an incompetent judge held on to his job (as actually Cosgrove did too, albeit just for a time).

But the fact is, it appears no one much quarrelled with the idea that something had to be done about Cosgrove. The argument was simply about how it ought to be done.

The issue ping-ponged about, first to the Federal Court, then to the Federal Court of Appeal and then to the Supreme Court (which refused to hear the matter) for four years. The sorry lesson, I suppose, is that virtually no one—not even a judge—is able to get a speedy hearing in this country.

But in the end, the inquiry proceeded, and after public hearings in Toronto and despite a last-minute mea culpa, the CJC panel found that Judge Cosgrove's "pervasive incompetence"; his threatening behaviour toward people "who had done no wrong" and who in some cases, as with Murray Segal, had no chance to answer his damning allegations; and the reasonable apprehension that he was biased against the police and Crown were of such grave concern that four of five panel members recommended his removal.

(The fifth, Chief Justice Allan Wachowich of Alberta, and in fact the inquiry's own independent counsel, Earl Cherniak, argued in vain that a strong tongue-lashing would suffice.)

The recommendation to remove was duly and unanimously endorsed by twenty-two chief justices of the full CJC in the spring of 2009, and two days later, on April 1, Judge Cosgrove formally resigned. Had he not, the matter would have gone to the federal justice minister, and then to a majority vote of a joint session of the House of Commons and Senate.

Giving a judge the boot isn't meant to be easy or simple—nor should it be—but this baby had gone through all the hoops and run its course.

Cosgrove stood on the brink of becoming the first federally appointed judge since Confederation to be removed from office. He saved himself from that ignominy—just as Quebec Superior Court judge Jean Bienvenue, the only other federal judge recommended for dismissal, had done—only by quitting in disgrace in the nick of time.

I never expected him to agree to an interview when I called him one day in late August 2012.

I told him I'd been covering the then ongoing inquiry into the conduct of another judge, Manitoba associate chief justice Lori Douglas; conveyed my interest in the CJC process; and expressed my sympathy for the toll the hearing must have taken on him.

I never dreamed he would reply that the inquiry itself, mortifying as it was, was nowhere near as traumatic as the police and Crown misconduct he'd seen in the Elliott trial and which, he said, "shook me to the core."

Now, there *was* no such misconduct, of course. That was by this time well established. It had been established by the appeal court, the inquiry and the full CJC, and to a degree, had been acknowledged by the judge's own nine-page apology-cum-mea culpa, which he'd delivered to the hearing panel on September 10, 2008.

In any case, I offered to come to his house in Brockville and asked for the address.

"Oh," said the judge, chuckling, "I think, as a former judge, I can probably get a witness room at the courthouse."

He had been forced from the bench, barely escaping with his pension.

His incompetence in the Elliott case had been wide-ranging and pervasive.

He had damaged the reputations of Crown attorneys and police officers—significantly so in the case of those who worked or lived, as he does, in Brockville, where the stay and the wide-ranging "misconduct" he purported to find had been reported as big news.

He had even treated Steven Foster, the son of the dead man, shabbily.

Yet here he was, not remotely chastened.

The Brockville courthouse is a beaut, completed in 1845 and topped with a quirky, 3.5-metre-tall statue of Justice, locally known as "Sally Grant," after the woman who posed for it.

I met Judge Cosgrove there on the front steps on the morning of September 7, 2012. Gone was the fellow who, almost four years earlier to the day, in an effort to save his job, had been on bended knee before the CJC inquiry and described himself as humbled.

(His was actually a pretty qualified apology and came very late in the day: The judge allowed that his efforts to control his courtroom in the Elliott case had had "only modest success," regretted his intemperate language, admitted to some errors and granted that his conduct "did not meet the highest standards. . . ." In truth, it hadn't met even the bonehead standards.)

He still had his security pass, and led me on a little tour of the courthouse, through back corridors and rooms where he had to swipe the card and where it still worked like a charm.

The building had been beautifully renovated and enlarged about a decade earlier, in part under his leadership, and he was justifiably proud of it.

He showed me where his office had been, where once, pre-renovation, he had parked his car, and we ended up in the jury room of courtroom No. 4, the so-called historic one where he'd presided, he said, on thousands of cases.

Courteous and agreeable, he was well prepared for my visit. He had ready a list of "talking points," a stack of CJC documents (which I borrowed) and even a recent photograph of himself (at seventy-eight he was still a handsome dog) as a handout.

He spoke fondly of his days on the bench, places he'd travelled in the province, what he'd done and whom he knew. He enumerated his disappointments in the CJC process—that the Supreme Court declined to hear his case; that the panel wouldn't accept the many letters of recommendation he had, from, among others, a great group of sitting or retired judges, former members of Parliament, childhood friends and locals in Brockville; and that there was, with an AG-generated complaint, no room for mediation.

"If ever there was one case where I thought pre-settlement discussions, informally, in a room—the attorney general, the offending judge, counsel, independent counsel, to roll up their sleeves
and say, 'What the hell's this all about?' that's the case . . ."

Did he really imagine that the case against him could have
been settled in that way? I asked.

Probably, he said. He acknowledged some of what he'd said
in his lengthy apologia at the inquiry. He admitted that, as such
conduct is described, he had descended into the arena of the
courtroom, or as he put it: "I got into it, with both of them
[defence lawyer Murphy and the Crowns] and I shouldn't have."
But in the two areas where he was found most wanting—the so-
called Charter violations and his finding of non-existent police
and Crown misconduct—all the admonishments and corrections had had virtually no lasting effect.

I asked if he meant what he'd said on the phone when I first
called him, about that purported misconduct being the most
traumatic aspect of the whole schmear.

"I mean that," he said, and referenced his fifteen years on
the bench pre-Elliott and the "dozens of jury trials" he'd heard.
"I had not before experienced the, what I perceived to be, the
modus operandi of the Crown and the police to obtain a conviction at all costs."

By way of explanation, he said that as a boy, after his family
had moved to Marathon, a small pulp-and-paper town in
Northern Ontario, the local police chief had taught him to
drive and licensed him for his guns, and that an assisting police
officer who lived across the street taught him "boxing, judo,
soccer, hockey."

Clearly, I was to take from this that he was a law-and-order
guy, likelier to be on that side than the other. Thus, with that
background, he said, "I could not see police operations doing
what happened in front of me in the trial" and sit idly by.

As for the non-existent Charter breaches, and his harsh condemnation by the Court of Appeal, Cosgrove appeared to believe it was all a semantic misunderstanding, somehow a question of clumsy language poorly used.

"I've had second thoughts about that," he mused. "I said there were 150 breaches. I should not have said breaches; I should have said there were 150 incidents of misconduct [and then written that that] led me to the conclusion that this is hopeless, that this person can't get a fair trial because of what police had done . . .

"If I had just said there were these breaches and it resulted in an unfair trial and one that could not be rescued and that's against the provision of the Charter that says everybody's entitled to a fair trial, I might have avoided [the whole mess]."

He added, in a breathtaking display of temerity given that it was he who had so badly misapprehended the Charter, that the police at that time "weren't ready for the Charter world and hadn't been properly educated."

When I stumbled upon a lengthy online story about Julia Elliott's trial and came to the first paragraph about Judge Cosgrove, I was gobsmacked.

"Justice Paul Cosgrove, an ex–Trudeau government minister and political appointee to the Ontario judiciary, later admitted that he was completely unprepared. . . . He not only allowed the defence to pursue its claims but openly fanned the flames, issuing hundreds of extraordinary orders to facilitate the inquiry."

I'd never read anything like that—frank and cheeky both—anywhere, except possibly in my own oft-criticized court prose, in Canada before.

We in my business, and those in the legal community, generally tend to adopt an highly respectful attitude to the courts and particularly to the bench. As Tom Zuber, who was a Superior Court trial judge before and after a fifteen-year stint on the

Ontario Court of Appeal, wrote years ago in a paper he couldn't even get published owing to its contrarian nature, "In this country, regrettably, nearly all of the scholarly legal community simply fawns over each new escalation of judicial power, looking upon it as something great and good."

Zuber, now well into his eighties, still rues the uncritical nature of Canadian media and legal literature, and the over-intellectualization of the law, as former Manitoba Court of Queen's Bench chief justice Marc Monin, now on that province's Court of Appeal, once called it.

"We've got a lot of legal scholarship going on in the courts," Zuber told me in the fall of 2012 in an interview at his Windsor, Ontario, office. "But the criminal law is a fairly blunt instrument. It's not nuclear science," he said with a trademark chuckle.

Lawyers, and in general the press, also appear to enjoy the notion that our judges are wiser and less political than others (certainly, say, than American judges, some of whom, God forbid, are crassly elected).

We confuse the respect the bench is due with unseemly deference to its occupants, and the effect has been to virtually preclude anyone ever calling the proverbial spade a spade.

I can't recall ever reading that any judge was a political hack, which is what this story baldly said. But of course, it wasn't written by a Canadian but by an Australian, and it wasn't written by a non-lawyer grunt like me, but rather by Jeremy Gans, a distinguished law professor at the Melbourne Law School who does a running analysis of Australia's Charter of Human Rights and Responsibilities.

(The 2008 story on the Elliott case was headlined "Charter of Frights." It was on both Gans's *Charterblog* and *Inside Story*, a quality online Australian magazine.)

In any case, what Gans wrote was entirely accurate, as Cosgrove himself cheerfully acknowledges: He *was* a political hack.

It was 1984. As Cosgrove tells it, Prime Minister Pierre Trudeau, having taken his famous "walk in the snow" on February 29, was winding things down and preparing for his imminent retirement, a key part of which involved taking care of his friends.

He asked his former public works minister, "'What are you going to do, Paul?'

"And I said, 'I'm not running again. I'm tired.

"So he said, 'What are you going to do?'

"And I said, 'I think I could be a good judge, a county court judge.' . . . And I was appointed as a county court judge. That's how I became a judge."

The county and district courts later became the District Court of Ontario and later still the government merged that court, the former High Court and the Surrogate Court into the Ontario Court of Justice (General Division), which is now called the Ontario Superior Court.

Cosgrove's was one of about 225 patronage appointments—to the Senate, government agencies and boards, and of course various benches across the country—that Trudeau controversially made in the dying days of his administration, and that were endorsed by his successor, John Turner.

During the English-language TV debate in the federal election that followed, Brian Mulroney famously deflated Turner when, during an exchange about his approval of the raft of Trudeau appointments, Mulroney snarled, "You had an option, sir!"

Predictably, not quite a decade later, when he himself was about to call it a day, Mulroney declined to exercise the same option, and went on a patronage tear of his own. In fact, he out-Trudeaued Trudeau, giving about 250 of his political friends and party faithful farewell gifts.

A lawyer by training, Cosgrove nonetheless spent more years as a professional politician than he ever did practising law. A 1960 graduate of the then new Queen's Law School, he was first elected to Scarborough council as an alderman ten years later, when he was just thirty-six.

Three years after that, he became mayor, which earned him a seat on the old Metro Council with other area mayors, and five years later, he began running federally for the Liberals in the riding of York-Scarborough, finally succeeding in 1980 on his third try.

That meant he ran—in total—in seven elections in nine years. He was a politician for fourteen years, a lawyer for all of a decade.

His practice seems to have been mostly family law and estates, and certainly, in the four-year hiatus between the AG's complaint and the CJC recommendation for removal, he kept working as the estate expert for the eastern region bench and as the table motions judge, logging full days, though he didn't venture into the criminal courts.

Though he had something of a pro-Crown reputation before the Elliott trial, there were troubling signs in two 1997 cases that Cosgrove was developing what the Court of Appeal later called "a suspicious attitude toward the government," that he had made unwarranted attacks on Crown counsel, and that he misunderstood the reach of the Charter.

These two decisions kick-started what the appeal court later described as "a procedural nightmare."

Both these cases, overturned on appeal, were mentioned by Attorney General Bryant in his letter of complaint, but the CJC panel didn't consider them, and in fact refused, quid pro quo, to also consider Cosgrove's many letters of recommendation.

Though he said he wishes, now, that when the Elliott Crowns asked him to recuse himself (it means to withdraw from the case, and Murphy had also asked him to do it in the early days of the trial) he had done so, he still clearly believes that he deserved to remain a judge.

"As I said," he told me, "I wish I hadn't said 'Charter breaches.' That aspect of it. For all that, in my mind I say, I had a different idea of the Charter, you're [the CJC] saying it's a way out, we disagree.

"But, I'm incompetent?"

He was at the time about eight months away from retirement age; it wasn't worth the candle to continue the fight, he said.

I asked what he'd thought when he heard that Elliott had pleaded guilty, after all those years and all that happened. I meant, was he stricken or chagrined by the realization that he was the instrument by which a pretty chilly killer had almost got off scot-free?

His reply: He suspected all along Elliott would plead.

It was a Friday night, he said, when he got a call from the trial co-ordinator in Ottawa, Mary Simpson, asking him to take the Elliott case. She said, he remembered, "It looks like this is going to be a guilty plea; will you take it?"

He told her that because he'd done the bail hearing, Elliott had testified before him already and that therefore, "I can't take that."

Then, because as he said "my reputation was, if there's something to be done and I had nothing else to do, I'll do it"—and because his vanity was such that he couldn't bear to pass up a case unless he absolutely had to do so—he reconsidered.

As a general rule, lawyers appear to believe that their capacity for fairness and their ability to credibly argue any position in the world despite personal or previous involvement in a file—or, well, anything else—is infinite.

Once, when a Toronto defence counsel, David Bayliss, was trying to have a judge cite me for contempt, my newspaper had to hire me a lawyer.

This was in the *Post*'s heyday, when, on every front, only the best would do. And the paper got me one of the best. They hired

Alan D. Gold, a famous lawyer whose most recent big case was in Saint John, N.B., where he was part of the team unsuccessfully defending Dennis Oland, accused (and convicted in December 2015) of second-degree murder in the bludgeoning death of his father, Dick, four years earlier.

Gold, as it happens, didn't feel it was necessary to even mention to me or the *Post* lawyer who contacted him that in the local criminal lawyers' newsletter of that very month, he had written an article hugely critical of me and my way of covering the courts.

It was only as court convened, when Bayliss had the decency to mention it, that my newspaper and I learned of it. We fired Gold shortly thereafter.

I mention it as an indication that massive self-regard is something of an occupational hazard for lawyers, and not confined to those, like Cosgrove, who are obviously unworthy.

As Cosgrove describes his exchange with Simpson way back when, "I said, 'I'll tell you what. I'll read the bail hearing, and if I've made a finding of credibility against her, I'm not taking it, because we thought it was going to be a guilty plea.'"

He read the transcript, he said, and found out he'd made no such finding, that he'd denied Elliott bail simply because as a non–Canadian resident, there was "a hazard of flight. And I called [Simpson] back and I said 'Yeah.'

"And that's how I got into it," he said.

As we left the Brockville courthouse that day, a blue-blazered court official, on seeing the judge, chirped out, "Hi, Your Honour!"

Judge Cosgrove was carrying to my car some of the volumes of CJC material I was borrowing. There was a ton of it, so I was glad of his help, but a little amused too—that here he was, schlepping a stack of documents for a lowly reporter the very way that for so many years he would have had a court officer ("the judge's man" as I always think of these fellows) carry his books from his chambers to the courtroom and back again.

But then again, who was I to be amused?

It was four years after he'd ostensibly been sent home with his tail between his legs, and Paul Cosgrove still had the keys to the castle.

The year Cosgrove was named to the bench, so was another fellow member of Parliament (Robert Daudlin, who also went to the old Ontario County Court and ended up in the Superior Court), and three former members of Trudeau's cabinet—Mark MacGuigan, Bud Cullen and Yvon Pinard, who were all given spots on the Federal Court of Canada, the national court that reviews the administrative decisions of federal government bodies and hears civil lawsuits against Ottawa.

Some of Mulroney's appointments in 1993 were no less nakedly partisan. Nathan (Nate) Nurgitz, for instance—the former Tory party president who had been languishing comfortably in the Senate since 1979—resigned from that dishy gig just before he was named to the Manitoba Court of Queen's Bench.

My favourite line from the stories of those glory days is from one about the appointment of Judge Yvon Pinard.

First elected in 1974, Pinard, a former government House leader and president of Trudeau's Privy Council, was as political an animal as there is. His appointment was among the last plums the then prime minister handed out on his last day in office, and surprising because Pinard apparently had been considered a possible future party leader.

A delightful piece by Jim Rusk in *The Globe and Mail* of June 30, 1984, quoted a Pinard aide saying that after ten years as a lawyer and ten in politics, Pinard "had chosen to achieve his lifelong ambition of a seat on the bench."

Oh, well then: He'd wanted it so very badly. Who could complain?

Pinard remained on the Federal Court until 2013, spending his last eight years as a "supernum"—short for *supernumerary*, or out of the normal rotation, which means he effectively worked part-time for full-time pay.

The telling thing about his appointment is that of all the openly partisan ones that year, it caused its own little ruckus.

At the time, there was an agreement in place between the Canadian Bar Association and the government, under which prospective candidates for the bench were to be submitted first to a CBA committee for approval. The committee would rate the candidates as "qualified," "qualified with reservations," "highly qualified" or "not qualified," and then, from the groups that got the nod, the government would choose.

It all amounted, frankly, to a pinch of coon dung, because all significant judicial appointments were then—and remain—the sole purview of the federal government, whatever that committee or any other had to say. It has ever been thus, since the Constitution Act (the old, now renamed, British North America Act) of 1867.

The justice minister of the day, in consultation with cabinet, appoints Superior Court judges, who under Section 96 of the act handle all the important criminal and civil trials, and Court of Appeal judges. (Under Section 92 of the same act, provinces pick judges for the much busier lower-level courts.)

And the prime minister gets to name the chief justice and associate chief justice of both trial and appeal courts, as well as the judges on the Supreme Court of Canada.

But in his leave-taking haste, Prime Minister Pierre Trudeau neglected to first submit Pinard's name to the CBA committee for the requisite rubber-stamping.

In July 1984, the *Globe*'s Jeff Sallot duly reported, "the judicial appointments committee has informally complained" about the "breach in the agreement." He quoted Bert Raphael, a Toronto lawyer and member of the committee, saying snappishly, "What was the big rush, this enthusiasm to protect people with jobs? If [Pinard] was qualified, we would have cleared him. So, what, he might have been out of work for maybe 10 days?"

A contrarian might have seen things another way.

What on earth is the point of such a committee, anyway (and now there's no longer just one CBA committee but rather seventeen different judicial advisory committees, or JACs, across the country) if all they do is dress up and slap a little lipstick on a partisan pig of a process?

That is pretty much, in fact, what two major studies of Canadian judicial appointments have concluded—that the process was in reality partisan before the advent of the JACs, which came in 1989 under Prime Minister Mulroney, and is only marginally better *with* them, meaning the percentage of judges with what the researchers term "major" political connections is a shade lower than it used to be.

The first study, done by Peter Russell and Jacob Ziegel of the University of Toronto, reviewed Mulroney's first-term appointments from 1984 to 1988, before the advent of the committees, and found that patronage was pervasive. Almost a quarter of appointees were deemed to have had major involvement with the Progressive Conservative Party, with about 23 percent having minor links, such as having made donations to the party.

The second study, conducted by four researchers—Lori Hausegger from Boise State University, Troy Riddell from the University of Guelph, Matthew Hennigar from Brock University and Emmanuelle Richez from McGill University in Montreal—reviewed appointments made after the committees were up and running. They examined selections made between 1989 and 2003, which encompassed Mulroney's second term as PM and Jean Chrétien's three terms.

The number of women named to the bench continued to rise under both men—likely, the researchers say, at least in part because of the increasing numbers of women in the legal profession.

The country's three major law schools—the University of British Columbia, Dalhousie University in Halifax and Osgoode Hall in Ontario—still got their share of appointees.

And just as about 21 percent of the judges appointed by Mulroney in his final term had either major connections to the now-defunct Progressive Conservative Party or major political activities for the party in their background, so, by God, did about the same number appointed by Chrétien in his three terms have connections to or activity on behalf of the federal Liberal Party in theirs.

As the authors noted, "partisanship still plays an important role in the process," especially in Prince Edward Island, New Brunswick, Saskatchewan and Manitoba, which have the highest number of appointees with major political connections.

In other words, things muddle along pretty much as they did in the days when there were no committees.

Really, what the JACs have succeeded in doing is allowing everyone involved—the government of the day, those who are selected and of course the bar itself—to feel better about themselves.

All of them can point to the screening process as evidence of the non-partisanship, professionalism and overall marvellousness of the Canadian system. Implausible deniability, you could call it.

But, point No. 1, it's not as if the judicial committees themselves are necessarily apolitical, though their politics may not be only those of big-P stripe, but also those forged in lawyerly comradeship.

As the Hausegger et al. paper points out, studies of other merit-based selection systems—in the United States, where some judges are elected and others appointed—show that these committees aren't immune to either run-of-the-mill partisanship or bar politics.

The Canadian JACs now are composed of eight voting members—one judge, and one appointee each from the local law society, the Canadian Bar Association, the policing community and the provincial government, and three from the federal justice ministry.

The committees each have one non-voting representative from Federal Judicial Affairs Canada.

The lawyer members tend to be from the civil side and from each province's dominant firms (and like the Canadian army, the legal elite in this country is remarkably small), just as the appointees themselves tend to be. In fact, the majority of federal judges—as of 2003, it was close to 60 percent—tend to hail from private law firms.

JAC members are appointed for a three-year term, renewable only once.

And in 2015, the last year for which figures were available at the time of writing, the JACs had received 403 applications across the country, deemed 150 as "recommended" and stamped another 220 as "unable to recommend" (the language has changed over time).

Ninety-six superior court judges ended up being appointed.

Were the chosen all recommended candidates? Probably, or as happened with Judge Pinard's appointment, someone in the bar would have squealed to the press.

Did any have connections to the governing Conservatives? Did any have direct connections to any of the committee members? The only ones who know are high-level ministers or JAC members, who are sworn to confidentiality.

Even those who apply for the bench are never told what the result was at the JAC—unless they're appointed—or whether, as the saying goes, they even "made it out of the committee."

Certainly, some don't: They're not "our sort"; they ruffled feathers in their practice; they didn't make the right friends.

As judicial affairs tells committee members, ". . . information on the process is subject to the constraints required to protect the identity of candidates and the confidentiality of the Committee's consultations, proceedings and reports to the Minister of Justice." In other words, while the names of those sitting on the JACs are publicly available on a government website, how they do what they do—how they decide who's recommended and who's not and even how they themselves are chosen—is still shrouded in secrecy.

And make no mistake. While the government of the day gets to pick from the JACs' lists, it's a brave—and rare—justice minister or prime minister who defies the committees and names someone who didn't get the seal of approval. The only one who appears to have outright thumbed his nose at the process was Trudeau, with the Pinard appointment. The PM was on his way out the door, so the scolding that followed from the bar really landed in Turner's lap.

Thus the JACs, about whose quiet processes so little is known, are mighty powerful.

One of the few pieces of information about the committees on the website of the Commission for Federal Judicial Affairs Canada is the number of applications they receive every year.

Interestingly, in the period from November 1, 2004, to October 31, 2005, the 17 JACs received a total of 562 applications, stamped 170 as "recommended," and were "unable to recommend"—the system dispensed with the "highly recommended" category the next year—a whopping 295 others, or fully 52 percent.

One such application was formally acknowledged by legal counsel Margaret Rose Jamieson, the then executive director of judicial appointments, on December 23, 2004. She wrote the applicant to say she had received the lengthy "personal history form" and was duly submitting the paperwork to the Manitoba JAC for review.

The big announcement from Irwin Cotler, the then federal justice minister, came five months later in a press release dated May 20, 2005: That applicant, Anita Lori Douglas, was now Madam Justice Douglas of the Court of Queen's Bench of Manitoba, Family Division.

She would go on to be caught up in a wretchedly public version of a messy private scandal involving her late lawyer husband, Jack King, and one of his clients, a grasping and litigious man named Alex Chapman.

It's a long and complicated tale, but in a nutshell what happened goes like this.

In 2002–2003, King began posting intimate pictures of his wife on a website focused on interracial sex, and in the spring of 2003, he also ended up sending Chapman, a black man he was representing in a divorce, some of those pictures and directing him to the website.

Chapman then, in essence, threatened through a lawyer to sue King for sexual harassment unless he was paid off. King, using his wife's money, coughed up twenty-five thousand dollars to silence Chapman and have him "return" all the pictures.

Predictably, this little deal held up for only a few years. In July 2010, Chapman, the perennial chip on his shoulder freshly irritated, marched off to the CBC with his stash of dirty pictures and the proverbial shit-show followed.

By 2012, when a Canadian Judicial Council inquiry was probing Judge Douglas's conduct and any role she may have had in the matter—she has always utterly denied knowing what King was doing with their private pictures—and the case was making national headlines, the judge was fighting for her career.

Yet for all the salacious details that emerged about King's fantasy sex life at the hearing, the significant window that opened, albeit just an inch or two, was the one into the opaque judicial appointment process itself.

The truly amazing revelation in this regard, especially since one of the charges against Judge Douglas was that she hadn't declared that there was such a cloud in her background, was that the JAC that appointed her knew at least the bare bones—and at least one key member, considerably more—of the story.

As one of the judge's lawyers said in an affidavit filed in court, "the material facts" of her husband's misconduct, the payout to Chapman and the existence of intimate pictures of her on the web "were all known both to Justice Martin Freedman of the Manitoba Court of Appeal," who was then the chair of the Manitoba JAC, and "the then-Chief Justice of the Manitoba Court of Queen's Bench Chief Justice [Marc] Monnin."

And Justice Freedman, who retired from the appeals court in the fall of 2012, testified at the inquiry that he told the other members because "it was something that the committee had to know about."

He was questioned about what precisely he knew of the scandal at the time the committee met on April 21, 2005. Before the meeting, Freedman said, he'd consulted with other judges, in particular with Chief Justice Monnin.

He said the chief justice told him that Douglas had applied before, and that during the summer of 2003 he'd heard rumours about the scandal and withdrawn his support for her application, mostly "because of the risk of embarrassment or blackmail because of the photographs that had been on the Internet."

But, Freedman said, by the time he spoke to the chief justice that spring, Monnin "had withdrawn his opposition . . . he confirmed his understanding that the photographs, whatever they were, had been both destroyed and removed, and it was on that basis that he was [now] prepared to see her application go forward."

Freedman said that, personally, he knew that photos of "a sexual nature" had been involved and that though he hadn't seen them, what he meant by this was that "they would depict Ms. Douglas either performing sexual acts or in a state of nudity."

He said he knew that the reason King had had to leave the firm where at the time both he and Douglas were partners was that he had tried to persuade Chapman "to have sex with Lori Douglas."

He said he knew that there had been "a resolution of this trouble" and that there was a confidentiality settlement with Chapman, and added, "I don't know that I knew the amount that had been paid, but I think I knew there was some money paid."

Douglas was the tenth on a list of thirteen applicants the committee was discussing, and when they got to her, Freedman said, there was general agreement that she was "an excellent lawyer, excellent or better than that, outstanding, and would be an excellent judge."

Only then did the discussion turn to "the incident involving her husband, the fact of the photographs . . . and the fact, that as we understood it to be the case, that Ms. Douglas was an innocent, I use the word *victim*, in this situation."

But while Justice Freedman maintained that he'd told the rest of the committee much of what he knew, the evidence of most of the other members is that something may have been lost in translation.

The committee decided, he said, it needed to "ensure that our understanding was correct." It wouldn't matter if they weren't going to recommend her, but "once it was clear that this issue apart, we were going to recommend her, the decision had to be, 'Do we recommend her or highly recommend her?'"

Douglas was then on her third try for the bench. The other two times, she had been "highly recommended." But on this occasion, Freedman said, someone else at the table said, "'With this situation here, we'd better not highly recommend her . . . we can only go so far as to recommend her.'" So that's what they did, in a truly spectacular exhibition of punch-pulling.

In other words, if it all fell apart, which they appeared to doubt would ever happen, no one could point a big finger of blame at them.

They also decided to "deputize" Jamieson to, in Freedman's words, "interview Ms. Douglas on behalf of the committee and to obtain verification that what we understood to be the case, in the manner I've discussed, was, in fact, the case."

In any case, Freedman said, the committee decided that if their collective understanding of the situation was confirmed, they'd recommend her to Minister Cotler. But, he added, "We wanted to flag this information for the Minister's attention because it was an unusual situation, to say the least."

Apparently it struck no one odd—neither Freedman, nor the other lawyer members, nor the deputized Jamieson—that they were looking to confirm a purported victim's victimhood by calling the victim herself and no one else.

Jamieson, Justice Freedman said, did follow up on April 25 with the call to Douglas—who mentioned it in her gardening diary—and then wrote a two-paragraph note, which she read aloud to the committee. The first graph, he said, was a "glowing" report on Douglas's qualifications. The second, he said, "was this flag about an incident with her husband, innocent victim, photos of a sexual nature, destroyed, removed from the Internet permanently.

"That's the summary," he told the CJC inquiry on July 27, 2012. "The recommendation went in with the information flagged for the Minister's attention. . . . The Minister had to be notified that if he was considering Ms. Douglas for appointment, this was something that should be brought to his attention."

But the hearing had been told that the anticipated evidence from Cotler's judicial affairs advisor at the time, François Giroux, was that while "he was generally aware that there had been an incident involving Ms. Douglas's husband," he had no knowledge whatsoever that there were sexually explicit photos of Ms. Douglas and "certainly no knowledge that photos had been on the Internet."

Asked if it was possible the report for the minister didn't mention the photos, Freedman replied, "I don't think so, no," and said he could be sure of that because it was the pictures that had been "the whole concern of the Chief Justice . . . the concern about blackmail and embarrassment."

Alas, the CJC hearing itself proceeded to go off the rails shortly after Freedman testified, with various lawyers applying for judicial review in other courts, one so-called independent counsel, Guy Pratte, quitting, and another, Suzanne Cote, being appointed to take his place.

After a year of spectacular brawling among the assorted parties, the hearing was set to resume in the fall of 2013.

Some in the Manitoba legal community always suspected that if all the court actions sufficiently delayed the proceeding, Judge Douglas would just give up the ghost and retire.

In fact, that's precisely how things unfolded: Through a deal announced in the fall of 2014, but that took effect only in May of the following year, the CJC called off the dogs and Douglas agreed to resign—having just reached the magic ten-year anniversary whereupon she was eligible for a lovely two-thirds pension.

Yet for most of this fight, Douglas showed she wasn't cut from the quitting sort of cloth, period. After all, whether through bad advice or bad judgment, or both, she had the rather staggering chutzpah to send in her third application little more than a year after she, hubby King and his lawyer, Bill Gange, had managed—barely—to get a cap on the simmering and volatile cauldron that is Alex Chapman.

Douglas made her first application to the bench on December 10, 1999. It was valid until January 24, 2002, exactly two years from the day the JAC assessed it.

Before it even expired, on January 8, 2002, she reapplied. That application expired on June 12, 2004—almost exactly a year after Chapman's lawyer, Ian Histed, sent what was effectively a demand letter to both King and the old Winnipeg firm Thompson Dorfman Sweatman, where both King and Douglas were then partners.

In fact, it was over lunch on June 16, 2003, the CJC committee learned, that King first told his wife what he had done.

The panel fell apart before it could hear from the judge herself, but King and the firm's managing partner, Michael Sinclair, both testified as to her shock and horror. Contemporaneous entries made in her gardening diary also reflect her profound sense of betrayal.

Yet not six months later, Douglas was writing in that same diary that her hopes of a judicial appointment were alive again; this after a couple of meetings with TDS lawyer Rick Adams and a friend identified only as "Nate"—Nathan Nurgitz, the former Tory senator who resigned that seat only to get on the Manitoba Court of Queen's Bench, where he was still. (After he turned seventy-five in 2009, Judge Nurgitz returned to TDS, and worked there until the summer of 2012.)

Douglas wrote on November 20, 2003, ". . . meeting with Rick Adams—raises my hopes of a judicial appointment again. Can't believe Jack was so careless—may have ruined my chances for good."

Five days later, she was still optimistic. "Lunch with Nate, Rick and Albina [Moran, Adams's wife and another TDS lawyer]," Douglas wrote. "Has got my hopes up again."

Those hopes were dashed the next day, when she met Gerry Mercier, then the associate chief justice of the Queen's Bench and first among her key references.

"Felt like I'd run a marathon," she wrote afterwards. "Frankly [have] had to reconcile myself that there is simply no chance. I hope I can really forgive Jack."

But Judge Nurgitz wasn't ready to cry uncle yet, and a year later, about six months after her second application had expired, in early December 2004, Douglas wrote, "Started off with a call from Nate, raising my hopes re: an appointment again!"

A couple of days later, when fellow TDS lawyer Karen Simonsen was named a judge, Douglas mentioned it and wrote, "Yikes—no hope for me." (Simonsen was replacing Marc Monnin, who had been elevated to chief justice.)

But by December 17, Douglas wrote that she'd got all her billings done "as well as the judicial application form. Gets my hopes up again and I feel so completely hopeless about it."

In late April 2005, a few days after the JAC meeting, Margaret Rose Jamieson (Douglas simply describes the call in her diary as being "from Ottawa") phoned her, as the JAC had requested, to confirm that its understanding of the situation was correct.

"Hope my answers will suffice," Douglas wrote, "but it is definitely like winning a lottery."

On May 19, she won it.

What she described in her diary as "the long-awaited call from the Minister of Justice" finally came. "Instant cloud nine," she wrote.

It's not known, because of course it's secret, how many of the thirteen candidates for the bench that year the Manitoba JAC recommended, highly recommended or was unable to recommend. But Lori Douglas was surely the only one who had had intimate pictures of her posted on the web and who was, even if as an innocent victim, at least peripherally involved in a sex-and-blackmail scandal that saw her lawyer spouse resign in disgrace.

And the chair of the JAC was keenly aware of all of these elements, and to varying degrees, the other committee members, the executive director of the appointments process and the justice minister's aide were aware of at least a sizeable shadow in her background.

How on earth did Douglas come to be recommended and appointed?

As it turns out, getting a seat on the bench isn't at all like winning the lottery. Luck has almost nothing to do with it.

Until 2006, when the number was upped to eight, there were only seven members on all the JACs, Manitoba's included. The chair in Manitoba for 2004–2006 was Justice Freedman. Patrick Riley, a well-regarded local civil litigator (and stepson of the late former Bank of Canada governor James Coyne), was the appointee of the Manitoba Law Society.

Ellen Olfert, a popular labour activist and New Democrat, was the appointee of the provincial NDP government, then headed by Gary Doer, and a non-lawyer, Kaye E. Dunlop, represented the Canadian Bar Association, but because Dunlop's husband, Chris Pappas, was a partner at TDS, where Lori Douglas then worked, she didn't participate in the Douglas discussion.

The remaining three members—Alain Laurencelle, Frank Bueti and Sharon MacArthur (née Appleyard)—were appointees of the federal justice minister. The first two are lawyers, MacArthur a paralegal—but just as important, each came with good, solid Liberal connections.

Laurencelle was the party's former riding association president for Saint Boniface; MacArthur, the former riding association president for former Liberal MP Anita Neville and a former president of the Manitoba wing of the federal party; and Bueti, a failed Liberal candidate in Winnipeg North Centre in the 1984 election.

In the *plus-ça-change, plus-c'est-la-même-chose* category, the three appointees of the federal justice minister on the 2012 Manitoba

JAC were also all lawyers, this time with good connections to either the Progressive Conservative Party of Manitoba or the federal Conservatives.

Marni Larkin, who owns a marketing company, is a long-time Tory strategist who once ran federally for the PCs; John Tropak, a businessman, is a former campaign manager for the Conservative MP for Saint Boniface, Shelly Glover; and chartered accountant Ken Lee is the long-serving chief financial officer for the PC Party of Manitoba.

In other words, even the members of the JACs—often used as shields to dismiss any suggestion that the judicial appointment process isn't entirely merit-based and clean as a whistle—frequently have political connections. It is evidence only that all political parties appoint their friends and that those people, in turn, tend to appoint those who are either like them or known to them.

This aspect of judicial appointment commissions like Canada's is their most potentially dangerous characteristic.

The University of Queensland law professor Jim Allan, in his essay in the book *Appointing Judges in an Age of Judicial Power* (2006), a global survey of judicial selection and appointment processes, described such commissions as posing "the risk of self-selection and perpetration of an insulated lawyerly caste."

And, Allan said, such people are inherently less likely to make a bold appointment. "The reason is simple, if paradoxical," he wrote. "Lawyers with noticeably divergent views about interpretation will appear too political to appoint. A politician could make such an appointment and be prepared to live with the political fallout; an unelected judicial appointments board would probably prefer to opt for a safer candidate." And a nation is better off hearing unorthodox views, he concluded, "judicial as well as generally."

On one level, Lori Douglas was probably a safer or more neutral choice than some of her legal colleagues, or even, perhaps, than some of her still-secret competition for the bench that year. She has no political involvement in her background. She was a member of no party.

And the two men who appeared to have been most in her corner—most notably Nate Nurgitz, the fellow who stoked the coals of her judicial ambitions—were both plugged in, but to the wrong party. Judge Nurgitz, after all, had been a PC senator and left that sinecure only when a better one came along.

Ditto for Gerry Mercier, the former Manitoba PC Member of the Provincial Legislature and cabinet minister in the government of Sterling Lyon.

Mercier was, throughout Douglas's three applications for the bench, always listed as her No. 1 reference. Nurgitz was always her No. 2.

But in Ottawa at the time of the Douglas appointment, the Liberals were still in power. It would appear neither man would have had any particular schlep there or with the then justice minister, Irwin Cotler.

If anything was at play within Liberal government circles, it might have been the perception that Douglas was the truly wronged party in the Chapman scandal and that she should not be made to pay for the sins of her husband.

In any case, the Manitoba JAC spent about a half hour discussing each candidate, Justice Freedman testified. He had a good independent memory of the meeting, aided by a couple of procedural notes.

During Freedman's time on the stand at the CJC inquiry, independent counsel Kirsten Crain put to him the "will-say" statements of the other five involved committee members, Kaye Dunlop having abstained from the discussion.

Sharon MacArthur's recollection was similar to Freedman's, Crain told the judge. Laurencelle, she said, couldn't recall specifics, but remembered the JAC "received information that her husband had been involved in questionable sexual conduct" but that it "was a private matter which had been settled and that Douglas was an innocent victim of her husband's lack of judgment."

But, Crain said, Laurencelle "did not know anything about any photos."

The remaining three members—Ellen Olfert, Patrick Riley and Frank Bueti—all said "there was no discussion of photos at the meeting" and had no memory of any follow-up call that was to be made to Douglas.

Bueti, Crain said, in fact had a "firm memory" that there "was no discussion of sexually graphic photos of Ms. Douglas." And Jamieson, who was the one "deputized" to call Douglas, recalled the phone call, but not why or how she came to make it.

What Justice Freedman didn't have were the "extensive notes" of every interview he conducted before the meeting—these were his discussions with fellow judges—and notes of what was actually said at the meeting. "We were required to shred every note of any substantive discussion about a candidate," he said.

All members of all JACs are still required to shred their notes and documents.

"I shredded all my notes . . . as, I think, every other committee member did. We were required to do that, so I have no such notes."

The notes would have been mighty helpful in determining exactly who knew what, who had what to say about Douglas's candidacy and how exactly the committee reached its remarkable decision.

But in the end, without the notes and given the disparate memories of those who were there, all that can be said about the vetting process is that it failed.

In fairness, the JACs are not investigative bodies. The committee's function, as Justice Freedman testified, was not to investigate Douglas but to assess her application.

Merely asking Jamieson to phone an applicant directly was apparently considered radical, or as Freedman described it, "a very unusual, unique step for us." And, according to him, if Cotler had had questions, "further investigation could have been done had the minister wanted that to happen."

The likeliest explanations for the Douglas appointment is either that now the appointment has blown up in their faces some members of the committee are misremembering, or that Freedman was not as explicit in briefing the JAC about the sordid details of the scandal as he thought he had been.

He acknowledged, certainly, that he personally believed the unpleasantness was settled, that at the time he believed things on the Internet could be removed permanently, and that Douglas was a victim of her husband.

Perhaps it was this feeling he conveyed most strongly to the committee members, whether he was aware of it or not, so that the message they took was that this bit of unpleasantness was dead in the water.

And perhaps it was this same feeling that most registered with Jamieson, and what she in turn conveyed to Minister Cotler's aide, François Giroux.

If that was the sense of things people in that room and at the minister's office had, and if they also shared Freedman's clear modern view that a woman was neither a man's property nor responsible for his misdeeds, that could have turned the tide for Douglas.

"Never underestimate the power of political correctness with Liberals," one of them, uninvolved in the Douglas story, told me.

It is probably stating the obvious to say that as a modern woman and a feminist, I share the view that I don't belong to any man; that I can't be blamed for what my husband, lover, brother or father does or how he conducts himself; and that none of those men can answer for my sins or I for theirs.

Thus, I was on Judge Douglas's side before and during the aborted CJC inquiry in Winnipeg, which I covered for the *National Post* and Postmedia newspapers.

I perceived the judge, whom I have never met or even clamped eyes upon, as a victim of her husband—or perhaps more fairly of his illness, for King claims to have been in a severe depression at the time he posted the infamous pictures and behaved like a teenager in the first throes of raging hormones.

I believed that he had acted without her knowledge and that she had not participated in his tawdry games with Chapman. That she did participate is the first allegation against her.

I know that she altered one line in her diary—this is another allegation, one she quickly admitted—but I regard that transgression as relatively minor. I believed that so long as she hadn't tried to hide the whole awful business from the JAC, and she clearly had not done that, then she had been appointed on a warts-and-all basis.

I believed that she answered "No" to the key question on the judicial application form—"Is there anything in your past or present which could reflect negatively on yourself or the judiciary, and which should be disclosed?"—probably because, first, she felt she herself had done nothing wrong; second, because, like lawyers everywhere, she can split hairs until the cows come home; and third, because she knew that since many in Winnipeg's small legal community already knew about her husband's misconduct, any formal disclosure of it was redundant and unnecessary.

And intellectually, I also believed that the mere fact that these pictures of her were on the web ought not to in and of itself render her ineligible to continue on the bench.

A little to my surprise, at the hearing I even came to rather like Jack King, whose testimony I heard. I found him warm, funny and sharp as a tack. I felt sorry for him too.

Whatever we do in the grips of whatever form our sexual desires take, most of us would look foolish afterwards, and that's putting it kindly.

It reminded me of what my friend Tracy Nesdoly, a former courts reporter, once said years ago in the midst of a Toronto hubbub over the release from jail of a notorious offender: Nobody ever chooses to be a pedophile.

King didn't choose to be sexually excited by taking pictures of his wife either, or by the prospect of having a threesome with a black man. He just was. That's what turned his crank—and that crank, the human sex drive, is so strong that it can roll over and flatten intellect, sense and will, as was so wretchedly proven in this instance.

Purely as one flawed person looking upon another, I empathized with him. And I was genuinely sorry to learn of his death from cancer on April 28, 2014.

But one aspect of the whole story has always bewildered me. It's this.

Why, when the scandal first surfaced in 2003 in its relatively contained fashion (that is, within Thompson Dorfman Sweatman and the local bar) and Douglas got away lightly, her job secure and her reputation largely intact, did she not just keep her head down, merrily bill away at her firm, live a quiet life, and give up her dreams of the bench?

If one question is, How could that committee have recommended her?, the other is, How in the world did she imagine that she could—no, should—still be made a judge?

The imperfect analogy I make is this. For people of my generation, who grew up in an age when drinking and driving was our parents' norm if not quite ours, the recognition of it as a serious crime dawned slowly or incrementally. Many of us of a certain age probably continued to occasionally drive when we shouldn't have—I certainly did—but when the light bulb over our heads belatedly lit up, we were awash in relief and guilt and gratitude.

We knew we had managed to get away with something. We knew we had been lucky. We promised to ourselves to never do that again, and I'd bet a lot of us have kept that promise.

It seems Lori Douglas never had that moment.

A friend of hers, a lawyer, says that from the moment you enter law school, your faith in it builds—in the processes, the system, the precedents, the predictability of outcomes, the desire to fix things, the apparent magic of the code that makes their world run.

Lawyers, this one says, come to believe they really can fix everything, that the documents they sign are actually as binding upon—and mean as much to—the ordinary people who sign them as they are to them.

Another friend says that Douglas was constitutionally ill-suited to the rough-and-tumble of family law, which is a hard and wearing practice area. She is by nature a conciliator, this person says, someone who always preferred to settle cases, unlike her combative husband, who absolutely loved being in court and thrived on it.

For that reason, Douglas had an excellent reputation in the family bar as a nice person in a nasty business.

For that reason, her colleagues may have concluded, she was a natural for the bench.

And for that reason, this friend believes, Douglas wasn't happy at the prospect of being a family law lawyer for the rest of her career. She wanted out and the only career out was the bench—and perhaps that allowed her to rationalize her way into applying again.

Couple that with lawyers' sense of specialness, and the fact that they move within an echo chamber, and you have a recipe for entitlement.

Even so, how did all those smart people with their big brains think that a man like Alex Chapman—and he is an easy read even if you're deaf and blind to that sort of thing, with a track record for suing and for feeling aggrieved—would actually destroy the pictures he said he would destroy, keep his mouth shut and go away forever for twenty-five thousand dollars?

How could none of them—but for Justice Monnin, whose concern was relatively short-lived, though at least he had it—not have imagined that Chapman would come back to the well for more?

And how, given that this all occurred over 2003–2005 and not in the first days of the Internet, did no one point out what was already understood in the real world (if not as well as it is understood now), that that which is put on the web lives forever?

In this one regard, Paul Cosgrove, the most thoroughly disgraceful judge in modern Canadian history, and Lori Douglas, the most thoroughly disgraced judge, have something in common.

He believes to this day that what he saw in his courtroom was improper police and Crown conduct; that if he made mistakes, they ought to have been forgivable; and that he should have been able to stay on the bench.

And she believes, or at least her lawyers have argued, that none of what has happened ought to have precluded her from continuing as a judge.

His was a nakedly partisan appointment. Hers emerged from the supposedly better JACs system. Both were disastrous.

Whatever the best way of picking judges is, electing them is not considered a viable answer by the legal establishment. It is unlikely to ever happen in this country, whatever Canadians themselves say they want.

In 2007, a Strategic Counsel poll done for *The Globe and Mail* and CTV found that two thirds of respondents supported the idea of elected judges. A 2002 Environics poll showed the same majority favouring electing Supreme Court judges. And a 2003 Ipsos-Reid poll reported that more than 70 percent of Canadians agreed that "it should be up to Parliament . . . not the courts to make laws in Canada."

But lawyers, the judiciary, and legal experts and scholars practically faint in horror at the prospect.

New York lawyer Bobby Holdman, a former prosecutor who was an appointed judge until he went into private practice, agrees.

"So while the average person would of course say that free election is the fairest way, in practice . . . in my opinion, it is the worst," he says.

To be fair, New Yorkers are understandably touchy on the subject, having seen first-hand what can happen with such a system in the sorry saga of the former Democratic assemblyman from Brooklyn, Clarence Norman, Jr.

In 2007, Norman was convicted of extortion in what was essentially a judgeships-for-sale scandal. That August, he was sentenced to three to nine years for leaning on two civil court candidates to pay thousands to his favourite campaign consultants or lose the support of the party machine.

As Holdman says, because judges don't have the name recognition of senators, most voters probably pick them purely on the basis of the political party backing them, so the lone-wolf, genuinely independent candidate is at a huge disadvantage.

It's no different in Canada, where, as Toronto defence lawyer Steve Skurka says, more people likely know the names of the characters on *Jersey Shore* than they do those of Supreme Court judges, let alone any others.

The other risk, he says, is that one likely would end up with an ultra-conservative bench. (That such a bench would have won only with popular support seems to count for nought, either with Skurka or most any other lawyer I know. As with most governing classes, the legal one in Canada knows better than the citizens what's good for the citizens.)

"You now have an agenda and you're beholden to the group which put you in," Skurka says, "and invariably it's the law-and-order side. No one gets elected because they're protecting the rights of the criminals. Never."

But the truth is, the current federal judge-picking system is Canada is badly flawed. There has to be a better way, but what is it?

Globally, there are three basic methods.

In countries such as France, the Netherlands and Israel, judges are professionals, specifically trained as such, and appointed, whether by the government or bureaucracy or through a sort of appointments commission.

Direct election, the means by which some but nowhere near all American judges get their seats (basically, all federal judges are presidential appointments with the consent of the Senate, while state judges can be elected, with or without party affiliation noted on the ballot, or appointed in a mix of ways), is an increasingly unloved method.

Appointment, with the involvement of a nominating or recommending committee, is gaining favour as the growth of judicial power becomes too obvious to ignore. Even the United Kingdom, where judges used to be appointed by the Lord Chancellor after what were called "secret soundings" in the legal community, moved in 2005 to a judicial appointments commission.

In Canada, the old "tap on the shoulder" method also used to prevail: One didn't seek the job, much less fill out a ghastly form to get it. One was invited.

In her essay "The Judicial Whisper Goes Around" in the collection *Appointing Judges in an Age of Judicial Power*, Elizabeth Handsley was quoting an Australian judge: "The judicial whisper goes around and someone ends up miraculously on the bench."

And in fact, at least some of Canada's most admired and best judges were appointed the very same way.

As the retired judge Thomas Zuber, formerly of the Ontario appeal court and trial courts, says, there used to be an advance man for the justice minister, who "knew when vacancies were coming up . . . [and] went to people who wouldn't have sought an appointment. People like Arthur Martin, Charlie Dubin [the advance man], went to them first and said, 'Look, will you take an appointment?' And they said 'Yes, if you offer it to me.'"

Even now, Zuber says, a candidate has "got to have some beginning sponsorship," either his local MP or someone else in his corner who is connected, to kick-start the process.

One of those very well-regarded judges, Zuber himself wasn't invited onto the bench, but actively sought it out. A native of Windsor, Ontario, he was the president of Gene Whelan's riding association, and he and Whelan went against the local tide by supporting John Turner over Paul Martin, Sr., a veteran area MP, in the 1968 Liberal leadership race.

"I was a pariah for not having supported good ole Paul," Zuber says with a grin, "and then Trudeau became the leader and within a short time, who was the minister of justice but John Turner?"

Whelan passed Zuber's name on to Turner, and, Zuber says, "That was it."

But in post-Charter Canada, with the Supreme Court leading the way, it is indisputable that judges are becoming more activist. As Jim Allan wrote in "Judicial Appointments in New Zealand," his essay in *Appointing Judges*: "I do not think it likely that any legal academic could, with a straight face, argue that the power of the judiciary has not increased—and increased mark-edly—across the common law world.

"Of course," Allan wrote, "that increase has not been uni-form. "Canadian judges seem to me to be at the forefront of activism today."

There's a solution that would improve the federal appointments system right under Ottawa's nose: Do it the way that Ontario picks its lower-level judges, and has been doing since 1989.

Though the name sounds like the federal JAC, the province's Judicial Appointments Advisory Committee (the JAAC) is a whole different kettle of fish.

The provincial committee is dominated by a majority who are lay members (seven of thirteen); it does the revolutionary thing of advertising judicial vacancies, which has opened up the field to women, minorities and all of those lawyers who somewhat work and play outside the traditional old-boy channels, and—imagine this—the JAAC actually interviews those who want to be judges.

All of these provisions are set out in legislation, the Courts of Justice Act.

The architect of the system, and the founding chair of the JAAC, is U of T professor Peter Russell. Now retired after a dis-tinguished career teaching political science, Russell is one of the leading global experts on the way judges are chosen, and a man who also knows a thing or two about civilian oversight—he designed the Security and Intelligence Review Committee, the SIRC, which oversees the Canadian Security and Intelligence Service, or CSIS. The SIRC's greatest feature is that each of the main opposition parties in Ottawa names a member to it.

As Russell puts it, "That gave that little review committee some greater legitimacy in Parliament, because they all knew—if you were NDP and it's usually the NDP that are supporting people who are getting bad treatment by CSIS—'No, we've got a person on SIRC. We've got a voice.'"

Russell has long been interested in the judiciary, but it was towards the end of Roy McMurtry's decade-long tenure as Ontario attorney general in the Bill Davis Progressive Conservative government that he first took the subject on in a big way.

The two men were friends from university and were on their way out to lunch one day, when, just before they went out the door, McMurtry said, "Peter, I wish you could tell me how to get this monkey off my back."

He gestured at a wall of files in his office. "It was an entire wall of files," Russell says, "and I said, 'What do you mean? What's in there?'

"He said, 'Those are letters from candidates for the Ontario judiciary [at that time, it was called the provincial court] and those are their fan clubs. And they write all these letters and I have to make appointments.'"

Russell was then working on his book about judges—*The Judiciary in Canada: The Third Branch of Government*, published in 1987—and put his mind to it.

In 1985, when the Liberals took over as a minority government, and by which time Russell had his model designed, it was another of his old school friends, the late Ian Scott, who became the new AG in a new Liberal government at Queen's Park.

(McMurtry, and this amuses me in the context of a discussion about getting the patronage out of judicial appointments, was the beneficiary of two such appointments himself. He was named Canada's high commissioner to Great Britain in 1985 by PM Mulroney. Three years later, McMurtry returned to his law practice, and three years after that, in 1991, Mulroney made him associate chief justice of the Ontario Superior Court.)

Scott, a distinguished lawyer in his own right, called Russell in, gave him space at Queen's Park, and told him to make his idea work.

In January 1989, with Russell as the first chair, the JAAC set up as a three-year pilot project. It passed with all-party support. The only recommendation that didn't fly—Russell still can't believe it—was the one that sought to have the lay people chosen on a multi-partisan basis.

"All three parties . . . turned us down," he says. ". . . we thought the opposition parties would want it, but anyway, no, they think they'll be in power sooner or later so then they can make the appointments! They wouldn't buy that, isn't it crazy?"

But virtually everything else he dreamed of was approved—even that, by statute, the JAAC would have a majority of lay people.

"That's Ian Scott," Russell says.

He himself had been prepared to yield on that one if push came to shove, but Scott told him, "'We will insist on it, Peter. It'll be in the statute.'"

Scott was right, Russell says, because otherwise, "you could just see lawyers and judges . . . taking it over." This way, "they couldn't take it over and they can't take it over, and that's worked very well."

The basic system has been copied around the world (notably in South Africa), and by five other Canadian provinces (British Columbia, Alberta, Saskatchewan, Quebec and Nova Scotia), as, the planet over, nations reform their justice systems.

"But not, unfortunately, in Ottawa," Russell says.

It was not for lack of trying.

He was even retained at one point by the Canadian Bar Association, which "was fed up with the quality of judges being appointed by Ottawa." At one of their annual conventions, Russell remembers, the CBA "took evidence in camera [that is, in secret] from lawyers practising in the courts about the problems.

"I remember it like it was yesterday," he says, this Prince Edward Island lawyer describing how he urged all his clients to settle, whatever the strength of the case, because the judges were "so lousy, so awful, they're totally patronage appointees . . . the outcome is totally uncertain.'"

The CBA then "started to make submissions to a parliamentary committee," Russell says, "and we did that for years, one government after another."

That last time, in 2005, they thought they were getting close "because we got all-party agreement on more or less the Ontario [model].

"Their bells and whistles are a little bit different, but basically, it was that, and they all said that's what we should do, including Vic Toews. And Vic was the Conservative guy." Toews was also the Opposition justice critic at the time, and vice-chair of the parliamentary subcommittee, whose stated noble goal was to eliminate "political partisanship" from the appointment process.

They were ready to go, but then came the election of January 23, 2006, and the Stephen Harper Conservatives won.

Russell, with naive optimism, was delighted when, the following month, Toews was named federal justice minister and attorney general (he later became minister of public safety). *Maybe now, at last,* Russell thought to himself.

"Absolutely not," he says. Toews "just dropped it. "He broke my heart," Russell says. "So that's the story, and we failed."

(In July 2013, Toews quit federal politics, and about eight months later, was duly appointed to the Manitoba Court of Queen's Bench by his Conservative colleague, the then justice minister, Peter MacKay, just as the close-knit Manitoba bar had been speculating way back when.)

In late 2006, the Harper Conservatives did tinker with the JACs, reducing the judge member's ability to vote only for the purpose of breaking ties; getting rid of the "highly recommended" category so that JACs were left to either rate candidates as "satisfactory" or "not satisfactory"; and adding a fourth member from law enforcement.

The latter change had an upside, in that it meant another non-lawyer was added to the mix, giving that sub-set the majority on the committee.

It also had a downside, in that this person, like the other three members, was appointed by the justice minister from a list submitted by the particular constituency, in this case, the police.

If these weren't inconsequential changes, the reaction from the bar and the judiciary was nonetheless near-hysteria. The CJC formally expressed concern over the fact that now the majority of JAC members were picked by Ottawa, and even Beverley McLachlin, chief justice of the Supreme Court, leapt into the fray to say that the independence of the judiciary was now "in peril."

PM Harper snapped back that his government wasn't going to leave the vetting of judges to "a private club of judges and lawyers. . . . That is why we included voices as diverse as victims and the police."

Russell himself is furious at the loss of the "highly recommended" category because it makes it more difficult to know if the appointments are top-notch or not.

But in practice, that the balance of power on the JACs now rests with those who are neither judges nor lawyers gives the JACs something in common with Russell's JAAC, where appointed lay members outnumber the lawyers and judges.

Just about everything else about the JAAC is different—better—than the federal JACs. The former produces lengthy and easy-to-access annual reports and a proud list of the three-hundred-plus judges who have been appointed in Ontario since 1995. By contrast, the federal judicial affairs website offers minimal information, and to put together a list of judges, a citizen would have to plow through all the announcements out of the justice ministry, assuming she could get them.

The JAAC even publishes a leaflet entitled, "Where do judges come from?", which gives Ontarians a brief history of the committee and how it works.

The web site of the JAAC says it all: They shred their notes of meetings, and "information about particular candidates is completely confidential unless released by candidates themselves." But, and it's a big but, "information about committee process is completely open to any person whomsoever."

As Russell wrote in his conclusion to *Appointing Judges in an Age of Judicial Power*, a book of essays he put together with U.K. law professor Kate Malleson, ". . . our choice is between a process in which the politics is open, acknowledged, and possesses some degree of balance or a system in which political power and influence is masked, unacknowledged, and unilateral."

Peter Russell taught political science for almost four decades; he knows you'll never take the politics out of picking judges. He doesn't even believe that's necessarily desirable.

To the electoral victor, in other words, shouldn't some of the spoils go?

As he puts the question he says he's often asked, "Shouldn't they [the party that wins] be able to put people of their orientation in the judiciary?

"Well, sure," he says, "as long as that isn't the only thing going for them. And that's just very natural. The government leans left, leans right . . . you're not going to depoliticize the whole thing totally. That's a sort of straw man we get."

But consider this.

When Russell was chairing that first-ever JAAC, there came before the committee a candidate. "In his interview," Russell remembers, "he told us about defending police officers in criminal cases because, he said, they've been pulling people in off the street and giving them a 'tune-up.'

"Giving them a tune-up."

It was shocking to everyone, he says, but particularly to the lay people: It could have been one of them whose "tune-up" was being so casually described.

The JAAC rejected the man.

"He subsequently got appointed federally," Russell says.

With the JAAC, he says, "You wouldn't get a Paul Cosgrove."

And if Lori Douglas had come before such a body, with its mix of relatively ordinary people and their life experiences outside the law, I have to believe that one or two of them might have disputed the proposition that you could remove things "permanently" from the web, or looked askance at the prospects of a shakedown artist like Alex Chapman quietly going off into the sunset.

As the Aussie Jim Allan cheerfully concluded in his piece for Russell and Malleson's book, the direct appointments process may pose the risk of too much politics, but that's "easier to combat than the too great homogeneity of outlook risk, and anyway is usually counter-balanced where governments are periodically removed by the voters."

It reminds me of a most wonderful story I heard about a Superior Court judge who works at 361, the University Avenue courthouse in downtown Toronto known to all who make a living there by its street number. This judge is one of those who kindly agrees, on days when he's not sitting, to host groups of high school students when they come calling every fall.

Inevitably, with him on the bench and the students in the bleachers, one or another will ask, "How do you get to be a judge?"

On at least two occasions witnessed by someone I know, His Honour, visibly preening, has replied, "Well, the prime minister and the minister of justice comb the land looking for the very best lawyers to appoint to the court. Only the crème de la crème. And as soon as you receive the call, you are from that moment on a judge.

"I remember I was working on a big file with a younger lawyer when the minister of justice called me and advised me that I had been appointed. I turned to my young colleague and said, 'Son, I can be of no further assistance to you.'"

There was no mention of the sucking and blowing he would have done; the friendships he would have cultivated as a lawyer; or the useful connections he had, either in government or among the lawyers on the JAC.

Kevin Murphy didn't escape unscathed from the Cosgrove affair.

In its December 2003 nuking of the judge, the appeal court also excoriated Murphy, calling his trial strategy "deplorable" and "reprehensible." The court recognized, though, that the real villain of the piece wasn't the lawyer but rather the judge who had let him run wild. Still, almost a year later, the Ontario AG formally complained about Murphy to the Law Society of Upper Canada.

Five and a half years after that, on March 23, 2010, a hearing panel found Murphy guilty of professional misconduct, suspended him for six months and ordered him to pay $10,000 of the astonishing $300,000 to $400,000 that the Law Society estimated as its investigation cost.

The panel noted that Murphy admitted his misconduct, or what it called his "egregious conduct and shameful behaviour as an officer of the court and a member of an honourable profession."

It found that his criticism of prosecutors was "outrageous, shameful and undermined the values of the administration of justice.

"This case was more than a case about incivility," the panel wrote. "It involved ethical misconduct that reflected adversely on the integrity of the profession and the administration of justice as a whole."

And while acknowledging his misconduct, Murphy always denied the allegation that his intemperate language had been part of any take-no-prisoners "trial strategy."

I think it is a peculiar Canadian touch that in May 2008, having been roundly and publicly spanked by the Court of Appeal, the man who had spent almost two years in court slagging cops and Crown attorneys was hired as a prosecutor.

At this writing, Kevin Murphy was still with the federal prosecution service, handling drug cases and based in Ottawa.

Still and all, what I love most about the Murphy part of the tale is that in his closing submissions on the stay motion before Judge Cosgrove, the hired-gun Crown, David Humphrey, nonetheless sang the lawyer's praises.

He said, in part, the following about Murphy: ". . . he has courageously, tenaciously, admirably discharged his obligations to his client."

Lawyers just can't help themselves; they indulge in that sort of flowery horseshit about one another all the time. And some of them, along the way, begin to believe it. And that's when it appears they decide they should be judges—and even that, you know, they deserve it.

R v BERNARDO

"They're [cops and prosecutors] like elephants; they never get un-pissed."

—AUTHOR STEPHEN WILLIAMS

MANY YEARS AGO, when I was packing up my desk and leaving the *Toronto Sun* for a newspaper that hadn't even started publishing, I found a big box of notebooks from the trial of Paul Bernardo.

I covered that damn trial from the first day of jury selection in May 1995 until the jurors returned with their verdict in early September.

I was at the University Avenue courthouse in Toronto most mornings by 7 a.m., usually first in the lineup, though Pam Davies and Marianne Boucher, respectively then the court artists for the *Sun* and CITY-TV, often gave me a run for my money.

To say that I liked and preferred the aisle seat in the first press row, near the front, is to rather understate the case. I insisted on it. I was completely anal about it and would fight my colleagues for it. I would never just shift over to make room for some-one else—"reasonable accommodation" may be a hallmark of Canadian institutional life but it ain't of mine—but would sit lumpenly in place until the person clambered over me.

This compulsion wasn't entirely irrational, because the acoustics in Canadian courtrooms are so appalling. Most have no amplification system whatsoever, with any visible microphones either decorative or only for the benefit of the official recording of the proceeding, whether that is made by human hands or, as is sadly increasingly the case, by machine.

But like most big trials and public inquiries, the Bernardo trial was an exception. Real media attention—i.e., lots of TV cameras—seems to penetrate even the thickest organizational skulls in government.

In courtroom 6-1, there were actual amplifying mikes. But experience had taught me that there are just a few seats, always close to the front, from which I'm most likely to not only make out what's being said but also best see the witness, the accused, the jurors, the judge and the lawyers.

Beyond that, in the Bernardo case, the competition for media places was ferocious because there was such a vast throng of us, from all over the country and beyond, covering the trial. And though there were rows reserved for the press, the seats within them were grabbed on a first-come, first-served basis.

Some days, reporters even paid students to stand in line for them.

So I had my reasons, but mostly I was and am just nuts about this sort of thing. It's for the same reason I arrive at airports at least three hours early.

As I was going through my box of notebooks, the Bernardo trial was almost three years back in the rear-view mirror. I was leaving the *Sun* to join the start-up *National Post*, which began publishing in September 1998; I think I was the second or third editorial employee hired. I usually keep notebooks for six months max. I had no reason to hang on to these particular ones any longer, but decided to flip through them before I tossed them. The case had occupied so much of my psyche and time. It had receded but not gone away.

I was curious to have a last look, auld lang syne and all that.

I was bewildered when I grabbed the first notebook and discovered a bunch of pages were stuck together. Maybe I'd spilled something? But it was the same with the next one I picked up and the one after that and the one after that. Then I remembered:

The glue binding all these pages was the snot that ran from my nose as I cried every day of that case.

Now, I'm an embarrassingly easy crier, and it's a rare day in the courts—and in life—that I don't get verklempt at least once.

My tendency to weep only gets worse as I grow older, just as it did with my late father. It's my norm, or as Sam Pazzano, the *Sun*'s veteran court reporter and the person I still most often sit beside at trials, will say with a deep sigh upon spotting the first signs, "Ah, geez. Here she goes."

But the Bernardo trial was different. There, I didn't just cry quickly and quietly, as you learn to do in court. I think I was still quiet about it, but I cried hard, regularly for part of every day, such that my nose ran pretty much all the time as I sat there, unable to wipe it as, barely able to breathe, I kept taking notes.

Once, when my ex and I were playing Trivial Pursuit with some considerably younger friends, the fellow read aloud a question about Malcolm X. We nearly fell off our chairs when he pronounced it as "Malcolm the Tenth," as though he were referring to the latest of an exotic line of kings and not a famous and fiery African-American civil rights activist who had been assassinated in 1965.

I feel the same way, now, to realize that there's a whole generation too young to know who Bernardo was, who didn't vicariously endure either his trial that long-ago summer or the bit of business that preceded it by almost two years, the secret, almost private, trial of his former wife, Karla Homolka.

As for the handful of good people who were utterly flattened in the Bernardo-Homolka aftermath, in what I think of as the Ontario government's Great Cleanup, no one much cared about them at the time, and so it is almost two decades later.

For a good long while, back when it all was happening, it seemed improbable that Canadians would not always recoil a little at the mention of those two names. The country had never before seen crimes quite like theirs, and probably was never more sharply reminded of a few uncomfortable truths.

The first was that girls and women could be every bit as venal and criminal as boys and men. The second was that murderers don't always look like the fellow who probably was then Canada's most infamous killer, Clifford Olson.

By he time the Bernardo trial started in 1995, Olson had confessed to murdering eleven boys and teenagers and was safely behind bars where he died in 2011. Conveniently, he was as physically repellant as he was morally. He might just as well have been wearing a sign that read, "Serial killer." Not so Bernardo and Homolka, with their conventional blond good looks and sheen of normalcy.

And the third thing, though I don't know if anyone realized it back then, was that the act that truly distinguished this couple— that they videotaped their protracted sexual assaults upon their victims—was but a glimpse of the tip of the record-it-all iceberg that was to come with the advent of cellphone cameras, webcams, selfies and the like.

They met when she was just seventeen, Bernardo twenty-three. Homolka was then living at home in St. Catharines, Ontario, with her parents and two younger sisters. At first, Bernardo commuted to see her there on weekends from Scarborough, where he was in school, working as an accountant-in-training (he never really shucked those career training wheels and soon turned to smuggling) and living with his parents.

He was already the so-called Scarborough Rapist at the time they met in October 1987, though he had just begun his vicious blitz attacks of young women in the pretty enclave, called Guildwood, of the Toronto suburb.

These violent assaults continued for much of his early courtship of Homolka, covering a period from May 1987 to May 1990, spawning a special Toronto Police task force and eventually resulting in a composite drawing being released, complete with a "Have You Seen This Man?" headline, which looked so much like Bernardo that his friends remarked upon the resemblance.

Still, he wasn't arrested for almost another three years, for a good part of which time the DNA sample he'd given Toronto Police in 1990 sat with DNA samples from more than a hundred other suspects in the rapes, untested at the then overworked and underfunded provincial crime lab.

If the assaults in Scarborough stopped about the time he moved to St. Catharines, first into the Homolka family home and later to a rented bungalow with Homolka in a part of town called Port Dalhousie, Bernardo didn't slow down, but in fact escalated.

Now working as a couple, Bernardo and Homolka embarked on the kidnapping-torture-rape-and-murder spree that would make them notorious.

As John Rosen, who represented Bernardo at trial, told me a couple of years ago, "Together they formed an entity greater than the sum of the individual parts."

They began in their own backyard, as it were, by zoning in on Homolka's baby sister, Tammy.

Bernardo had an obsession with virgins that would have been ridiculous, even cartoonish, if it wasn't also lethal. As his former best friend told former *Toronto Sun* reporters Scott Burnside and Alan Cairns, as quoted in their 1995 book about the case, *Deadly Innocence*, he dreamed of a "virgin farm" where beautiful, innocent girls would roam free, their only goal to service him.

Bernardo also had a fetish for schoolgirls in their kilts-and-knee-socks uniforms, a harmless enough fantasy for most of the men who share it, but for him, it constituted an action plan.

In fact, his greatest complaint about Homolka was that she'd had sex with a boyfriend before him. And sometime before Christmas of 1990, Bernardo suggested to Homolka that he wanted Tammy—to have sex with her, or as the couple always put it, "to take her virginity"—as a Christmas present.

Tammy was then just fifteen, a pretty kid who presumably trusted her big sister and had grown used to her boyfriend, who was by then squatting in the family home and being treated like the son-in-law he would soon become.

Homolka was in the very bosom of her family. She was finishing high school, though she dropped out for a time. She had a job, at an animal clinic. She had friends of her own, money of her own. She was considered to be, and was by most accounts but her own revisionist spin delivered much later on, a feisty, independent free spirit.

Yet the only explanation she has ever offered for what she did to her little sister was that Bernardo had been nagging her about it and that she was, inexplicably in these circumstances, somehow in his thrall.

In addition, Homolka said, he promised to wear a condom when they went at Tammy and that the assault would be over fast. Besides, as she inimitably put it in her testimony at his trial, "it would be a one-time thing."

As I wrote that day, in one of only a handful lines I remember from a forty-year career of newspaper writing, "Oh well, then."

Once she agreed to it, Homolka went at it full-bore: She was the planner, the one who made it happen.

In early December 1990, she and Bernardo were also formally engaged, so she was a busy, busy girl. As the author Stephen Williams dryly wrote in *Invisible Darkness*, the first of his two excellent books about the case, "Now, she had two big things to plan: her wedding and her sister's rape."

Homolka studied her drug compendium for the right sleeping pill (the pre-drug drug) and the right inhalant anesthetic (the drug proper) to use on Tammy. For the latter, the one she picked was halothane, which is meant to be used with a face mask or vaporizer. She stole some from the clinic where she worked.

A video camera, she said, using that strange passive voice she adopted in court, "was purchased," as though it had been purchased by passing random strangers and not by her betrothed, who wanted to video what Homolka called "the acts with Tammy."

Note: The acts *with* Tammy, not against her. Homolka always described the assault that way, as though Tammy was somehow a willing participant or had waived her minor objections.

The pair got their chance on the evening of December 23 that year.

The Homolka clan—Karla, Bernardo, Tammy, middle sister Lori and the parents—was gathered in their basement rec room, drinks at hand (only Tammy's were laced with crushed sleeping pills), to watch some TV.

Bernardo was videotaping everyone with his new camcorder.

Video-ing the family at Christmas in the rec room: I've always found it an indescribably creepy practice—the modern equivalent is the selfie—but recognize that for many people, it was both familiar and benign. It's just one illustration of how this couple could touch the ordinary or mundane and spoil it for everyone else.

Eventually, Lori and the elder Homolkas went up to bed, but Tammy, a little drunk and sleepy, thanks to the doctored drinks she'd been fed, stayed put to watch a movie with Bernardo and her big sister.

As soon as she fell asleep, the couple got down to business.

Homolka got the halothane, put some on a cloth and held it over her little sister's mouth and nose, while Bernardo with one hand pulled down Tammy's pants and with the other began taping the assaults, which culminated with him putting his penis in her.

"Keep her down," he told Homolka at one point. "Here we go."

He raped her, and at his direction, Homolka performed cunnilingus on Tammy, pushed her fingers inside her and then, at Bernardo's hissed direction, reluctantly licked them. Tammy had her period, it turned out, which Homolka pronounced "Fucking disgusting" even as she continued to do what Bernardo asked.

He had just switched his attention to Tammy's anus when the teenager suddenly vomited, probably the result of her having aspirated her stomach contents—as Homolka, the veterinarian's assistant, knew full well was always a risk when a patient, animal or human, eats before anesthesia.

Tammy had stopped breathing.

In the panic that followed, Homolka and Bernardo dragged her across the floor, put her clothes back on. He started doing mouth-to-mouth; she called 911.

But it wasn't all hysteria for Homolka: By the time Niagara Regional Police arrived, she'd had the presence of mind to dump the drugs and get the vomit-stained blankets into the wash.

Tammy was formally pronounced dead at hospital, but she died in the first hour of Christmas Eve day in her own rec room at the hands of her sister and her then boyfriend, under the noses of her mom and dad and sister Lori.

Her death was remarkable in almost every way.

For one thing, it was a huge missed opportunity—one of several—for the police.

There was a strange red blotch on the left side of Tammy's mouth, chin and neck. It looked like a burn, but it's unlikely that it was caused by either the halothane or by her being dragged. It should have screamed in neon lights that this was a death worth a good hard look.

But only one Niagara Regional Police officer, a rookie, was suspicious. He was promptly overruled, and Tammy's death was briskly written off as accidental.

Within weeks of her sister dying, as Williams wrote, ". . . Paul and Karla decided the best thing to do was for Paul to go out and get another girl and rape her."

He did just that—neither of them knew her name, so they called her the January Girl. Bernardo had sex with her; Homolka watched. He then drove the girl to a deserted road and let her go. It was the couple's version of getting right back on the horse that threw you: If an attack goes bad, best to do it again straight away, or you may lose the knack.

And a few days after that, with Tammy in her grave less than three weeks, Homolka dressed up in Tammy's clothes and pretended to be her, covering her face—now with her hair, then with a picture of dead sister—to complete the effect.

It was all videotaped, of course.

"I loved it when you fucked my little sister," Homolka told Bernardo. "I loved it when you fucked Tammy. I loved it when you took her virginity."

This was the crime that really told the tale about Karla Homolka. It may be that she wasn't trying to kill her sister, but, as the Criminal Code of Canada puts it in the very definition of murder in Section 229, she was certainly "reckless whether death ensues or not."

Homolka was indifferent whether Tammy survived and woke up with a major headache and a mysterious ache in her privates, or not. She just wasn't much invested in either outcome.

There were other crimes that followed.

Before their wedding, and for about two years after, the couple engaged in their version of courtship with a fifteen-year-old girl who can only be identified as Jane Doe.

Critically, Jane was Homolka's friend, her "project" as Stephen Williams put it: They met at the animal clinic where Homolka worked and bonded over their love of animals, and it was Homolka who phoned to rekindle the friendship after a three-year lapse.

Using the same drugs she used to fatal effect with Tammy, she twice knocked Jane out.

The first time, in June 1991, it worked like a charm: The girl was successfully drugged and Homolka and Bernardo took turns sexually assaulting and videotaping her, and Bernardo was pleased as punch to discover Jane was a virgin.

The second time not so much. It was two months later: The thoughtless Jane started to choke, just as Tammy before her had done, and Homolka again called 911. But Jane recovered, and though still unconscious, started to breathe again.

Homolka called back to cancel the emergency; who even knew you could do that and that the emergency responders would agree to be called off?

The couple also wooed Jane with presents, dinners out, both of them pressuring her all the while to have sex—in the traditional manner, that is, while she was conscious—with Bernardo.

And on their big day, June 29, 1991—it was in Niagara-on-the-Lake, one of those ghastly, over-the-top weddings with the happy couple even parading about in a horse-drawn carriage— Leslie Mahaffy's body parts were found encased in cement blocks not far away in Lake Gibson.

(I saw the lake for the first time in 2015, while hiking the Bruce Trail with some friends. I told them about Leslie then, and grimly added it to the death and destruction tour that grows in my head.)

Bernardo had abducted Leslie from her own backyard in Burlington, Ontario, just two weeks before, then raped and sodomized her while Homolka alternately slept or read upstairs. Then he invited Homolka to join in, which she did.

The fourteen-year-old was killed two days later, her body wrapped in a comforter and stored in the basement because, after all, Homolka's parents were coming over for a Sunday Father's Day dinner.

The next day, Bernardo or Bernardo and Homolka (she denied taking part) dismembered Leslie's body and encased her parts in cement, with Bernardo marvelling at how "light" a human head could be.

On the Thursday before Easter of 1992, the pair went shopping for another girl, and this time, Homolka came along to help.

They settled on fifteen-year-old Kristen French, spotting her as she walked home from Holy Cross High School in St. Catharines. Homolka called her over to ask for directions. The polite and friendly girl obliged, and as the two young women stood by the passenger door, bent over the map the couple had brought precisely for this purpose, Bernardo got out of the car and forced Kristen inside at knifepoint.

Then followed the couple's usual menu of videotaping, feeding their captive drinks, rape first of all by Bernardo (Homolka was downstairs cooking dinner) and then sexual assaults by both of them.

This time, Bernardo also had Homolka enlist Kristen in an elaborate game of let's pretend: Wearing school uniform kilts, they pretended to be schoolgirls getting ready for a night out, while Bernardo taped them.

For four days, they held Kristen, degraded her, bound her, assaulted her separately and together (using hands, mouths, penis and a wine bottle), drugged her, and forced her into all sorts of sex.

Homolka was alone with her twice, while Bernardo went out to run errands or get takeout, and lifted not a finger to help her.

They let her watch her beloved father, Doug, beg for her safe return in a televised press conference not long after she was snatched from the street, an unspeakable cruelty even for specialists like these two.

Shortly before her death, Bernardo urinated on Kristen's face as she lay, defeat in her eyes, in a bathtub.

On that fourth day, with an Easter ham awaiting the young couple at Homolka's parents' house, they killed her.

As Homolka testified in court, "I knew she was going to be killed that day. Paul and I had to go to my parents' for Easter dinner."

At the end of that long trial in the summer of 1995, Bernardo was predictably convicted of two counts of first-degree murder and a slew of other charges from his Scarborough Rapist days and sentenced to life in prison. For good measure, he was later also declared a dangerous offender.

There's little doubt that, like Clifford Olson, he will die in jail; in 2015, he applied for parole, setting off a bit of a public panic, but there's not a parole board in this country that would dare let him out.

The same can't be said for Homolka, who was out of prison in a dozen years, and soon married with kids of her own.

And the damage inflicted to the processes of the criminal justice system along the way—the various proceedings with Bernardo and Homolka at their heart spanned a decade—may also be permanent.

Karla Homolka's "trial" in St. Catharines, Ontario, in the early summer of 1993 was nothing of the sort. It was a plea bargain, with prosecutors and defence presenting to the presiding judge what's called a joint submission, painstakingly worked out in advance.

The practice is so pragmatic that it is still sometimes considered to be, even by those within the profession of law, just a little greasy.

"Much of the controversy surrounding plea bargaining results from disagreement as to what the practice is," the Law Reform Commission of Canada, an independent law review body that is now defunct, wrote in a working paper on the subject in 1975.

The Commission went on to define it as "any agreement by the accused to plead guilty in return for the promise of some benefit."

Back then, the Commission found that the drawbacks—among them, that plea bargaining unfolds in secrecy, which may in turn provide a shield for unethical conduct—were overwhelming.

Its conclusion: "Justice should not be, and should not be seen to be, something that can be purchased at the bargaining table."

But that view began to soften, and by 1989, noting how the system itself had changed (in particular the enhanced protections offered the accused under the Charter of Rights and Freedoms), the Commission reversed itself, did a 180-degree turn and was now solidly in favour of plea bargaining.

This ability to change their minds on a dime, marshal new and different arguments as though for the first time, is another special gift of lawyers.

"Plea negotiation is not an inherently shameful practice," the Commission now said in a 1989 working paper on the matter. "It ought not, on a theoretical level, be characterized as a failure of principle."

By the time the great former defence lawyer and judge G. Arthur Martin presented his five hundred-page *Report on Charge Screening, Disclosure and Resolution Discussions* to the then Ontario attorney general, Marion Boyd, in 1993, it was really all over but the shouting: Plea bargaining was already an integral part of the justice system.

Though there are no available national statistics, in Ontario in 1992, the year the Martin committee was doing its research, fully 81 percent of all charges in the Ontario Courts (the old provincial division where most cases even now are handled), were resolved by way of guilty plea.

And two years before that, in an infamous case called *R v Askov*, the Supreme Court of Canada had formally blessed the practice. So too had provincial and federal lawyers' associations.

Martin went on to endorse plea bargaining as essential, though he never lost sight of the fact that because such deals are the result of conversations held among lawyers behind closed doors, there always remains the potential for abuse.

As he noted, "A case that proceeds to trial creates a record which is subject to careful scrutiny on appeal to ensure that the result at trial was appropriate and just. Resolution discussions, by and large, create a much more limited record."

So, the fact of Homolka's plea was hardly unusual. This was the way the vast majority of cases—one legal author cited by Martin estimates that between 70 and 95 percent of all cases are resolved by guilty pleas—were and are settled in Canada.

But what was unusual about this particular plea was that it was so steeped in secrecy. Parts were variously banned, sealed or otherwise controlled, and to some considerable degree, parts remain banned, sealed or controlled to this day. Details of Homolka's deal would be revealed only two years after it was done, not during her own quickie proceeding but in the middle of her testimony at Bernardo's lengthy trial in Toronto.

All that could be contemporaneously reported from her "trial" was that she was convicted of manslaughter in the deaths of Leslie and Kristen, that she was sentenced to twelve years for each, and that the sentences were to be served at the same time.

The term *plea bargain* couldn't even be used to describe what happened.

The deal would be reviewed—in a lengthy report by retired Ontario Court judge Patrick Galligan, who then had just stepped down from the bench—only in 1996 and only then because, as Galligan put it with magnificent judicial understatement, there was a "sense of public disquiet" at Homolka's sentence.

In fact, well before the details of the plea were revealed at Bernardo's trial in 1995, the Canadian public had roared with fury at news of Homolka's sentence: The maximum penalty for manslaughter is life in prison, so why on earth did she get just twelve years in the homicides of those two lovely girls and the death of her own sister?

Only a judge could have called that kind of visceral reaction "disquiet."

Galligan's report, however, was enormous and thorough, in that he interviewed most of the architects of the deal, within and without the government, including Murray Segal, the then director of the Crown law office, criminal; assistant deputy attorney general Michael Code; AG Marion Boyd, the various trial prosecutors and senior police officers; and Homolka's lawyer, George Walker.

Galligan satisfied himself that one thing was undeniable: If from the get-go the authorities had been in possession of the videotapes made by the couple of their assaults upon Tammy, Leslie, Kristen and Jane Doe—which showed Homolka as a participant—she would almost certainly have been in the prisoners' box beside Bernardo.

But they didn't have the tapes.

It wasn't until September 1994, sixteen months after the government made its so-called deal with the devil and Homolka was already in prison serving her sentence, that Ken Murray—a lanky, bitterly funny, oft-profane fellow—abruptly quit as Bernardo's lawyer, handed the tapes to his successor John Rosen, and Rosen, a couple of weeks later, handed them to police; Murray had kept the tapes to himself, intending to use them to defend Bernardo.

His plan was to get Homolka on the record minimizing her conduct, this at one or another of Bernardo's preliminary hearings, then go to prosecutors and say, "I have evidence that blows that out of the water. Let's make a deal."

Having revealed her as a liar and possible killer—the actual deaths of Leslie and Kristen weren't caught on tape, so it could have been either Bernardo or Homolka who did the killing, or both—Murray believed he could wring a concession or two for his client.

It would be nothing like the deal Homolka got, of course. Murray knew that. But he thought perhaps he could get enough—perhaps a cell with a view, for instance—that Bernardo would plead guilty.

Of course, none of that happened: The government cancelled both of Bernardo's preliminary hearings, sending him to trial on what's called a direct indictment preferred by the attorney general.

Murray lost his opening to have at Homolka. So he switched gears and planned to ambush her with the tapes at Bernardo's trial. It was then that his client had a change of heart and ordered him to bury, or lose, the tapes, and suggested he would lie on the stand. Murray realized he couldn't continue without suborning perjury and had to get off the file.

It was during May 1993, when only Murray knew about the tapes, that the government closed the deal with Homolka and Walker.

It had little choice—so far as the powers-that-be knew, there was virtually no evidence linking Bernardo to the murders of Leslie and Kristen.

But that wasn't Murray's fault.

He didn't discover the tapes by doing anything sneaky or underhanded; it wasn't even that he had outfoxed the authorities. All he'd needed to be was marginally less inept than the police had been, and that he managed, if only just.

Bernardo had given him an envelope a few days earlier, to be opened, he said, only when the defence team briefly got access to the house. Murray had tossed it into his slipcase and promptly forgotten about it.

It was only when he got lost, and was trying to phone his junior for directions, that he spotted the envelope.

Inside was a map of the upstairs bathroom ceiling showing the pot light above which Bernardo had hidden the six mini-cassettes.

It took Murray almost two weeks to summon the will to retrieve the tapes from a safe in his office. He didn't know what was on them, only that Bernardo said they'd be useful. As he put it in an interview in November 2012, "And I had been assured by my ever-reliable client it was not a snuff tape."

A technological klutz, Murray was terrified he would erase the tapes by mistake.

Carefully, he made one working VHS copy of each, as lawyers usually do with this kind of original evidence.

Inarguably, the only real reason Murray found the tapes was because the police in their seventy-one-day search of the Bernardo/Homolka marital home, didn't.

In any case, what Judge Galligan fairly concluded is just what the authorities had concluded: They had to hold their noses and do the deal at the time they did the deal.

But by September 1994, at which point Bernardo's trial was still a half-year away, the government had the tapes.

Within a month, having reviewed them in detail, police and prosecutors knew just who their star witness really was—and that this was no simple case of he-made-me-do-it.

The tapes showed Homolka as a keen, lip-licking partner in the assaults upon Leslie and Kristen and in Kristen's abduction. As Galligan wrote, "The Crown no longer had to rely essentially on the evidence of Karla Homolka to prove that Leslie Mahaffy and Kristen French had been taken to 57 Bayview Drive . . . that Paul Bernardo sexually assaulted each of them. . . . had unlawfully confined both of them."

The tapes also revealed that contrary to Homolka's disclosure, there had been not one but two sexual assaults upon Jane Doe and that Homolka had been at least as involved in them as Bernardo.

Still, Galligan concluded prosecutors were right when they decided not to charge Homolka with the newly discovered attack on Jane—even though, he acknowledged, at first he believed the assault wasn't covered by her plea deal and even though at least one senior police officer and one prosecutor in the province were champing at the bit to charge her.

These respectively were Niagara chief Grant Waddell and Mary Hall, who was handling the Scarborough rapes charges. The two believed Homolka had breached her deal by not disclosing the June 1991 assault on Jane and that she should be charged, either with sexual assault or aggravated sexual assault.

But Galligan sided with those at the attorney general's office who ruled against it.

The judge even endorsed the solicitous kid-glove treatment that had been given Homolka by prosecutors throughout her testimony at Bernardo's trial.

There are two methods, Galligan said in his report, of dealing with an accomplice witness like Homolka. "One is to treat her with disdain. The other is to deal with her as the prosecutors did in this case." He pronounced criticism of that approach as "somewhat droll."

Actually, there's a third way the Crown can handle an accomplice witness—and that is, treat her as a flawed but fully capable and hard-nosed adult. After all, jurors don't have to be convinced of her moral worth—not someone who has rolled over for the state to save her own skin. They merely have to believe her, or not.

As John Rosen put it, the smart prosecutor will "say to the jury—'I had to call her, you take what you want out of her, but let's look at the rest of the evidence and see how it all fits in.'"

But Galligan concentrated on the evidence—chiefly, the psychiatric reports—that supported the Crown's view of Homolka as a battered woman.

What he didn't appear to do was study anything that opposed the wisdom already entrenched within the attorney general's office.

A small example will suffice.

In the official chronology attached as an appendix to his report, Galligan noted "Summer, 1984" as the time Bernardo began a very abusive sexual relationship with a young woman.

"You see? Bernardo was violent and sadistic already," the judge might as well have been saying.

But he took no comparable notice of a comparable event in Homolka's life—"Summer, 1987," the time she zipped down to Kansas to visit a boy who had briefly gone to her high school in St. Catharines.

There, as she told a number of friends upon her return, the two had done cocaine and had rough sex, during which the boy had tied her up with a belt.

And Galligan didn't even glance at the videotapes—not even the segment that revealed the Jane Doe assault in June—that shook, if not shattered, the formal prosecutorial view of Homolka. As he told me in the summer of 2013, at the downtown Toronto office where he was still working as a mediator, he didn't believe the deceased young women would "want anyone who didn't have to see" the tapes to view them.

He agreed they were relevant to the issues he'd been asked to review, but said the detailed police transcripts of what was on the tapes did the trick. "There was no need to look at them in order to know what had happened."

He interviewed fifty-three people, many of whom were intimately involved in making the deal with Homolka and whose reputations, whether they acknowledged it or not, were inextricably linked to it.

Of the fifty-three, nineteen were prosecutors or senior officials in the Crown law office, four of whom, including Michael Code, went on to be appointed to the bench.

Another twenty-three were leading lights of the criminal bar, two of whom also later became judges.

Essentially, the position of the key players Galligan talked to was: *Of course we were working in the best interests of justice. Of course the deal was a necessary evil.*

And his starting point, of course, was that these were people of the highest integrity and finest calibre.

Indeed, he described for the reader the stellar qualities of each in the florid language—Walker was "highly competent, ethical and responsible"; Segal had "extensive experience" and had written or co-written many scholarly articles; Code was "a prominent and respected member" of the bar, etc. etc.—that lawyers so often use when referring to one another.

Given the sterling characters of those to whom he spoke, it was hardly a shock that Galligan accepted what they told him. That he was one of them—lawyer, judge, part of that strange unelected governing class whose members invariably believe the very best of themselves—appears not to have crossed Galligan's mind or caused him a whit of self-doubt.

He hired as his counsel David Humphrey, to whom Galligan was profuse in his thanks in his report. Why, he said, Humphrey had rearranged his busy schedule to help him; his assistance was "invaluable"; he'd brought to the task "a broad and thorough understanding of the criminal law"; he had experience in the Crown law office and in private practice; he gave "good counsel, boundless energy and a keen sense of humour."

No doubt all of that was true, but Humphrey's experience in the Crown law office was working for Murray Segal, who had been significantly involved in the Homolka plea, the merits of which, or not, Galligan was purportedly evaluating.

Asked about his choice eighteen years later, Galligan said simply he knew Humphrey to be "a splendid lawyer" who "knew his way around. . . . I am not at this late date prepared to say what decision

I would have made had anyone challenged my choice of counsel.

"I suspect that my answer would have been short and blunt," he said. He meant it as a slap to my face for having questioned him about it.

As Stephen Williams wrote in his second book on the case, *Karla: A Pact with the Devil*, Galligan didn't critically analyze the evidence of Homolka's purported abuse by Bernardo, or anything that would contradict it.

"Instead, he just accepted it verbatim because the people, whose actions and motives he was supposed to be investigating, accepted it themselves.

"Where I come from, this sort of tautological ellipticum constitutes whitewash."

That latter was classic Stephen Williams—wordy, a bit pompous, and, as I was to come to appreciate, absolutely dead on.

At least on paper, there's a good reason for slapping publication bans on proceedings in trials where two people are facing separate trials on charges stemming from the same set of facts in the same crimes—ostensibly it's to protect the jury pool in the case that is tried second.

That was precisely the situation with Bernardo and Homolka.

In late June 1993, he was facing two counts of first-degree murder in Leslie and Kristen's deaths, as well as a slew of other charges in connection with the Scarborough rapes. She, on the other hand, was charged with manslaughter in the same two deaths, and it was her case, not his, that was racing to the finish line.

Thus, Bernardo's fair-trial rights—including the right to jurors untainted by the enormous publicity against him, which is the argument always made—were important and theoretically at risk.

As it turned out, though two weeks were set aside for jury selection at his trial, the lawyers managed to do the job within three days, just as they might have done with a nice, quiet, run-of-the-mill murder.

In fact, that's most often the case.

Whatever the pretrial publicity—and in this instance, the web with all its reach wasn't yet a force to be reckoned with—ordinary Canadians selected for jury duty usually rise above it.

In the selection process, they either readily admit to a bias if they have one (or, if they really want out of jury duty, admit to a bias they don't have), or explain frankly why they can't serve (as one candidate in the Bernardo pool volunteered, "I got some mental disorders, Your Honour") or they are quite smart enough to realize that what they have read or heard in the media doesn't matter and are perfectly capable of discarding it.

I was once involved in a trial where the defence lawyer demanded the jurors be polled to see if they'd been affected by a colourful headline that appeared on one of my stories (editors, not the reporters, write the headlines in newspapers).

The first eleven hadn't even read the offending piece. The twelfth had, but as he cheerfully told the presiding judge, "I never pay attention to anything Ms. Blatchford writes." Never was I so delighted to be so handily dismissed.

The point stands: People are more than capable of making up their own minds, which is what that juror was really saying.

When the Homolka proceeding began on June 28 in St. Catharines before Ontario Court judge Francis Kovacs, representing Bernardo was Tim Breen, part of what was then the small team headed by Ken Murray.

It would have been unsurprising for Breen to ask for a publication ban.

It's so the norm that defence lawyers seek these bans—and if the defence asks for a pub ban at a preliminary hearing or bail hearing, it's mandatory—that it's part of the courtroom furniture.

Years ago, I was in court for a prelim on a case I now can't remember, and the defence lawyer forgot to ask for a ban, and the prosecutor forgot to remind him. I was beside myself with joy, composing my story in my head, thinking that for once, I'd be able to write about something as it happened, not months or years later.

Court was minutes away from finishing for the day when, to my horror, I watched as my competition from the *Toronto Star*, an old hand named Gary Oakes, got up and whispered something in the defence lawyer's ear.

In the next minute, the lawyer was on his feet, thanking Oakes for the favour, and demanding the usual ban.

But this day in St. Catharines, it wasn't the defence asking for a pub ban.

In fact, Tim Breen was vociferously arguing against it.

He pointed out that all the publicity—and there was plenty— about the case thus far already had cast Homolka as the victim, his client as the monster.

In effect, Breen was saying, either there was nothing left of this aspect of Bernardo's rights to protect, or he had faith a fair and impartial jury could be found for him in any case.

This, Breen suggested, was all a sham, designed to protect something or someone else. So, he said in essence, let's let the light in.

Joining him in arguing against a ban were lawyers for various media organizations.

And the guy fighting hardest for the ban, though he was joined by Homolka's lawyer, was none other than Murray Segal.

These arguments ate up two days, the judge's decision another, and when it was all over, Kovacs gave Segal everything he asked for and more.

The general public was banned from the courtroom outright, an astonishing and unprecedented move. This, after all, was no mere prelim or bail hearing. This was a criminal trial, the critical proceeding in the justice system and a jewel in the crown of any democracy.

Its single greatest attribute is that it is held in the open, that people can walk in off the street, and there are always a few who do just that, to see for themselves the wheels of justice turn, or to grab a few winks. In theory, members of the public are even entitled to see the exhibits, though almost no one ever asks.

But Kovacs not only closed the court to the public but also outright banned the American media, who as non-citizens weren't subject to his ruling about what was publishable (almost nothing) and what wasn't (virtually everything).

He put under seal all but the most inane of court documents, including the transcript of the proceeding. He sealed the victim impact statements delivered by Leslie's mother, Debbie, and Kristen's mother, Donna, not merely for the eighteen months to three years it was then estimated it would take the courts to deal with all of Bernardo's charges, but forever, or until another judge unsealed them.

The entire proceeding lasted less than four hours.

Murray Segal spoke for twenty-seven minutes, an astonishing soliloquy, almost a gaseous outburst, for this ultra-cautious man.

Homolka's lawyer spoke.

Debbie Mahaffy's reading of her victim impact statement lasted thirty-two minutes, Donna French's a little less time.

The judge spoke for seventy minutes.

And in the end, about fifteen minutes of the whole shebang could be reported for the public who weren't allowed in.

In the days immediately after, as, despite the secrecy or perhaps because of it, the public furor over Homolka's sentence grew, the non-lawyer Ontario attorney general Marion Boyd, told reporters, "I don't think people understand very well how the justice system operates . . ."

And how bloody could they, when they were banned from even attending a public trial in a public courtroom?

———

An explanation of how the videotapes were found, or rather how they were missed, is now in order.

Homolka left Bernardo, and their bungalow in Port Dalhousie, in January 1993.

He was off on a cigarette-smuggling run, and the house was empty.

He had been beating her with a heavy flashlight over the course of several days, and she had terrible raccoon eyes and bruises to her arms and legs.

That said, it was only with her parents roused to action and leaning on her to end the marriage that she fled, first to friends of her sister and then to the apartment of an aunt and uncle.

In short order, Niagara Regional Police were called, and when Bernardo came home, he was duly arrested and charged with assault with a weapon.

About the same time, in Toronto, forensic scientists had finally run Bernardo's DNA and discovered he was the Scarborough Rapist, sending the Toronto cops into a frenzy of activity—arranging surveillance on Bernardo, getting judicial approval for a tap on his phone, and checking the national police computer system, CPIC, only to discover he had been recently charged with assault.

In the way of police forces then, Niagara and Toronto didn't tell one another what they were doing until early February (by which time Toronto cops were actually following Bernardo), let alone share the fruits of their separate investigations.

Also that February, two Toronto officers went to St. Catharines to interview Homolka, and even fingerprinted her.

It was ostensibly all about Bernardo, but the cops' visit spooked her; the net was clearly closing in and she knew it.

Homolka called George Walker, whose wife she knew as a customer from the vet clinic, and made an appointment.

As Williams wrote in *Invisible Darkness*, what Homolka told the lawyer left him reeling. "In such disarmingly matter-of-fact terms, she had told him what no one else in the world yet knew: a tale of such nightmarish, unimaginable degradation, sex, death, lies and videotape as to defy the imagination."

The next day, Walker went to see Ray Houlahan, the local regional prosecutor, and told him what his new client had told him (that is, that Bernardo had killed Leslie and Kristen, that she had been there, and that the assaults, though not the murders, had been videotaped).

She was willing to testify against the man she was now in the process of divorcing, Walker said, but she wanted immunity.

Recognizing he might be involved as a trial prosecutor, Houlahan immediately handed the matter off to his boss, who called in Murray Segal.

Bernardo was in custody by February 17, 1993, with members of the Toronto force and the Green Ribbon Task Force, as the Niagara team investigating the murders was called, inside the couple's house shortly thereafter.

The police were there for ten weeks with a team of specialists. They searched almost every inch of the place, but the critical few inches they missed—in that upstairs bathroom ceiling—was where Bernardo had hidden the videotapes.

The officer who had reached up and felt along the ceiling above the pot lights with his hand was simply too short, or at least, his arm was.

The search warrant expired on April 30, 1993. Cops from the joint Toronto–Green Ribbon team gave up custody.

Thus was the stage fully set: The police had left with all kinds of hair, fibre, books and other items, but little of it was incriminating, let alone damning, of Bernardo.

Now, the authorities really needed Homolka's testimony.

The discussions among Walker, Segal and Michael Code, who was pulling the state strings throughout, had been proceeding throughout the house search. These talks intensified.

The first proposal from Walker sought "blanket immunity," and the second would have seen Homolka receive a total of ten years for her role in the slayings of Leslie Mahaffy and Kristen French. Three months later, the name of a third victim—Tammy, for by now Homolka had told Walker about her sister and he had informed the prosecutors—was added for the first time and two extra years tacked on.

Homolka had her deal. It was inked on May 14.

By its terms, she would give a cautioned statement to police, testify against Bernardo and plead guilty to two counts of manslaughter in Leslie's and Kristen's deaths and acknowledge her "involvement" in Tammy's death.

If it was discovered that Homolka lied, she was guaranteed no immunity from prosecution, and the deal itself would be off if it was learned that, in the inimitable language of the law, she "had caused the death of any person, in the sense of her stopping life" (as opposed to her causing death in some other sense known only to lawyers, I suppose).

As Stephen Williams wrote in *Invisible Darkness*, "Karla would 'take two' for Tammy—instead of two 10-year terms for manslaughter, she would get two concurrent 12-year terms. Effectively, Karla had been completely exonerated in the death of her sister and had escaped any sexual assault charges whatsoever."

Throughout all this, Homolka herself, Walker and the psychiatrists he arranged for her to see, the prosecutors and even the police were growing ever more determined to view her not as Bernardo's partner but as his victim.

If she wasn't a battered spouse, she was the "compliant victim of a sexual sadist," or she had PTSD (post-traumatic stress disorder), or she had traumatic amnesia or, by God, she was, well, depressed.

Even the families of Leslie and Kristen implicitly gave their blessing to this vision of Homolka by their approval of the deal.

The families never saw Homolka as a victim, their lawyer Tim Danson said. But they were emotionally devastated; they trusted the police and Crowns. And at this stage, no one had much of a choice.

"I think the starting point is we accepted the information that was given to us on the plea bargain," Danson said in a July 2013 interview. "It was all they had, and what was also being presented was that this was escalating and there could be more victims and it was pretty frightening, and that's all they had.

"So, holding your nose . . ."

But, Danson said, the most critical aspect of the deal for the families, what gave them a smidge of comfort, was the promise that "if she lies in any way, then the deal's off, and if the videotapes confirm what she said, then okay.

"We still might not like it, we certainly don't buy into the battered-woman syndrome," but like everyone else, the families would suck it up for the greater good of nailing Bernardo.

Days before the plea was finalized, Murray Segal and Vince Bevan, then an inspector with the Niagara Regional force and the head of the Green Ribbon Task Force, met the families to break the news that there might be a deal in the works.

As Patrick Galligan wrote in his review, "It was explained to [the families] that the crucial videotapes had not been found and, that at that time, without Karla Homolka's cooperation, there was really no case against Paul Bernardo. They understood the difficulty of the Crown's position and reluctantly acceded to it."

The families were far less keen when, well down the road, they learned that there had not been just the one drugging and sexual assault upon Jane Doe—which Homolka admitted to only when she gave an induced statement to police as part of her deal—but two.

By the spring of 1994, the police had been able to figure out that there had been multiple distinct attacks upon the young woman.

From the short bit of videotape that had been found in the police search of their house—it showed a sexual assault upon an unconscious young female at first believed to be either Tammy or Kristen French—and from Homolka's statement that she had once called 911 when Jane had stopped breathing during an attack, detectives were able to date the assaults to June and August of 1991.

Yet when the six tapes were handed over in the fall of 1994, one of them clearly showed Homolka applying halothane to Jane Doe, and both Bernardo and Homolka sexually assaulting her.

The issue of whether Homolka had breached her deal and should be charged went to the management committee in the AG's office.

Composed of three veteran regional prosecutors and chaired by Michael Code, the committee decided on May 18, 1995, against charging her—just before she took the stand at Bernardo's trial.

There was first of all the difficulty that in Canada, courts prefer that all charges against so-called accomplice witnesses such as Homolka be finished, with sentence imposed, before they take the witness box. That was unlikely to happen, even had the management committee made its decision in less stately a fashion than it did.

As well, George Walker said Homolka would never have pleaded guilty or discussed a plea to any new charge, which would have meant a hotly contested case and a lengthier proceeding. Walker's view was that a charge would have violated the spirit, if not the letter, of her plea bargain.

Ultimately, the management committee agreed, as did Judge Galligan in his review.

In short, the prevailing wisdom of the day was that a) Homolka was genuinely suffering from amnesia and had not lied about the June assault on Jane, just failed to remember it; b) it was too late in the game to charge her and have the charge get through the courts before Bernardo's trial; c) even if she were to have been convicted for the assault upon Jane, it might not have added significant time, if any, to her sentence; and d) if Homolka had been charged and become a less than cooperative witness, the prosecution against Bernardo might have been jeopardized. (Jeopardized? There was not a chance, not with those tapes.)

The decision was made within the usual echo chamber at 720 Bay Street, the office of senior Crown law officials.

In fact, plea bargains aren't carved in stone—and can be broken if the accused person signing on to the deal breaks it.

There's no question that breaching Homolka's deal would have been controversial, but probably half the on-the-ground trial prosecutors in Canada would have agreed with Mary Hall that she should be charged, and half would have disagreed.

As just one illustration that deals can be unmade, and sometimes are, consider a 2007 case that mirrors the Homolka bargain.

A man named Adrian Roks was charged with second-degree murder, arson and conspiracy to commit arson in connection with a massive explosion and fire on Christmas Day of 2001 at a building supply store in east-end Toronto. One of the other arsonists involved, a fellow named Tony Jarcevic, died in the fire, while another was badly burned.

Roks had made a plea deal and now was claiming an abuse of process, saying he shouldn't ever have been charged. But his deal, like Homolka's, was contingent on his telling the truth about the arson and giving a full statement. That, he didn't do.

While his statement to police was lengthy, it was hardly complete. In Homolka-esque fashion, Roks minimized his own knowledge of and role in the fire and that of his friend, John Magno, the man who was the architect of the plan. Despite having a lawyer at his side to huddle with throughout, and despite repeated prompts from the officers for more straightforward answers, Roks lied.

So police and prosecutors tore up his deal and charged him—and, as Ontario Superior Court judge Gloria Epstein ruled, for good reason.

"[Roks] is only protected by immunity from this prosecution if he fulfilled his end of the bargain," she wrote in an April 4, 2007, decision. "All he had to do was tell the truth; the police and the Crown reasonably concluded he did not."

Roks was eventually convicted of manslaughter and given six years in jail; in 2011, Magno was convicted of the same offence and given ten years.

But there was no similar will at 720 Bay to see Homolka's deal—for two murders and the death of her sister, remember—undone.

As soon as Tim Danson saw the tapes, he knew immediately Homolka had lied, and, as he told the families and Jane Doe herself, whom he was also representing on the tapes' issue, he believed she had breached her plea.

What he told prosecutors and the AG brass was: "You breach, you breach. There's no middle ground here, there's no cushion here." The families wanted Homolka charged in the assault on Jane.

"It culminated in a meeting in my boardroom," Danson said, with the families, all the top people from the AG.

"They're basically saying, on the Jane Doe, our experts say that Homolka did not lie, because she was suffering from post-traumatic amnesia," Danson said. "I'd like to see the literature on that. I'll say that in a measured way, I lost it—lost it, and I just said this is outrageous and this is totally unacceptable."

But the AG's people were, he said, "so afraid of not getting Bernardo that they became unusually paranoid, and I was surprised, given the brainpower and experience of this group, that they really believed that."

What Danson was saying came down to: So if you'd had the videotapes to begin with, you would never have entered into a plea bargain? Then how can you still believe you need that plea bargain?

As he put it, "How it is that Karla Homolka remembers all of these details that go on and on and on, how is it that post-traumatic amnesia doesn't affect the big story?

"And somehow, just right here with Jane Doe, it just slipped her mind?

"No," Danson said. "What happened was, she knew you didn't know, so she kept [the information to herself], because she's a psychopath.

"And she's a manipulator of the highest degree and she had you, and that's the way she is, and you know that's the way she is, so don't give me this bullshit."

While Danson said he believed prosecutors were acting in good faith, he said upon the families, "the effect was very coercive: 'You guys better be careful or Bernardo may walk free' . . . It was like, 'You could prejudice the prosecution of Bernardo, you guys gotta be careful, we've got to keep together.'"

Now, if informing victims and even asking for their input wasn't entirely new, such naked consultation was.

Since 1988, when provincial and federal justice ministers first gave the nod to the Canadian Statement of Basic Principles of Justice for Victims of Crime at a meeting in Saskatoon, the victims' rights movement had been gathering strength.

As Carol Cameron, then the president of the Toronto-based group Victims of Violence, told the *Toronto Star* at the time, "The politicians long ago recognized the needs of criminals, but they forgot about us.

"A justice system that doesn't want fair treatment for both sides is not a fair system," she said.

But victims of crime were never meant to be one of the "two sides."

Justice in Canada, and most Western democracies, isn't supposed to be a matter between victim and perpetrator, but rather between state and perpetrator. The broader societal interests of public safety and protection incorporate, of course, the narrower interests of those who have been hurt or damaged by crime, but traditionally that's where the victim's role begins and ends.

Even the bill itself—it came into force in 1989 and would have been the governing piece of federal legislation at the time of the Homolka-Bernardo prosecutions—required only that victims "be given information" about the process and that their views and concerns should be "considered."

(Ontario didn't establish its own Office for Victims of Crimes until 1998, through the Victims' Bill of Rights, which says only that victims "should have information" about such matters as plea bargains.)

It was meant if not as a sop to victims then as not much more than a nod of acknowledgement: You exist; we will keep you up to speed about the case; we will hear you out.

Nowhere was it written in the legislation that victims' families must be consulted about plea agreements.

Certainly, nowhere was it even contemplated that victims or their families would ever call the shots.

Yet, to some considerable degree, that's what eventually happened.

Homolka spent seventeen days in the witness stand at her ex's trial, eight in cross-examination with John Rosen, one of the best criminal lawyers in the country.

He was at the top of his always very good game then, but she kicked his ass around the block, growing stronger every day she was in the box.

The trial itself went on and on and on, providing a battering for all the participants and even those at a distance, the Canadian newspaper-reading and TV-viewing public. There really was no safe remove from the daily fare of rape, casual cruelty and degrading violence, always directed at young females.

That summer was notably hot and sunny, but I remember virtually nothing of it. I suppose other things must have happened, and that I myself must have done other things, at least during the twelve-day trial break, but I have no memory. Every centimetre of my being was consumed by the case.

I was at the courthouse by 7 a.m. or so to get my favoured seat, in line or in court until about 4:30 or 5:00 p.m., and then, as was the case in the pre-web era, the working day for us reporters would really start.

Back then, most daily newspapers had final deadlines that ranged between about 7:30 and 10:00 p.m.

Because of a ruling—it's always called "controversial" but it wasn't anywhere near controversial enough for my dough—from Ontario Superior Court judge Patrick LeSage, the media and public weren't allowed to see what I came to call the attack videotapes.

We could watch all the others, but not those that documented the couple's assaults on Tammy, Jane Doe, Leslie, Kristen or the other girls he covertly videoed on toilets or badgered into what for him passed for consensual sex.

We could stay in the courtroom while the attack tapes were played, we could listen to them, but the monitors that faced the public gallery were turned off.

One of the peculiar side effects of this ruling was that we sat there, straining to catch what Bernardo or Homolka or their victims were saying, without having any pictures to help us understand it.

You don't realize how linked the two senses are, how interdependent, until you're deprived of one. It felt like the sudden onset of blindness.

It was so creepy-crawly, the music Bernardo liked (a lot of early good rap like Ice-T, but some great rock 'n' roll classics too, and even some Tragically Hip and Talking Heads, two of my favourite bands) floating in the air as background noise, the whir of the video camera, and over the familiar grunts and sounds of sex, young girls crying or screaming.

We had no transcripts of the tapes, of course.

There were transcripts—the lawyers and jurors had copies and we could see them flipping pages—but the press rarely gets such consideration in Canadian courtrooms, certainly not when it would actually be useful.

As I remember it, one of our number told the judge we could make little sense of what we were hearing, let alone even agree upon the words being said. He arranged that the court clerk, a sweet young woman named Bibi, would read to us whatever words had been spoken in whatever segment of video had been played that day.

To do this, of course, Bibi had to read from the very transcripts that we couldn't actually have in our hands—a typical bit of court-imposed lunacy.

It was a massively cumbersome process.

As soon as court ended, all of us reporters would crowd into a small windowless room set aside for this purpose, and there, sweating cheek by jowl in the heat, take notes as poor Bibi read aloud, demanding here and there that she repeat herself when we missed a word.

(As an illustration of the sort of exchanges we had, I give you this. Reporter: "Did he say 'Shove it in hard' there? or 'Shove it in harder'?" Bibi: "Shove it in hard.")

It also took time, upwards of an hour depending on how much video had been played, and elongated already wearing days. Still, that was but an unintentional consequence—an irritating inconvenience only to journalists—of LeSage's ruling on the videotapes.

The real consequence was barely acknowledged yet was transformative for the criminal justice system. That system was always meant to be a contest between the accused person and the state. It's for this reason cases are known as, for example, *R versus Bernardo*, the "R" for *Regina* (the Queen being, in the case of a constitutional monarchy like Canada's, the head of state). In the United States, depending on geography, the same prosecution might have been called *The State of New York v Bernardo* or *The State of Florida v Bernardo*.

It isn't just about nomenclature, either. It's really about a big idea and an ancient ideal—what constitutes justice, whose concerns ought to matter and what the best processes are to achieve those good things.

At the heart of it are a couple of ringing principles.

The first is what's called the rule of law. That is society's collective agreement that we will not seek to avenge criminal wrongs done to us as individuals, but rather leave it to the state to mete out justice, even and dispassionate.

As prosecutor Paul McDermott once told me, over many drinks, what the rule of law really means is: If you burn down my house, instead of burning down yours in retaliation and maybe beating up your kid too just to up the ante, I'll call the cops and let them sort it out.

As someone who was in the former Yugoslavia at the time of selective house-burning—Serbs torching Croat homes, Croats burning Serbian ones, pretty much everyone having a go at Muslim houses—that has palpable meaning for me.

The rule of law is the best pre-emptive strike there is against that sort of bloody cycle.

But to leave justice to the state with any equanimity, people have to have faith that we're all equal under the law and will be treated the same.

The second principle, the one that judges and lawyers are so fond of quoting if not putting into practice, is that justice must not only be done but also be seen to be done.

In other words, the whole schmear should be as public and as transparent as possible, so that we who in effect have agreed to stifle our individual desire to extract our own brand of justice can see how well, or not, the system and the rule of law are working.

Yet in this case, both those principles took a savage beating.

First, the heavy curtain of secrecy dropped over Homolka's plea bargain and trial.

At the same time, the straight line that ran between the accused and the state was morphing into a sort of triangle, with victims—in this case, the victims' families—forming a wobbly third leg.

It was solely out of concern for the families that at Bernardo's trial Judge LeSage decided against letting public and press see the tapes.

The first arguments were heard before him in St. Catharines in February 1995.

Tim Danson, the Toronto lawyer and son of a former minister in Pierre Trudeau's cabinet (defence minister Barney Danson) who already was making a name for himself as a victims' advocate, was there on behalf of the two families and Jane Doe.

Supported by prosecutors, Danson was seeking to win "intervenor status," so he could make submissions and potentially even call evidence in the later arguments about who should and should not be able to see the videotapes.

It was in essence a Charter argument: Danson argued that if the tapes were played in open court, it would violate the families' (and their daughters') Charter right to privacy.

Three media lawyers argued that victims and their families should provide their perspective via the Crown, in the manner that had worked so well for years.

One of them, Peter Jacobsen, then representing the *Globe*, the

Star and the *Sun*, told LeSage that in his research, he couldn't find a single case to suggest that victims can even bring Charter applications during a criminal trial.

With evident reluctance, LeSage nonetheless granted the families intervenor status, though he stressed it was only "as an indulgence," and only for the purposes of the coming publication ban arguments.

Patrick LeSage is a lovely human being—my pal, the *Star* columnist Rosie DiManno, once said, and I believe wrote in a column, that she didn't know whether she would rather have his child or be his child—but he could no more muster up the nerve to look those bereaved parents in the eye and deny them than could any of his fellows on the bench.

His decision, which at first blush seemed a fine Canadian compromise (and I hailed it as such at the time in a moment of weakness), was in fact another example of the state in essence caving to victims.

A key plank of Danson's oft-emotional argument was that if the tapes were shown in open court, the girls' families would have to see them too.

That ignored the fact that most of the time, those who survive someone who is murdered are internally compelled to come to court, regardless of how disturbing the evidence is or who does or doesn't see it. I can hardly remember a murder trial where that didn't happen; it's as if it is an unwritten final duty or last rite. (Who else but victims' relatives do you imagine are yelling, as many court stories report, "Rot in hell!" as the accused is led away to start serving his sentence?)

Two months later, as arguments about the tapes themselves began, reporters learned that the families also had been consulted in failed plea negotiations with John Rosen. As it turned out, they had a significant say—if not the most important vote—in turning down a deal for Bernardo.

Prosecutors—the state, in other words—had essentially del-egated to Danson a slice of their role.

Danson himself says it was unprecedented. Even so, many years later, he could hardly believe that it happened.

"I think that the discussions between John Rosen and I were extraordinary," he told me in a lengthy interview at his Bay Street office in downtown Toronto. "Even I who advocates for victims' rights," he said, would never extend that role to a third party like him.

What happened, he said, is that Rosen approached prosecu-tors and said, "I got a deal for you."

The proposal on the table was that Bernardo would plead guilty to two counts of second-degree murder, in exchange for which he would get a slight break on parole eligibility, a theo-retical construct because no one expected then or believes now he will ever be paroled.

It would mean only that he might be able to make his first unsuccessful application earlier.

But, most important, as Danson said, the video problem would disappear and with it, for the families, the heartache of having to deal, one way or the other, with the evidence of their daughters' destruction.

Rosen pushed all the right buttons, said Danson: "He's saying whether Paul Bernardo is convicted of first-degree or second-degree, he's not getting out, so it's an academic distinction."

Someone senior in the attorney general's office then called him.

Danson was very careful how he described the next bit. "My view was, is, that, and this is only my personal opinion, no one said this," he told me. But, "You know when you have discus-sions, there's tones of voices, there's breathing? You sense things, right? Instinct, rightly or wrongly. I believe that the govern-ment would absolutely have done the deal, if the families would support it.

"And in view of the Homolka deal and in view of the decision not to breach her [i.e., void the plea because she had lied about Jane Doe], they knew that they could not do this plea bargain without the support of the families.

"So, basically, the way it worked, like wink-wink, 'John, you've got to speak with Tim and see what you can do.'"

At the Criminal Lawyers' Association annual convention in the fall of 1994, the two sneaked off for a first word.

"Extraordinary," Danson said. He grinned at the memory: "I'm thinking to myself, this is bizarre. I mean, I liked it, you know? I want to be involved; my job is the families, so if you're going to give me this, absolutely."

Rosen's memory is quite different.

While he said he probably had "casual conversations" with Danson, it was "not at the direction of the attorney general," nor were there formal discussions. Rosen said the position of the families was "not determinative" in the decision, just a factor.

"So I disagree with Tim that this was strictly the families telling the AG what to do," he said in an interview at his office in July 2013.

But, Rosen said, he accepts "maybe the families' position was the tipping point."

And in the bigger picture, he said, it was not a case of the victims pulling the government's strings, but rather one of the government allowing it to appear that way for its own reasons.

"The victims were the excuse for the exercise of the power," Rosen said. "Everything was done in their names. It's like when you have a martyr, and everything's done in the martyr's name."

The families weren't telling the government what to do, Rosen said.

"It's the other way around: 'We are going to do this and use them as the excuse. We have our other agenda for doing it.' That's a different way to look at the problem."

In effect, he said, the government had decided, "'We are hiding Karla, we are hiding the deal, none of this is going to be subject to scrutiny, we won't have to be accountable to anyone and we're going to use [the families] as the excuse, and we're not going to say that's really why we're doing it.'"

Whether because the families actually were so empowered or the government was just letting them think they were, Danson certainly believes he held all the cards, and for him and his clients it meant an agonizing decision.

He had filed his motion for intervenor status and to restrict the videos in early January of the new year, 1995.

The families were keenly aware of what was at stake, he said. Over their many discussions, "They kept saying, 'Do you really feel confident that you'll win?'

"I said I do feel confident, but being right doesn't mean you win in this business. It's always a crapshoot."

Finally, he gave them his opinion: "I said no [deal], because [Bernardo is] going to get convicted and I just said, after the Homolka deal, I can't stomach it, I think it's wrong. But, there's a risk. The risk is that I lose the motion, because I think they would have done anything to protect their daughters from public viewing."

In the end, the families agreed: No deal.

"I called someone in the AG's office and I said I've had my meeting with Rosen, and here's what we talked about. I've now met with the families, and the answer's no.

"And he said, fine. No discussion, no attempt to persuade, just fine."

Danson said prosecutors and the big guns at the AG knew "we would have blown"—a gasket, that is—and gone public—had the government made a deal with Bernardo.

Yet just months later, there he was again, attempting to dictate some of the terms of the trial he and his clients had insisted Bernardo have—chiefly, who should or shouldn't see the tapes.

It was beginning to be clear that not only would this case set a record for most publication bans and court seals, it was also establishing a new standard for the inclusion of victims and/or their survivors in the vital processes of the justice system.

Curiously, for an institution that traditionally prefers reason over emotion, the courts imbued the Mahaffy and French families with enormous clout precisely because judges were convinced at every turn to consider and spare their feelings.

Judge Kovacs, at the Homolka proceeding, perhaps inadvertently set the tone when, as a courtesy, he allowed the French family to wait out a recess in his office, the Mahaffys in the office of his colleague on the bench, the late Patrick Gravely.

Undoubtedly, it was a thoughtful gesture, born of kindness, but there are thousands of crime victims who haven't had such a benefit, who have instead emerged from a courtroom into a lonely hallway, too shy to even ask where they can buy a coffee or where the loo is, or who have stumbled out of courthouses into the waiting arms of rapacious reporters.

The entire argument about the tapes centred on how the families would feel if they were played in open court.

Yet there was little unusual about the case.

No one knows better than judges and criminal lawyers that sexual sadists are a dime a dozen, that all violent crime creates victims and that all victims hurt and bleed.

What set this case apart is that the victims' families were among the decision makers.

LeSage gave his ruling early on in Bernardo's trial, telling jurors that any benefit that might be gained from playing the tapes in open court would be far exceeded by the harm done to the families, and that the monitors that faced the body of the court therefore would be turned off.

The message was unequivocal—the new royalty in Canadian courts were victims, or their survivors.

In case anyone missed it, what happened a few days earlier underlined the practical reality of this new world order.

Every time there was a witness on the stand who was identifying graphic crime scene pictures for the prosecutors—one day pictures of Kristen's nude body, the next the concrete blocks in which parts of Leslie's dismembered body were encased—the public monitors were turned off as per an earlier LeSage ruling.

This wasn't unique, in that courts rarely attempt to accommodate the public in seeing crime scene photos—or anything else.

Usually, remember, there are no public monitors, but given the equipment that had been trucked into court especially for this multi-million-dollar sucker, the ruling was a little jarring. After all, the monitors were already there, so why not use them?

More important, every day in courthouses and coroner's inquests across Canada, equally terrible pictures of human ruin—battered infants, slain children, raped women, destroyed men—are shown, and at coroner's inquests at least, often publicly.

The mainstream media rarely uses—that is, publishes or shows on TV—any of this material. In my view, often we ought to have done so, because this is what the courts call the best evidence and because readers and viewers are adults, able to protect those in their midst whom they deem to be in need of protection.

Sometimes, reporters like me have argued hard for publication or broadcast. But almost all the time, we lose these battles. Our editors, creatures far more delicate than we are, less invested in the nitty-gritty of the process and perhaps better able to see the big picture, inevitably decide that such photos are too awful for the breakfast table or the morning news.

(They may well be right too, but worth noting is that these editorial delicacy standards may shift. For instance, it's all fine and dandy for Canadian newspapers to publish photos of starving babies, so long as they're starving somewhere else, whether

Africa or Afghanistan. But let a Canadian coroner release a picture of a Canadian child who was starved to death in the midst of plenty, which is exactly what happened at the inquest I covered into the aforementioned starvation of baby Jordan Heikamp, and it suddenly becomes a matter of taste. Your dead kids okay; our dead kids not so much.)

But the fact is, there simply is no journalistic tradition of, and little appetite for, mainstream media publishing graphic video or photographic evidence of crime.

That may be changing on the web, where there are all manner of crime blogs and even sites for the "gore" aficionado, and that may change the rapidly shifting landscape for the traditional press too.

But it hasn't happened yet, and it sure hadn't even loomed as a possibility when the Bernardo trial was going on.

Besides, and this is more important, every day in courts across the land, the living victims of abuse and cruelty and violation take the witness stand to testify about what happened to them—and with few exceptions, though their numbers are growing, and these usually based on age or religion, in full public view.

Not this time, not with this case.

At the prosecutors' table at the front of the room, where they were accustomed to deferring to the families' feelings, they quickly tucked their small monitor into a desk so no one else could see the crime scene photographs.

But at the defence table on the other side, their monitor stayed on, though it was turned to face the lawyers.

And every time one of the graphic pictures was on that monitor, Debbie and Dan Mahaffy would rise from their seats in the rows reserved for the families, make their way to the other side of the courtroom, and sit behind Bernardo and the defence team, deliberately trying to prevent anyone else from seeing the screen.

It was a protest.

The Mahaffys might just as well have been carrying signs and chanting, so unmistakable was their pain and rage.

Of course, they were trying to protect the dead girls from what they believed was further indignity. Of course, it was poignant to watch, and awful that they had to endure this.

But then that *is* (or was) the criminal trial—wrenching, merciless in the ice at the centre of its heart, and in the modern lexicon, re-traumatizing. And it's the same at every serious criminal trial and for every victim's family because the victim isn't the focus; the accused is.

It appeared the Mahaffys were trying to intimidate or shame Rosen and his co-counsel Tony Bryant into hiding their monitor too.

"For what?" I wrote at the time. "Daring to defend an accused murderer?"

I thought then and believe now that Rosen, who refused to be cowed by this calculated show of disdain and who continued to hold in his hand copies of the pictures as he questioned these witnesses, just as he would have done in every other case, was defending at that moment not just Bernardo but also the very integrity of the system.

It was when both trials were done that the powers-that-be really got serious.

The state, which had been so considerate of victims' feelings, which had positioned itself as the repository of kindness and empathy if not moral rectitude, then moved against some of those on the periphery of the story with more vigour than it had ever directed against Karla Homolka, and certainly with more viciousness.

For years afterwards, Tim Danson and/or the two families were like Woody Allen's Leonard Zelig, the nondescript human chameleon who kept popping up beside famous figures in old newsreel footage in Allen's eponymous 1983 movie.

They were here, there, everywhere.

There they were at the side of David Young, the Ontario attorney general in the then new Mike Harris Conservative government; there they were in Patrick Gravely's courtroom in St. Catharines, seeking a destruction order of the physical evidence introduced at the Bernardo trial; there was Danson in Joliette, Quebec, demanding to be heard about what conditions ought to be imposed upon Homolka when in June 2005 she was poised to get out of prison.

By this point, the two families were well and truly embraced, even beloved, by Canadians.

Nothing better illustrates this than the fact that two separate public fundraising campaigns—the French/Mahaffy Legal Assistance Fund, which ran between 1995 and 1997, and the French/Mahaffy Victims' Integrity Fund, which took over in 1998—had brought in almost $1 million from people across the country.

The bulk of the money—about $850,000—went to Danson.

He told me that at some point he stopped "docketing"—simply stopped keeping track of all the time he put in on the case, because there was no point. From that total, he said, he had to pay his expert witnesses and cover office overheads and the cost of transcripts. He noted that his work was spread over six years and that he paid some bills, particularly in the later years, from his own pocket.

In the final analysis, Danson said, "I lost my shirt, financially. I've lost millions of dollars and I was a successful lawyer. This is not me sitting with nothing to do. I could have taken any of my corporate clients and I would have been getting my bills out every thirty days and I'd be really good."

Still and all, the fact that he acknowledges receiving about $850,000—or more than twice what John Rosen earned from

Legal Aid for representing Bernardo—lends a rather generous new meaning to the phrase "pro bono," which is how Danson often has described the work he did for the families and how he still framed it to me in 2013, saying, "This was basically a pro bono case."

Pro bono is short for *pro bono publico*, Latin meaning a service provided, without compensation, "for the public good."

Pro bono publico, this case was not.

(One of the reporters who first wrote about the financial details of the two funds was Heather Bird, then of the *Toronto Sun*. Amusingly, Bird herself went on to attend law school, and is now a criminal lawyer licensed to practise in New York, Connecticut and Ontario. Just what the world needs—one fewer reporter and one more lawyer.)

But whatever else, as the fundraising campaigns showed, Canadians felt for the families and supported what Danson always cleverly branded as their fight to protect their daughters' privacy.

One of the unexpected places they all showed up—Debbie and Dan Mahaffy, Donna French and of course Danson—was at Ken Murray's criminal trial.

Murray was first on the government's hit list.

In January 1997, about sixteen months after Bernardo's trial ended, Murray got a call from the legendary Austin Cooper, the lawyer he had first consulted about how to get off the case and what to do about the tapes.

Cooper, who died in 2013, was a giant, both physically (he was about twelve feet tall—well, tall enough that he was a loomer, anyway) and within the Canadian defence bar.

Cooper told Murray he and his junior, Carolyn MacDonald, were going to be charged with obstructing justice. Murray was furious that MacDonald, a then promising young lawyer of thirty-five, was charged: She was his junior; she took instructions from him; as he saw it, he was responsible and no one else.

Their bail conditions precluded them from speaking to one another, but Murray knew MacDonald was devastated. She "saw the law as a perfect vehicle," he said years later, and was both charmed by it and blithely confident in it. "She had a belief in the system, that everybody plays fairly."

In fact, after the bruising delivered to her by the charges, MacDonald quit the law and has never returned.

Though she's still registered with the Law Society of Upper Canada, she's not practising and runs a dog-walking service.

But that aside, for himself, Murray wasn't entirely surprised that he was being charged.

He'd made his decision about the tapes in a vacuum—there simply were no hard-and-fast rules telling lawyers how to handle physical evidence—and his call was controversial even within the bar.

Rosen, for one, always thought the "obstruct" came not in Murray's retrieving the tapes, not in his holding on to them, but rather in what appeared to be an effort to "hide" them in the sexual assault file and, in Rosen's words, "let the murder case proceed and nobody would know the difference."

But that isn't how prosecutor Ian Scott saw it; he argued that the "obstruct" came in Murray holding on to the tapes.

That was a complex issue for lawyers, if for few others.

The videotapes were what lawyers call "physical objects of crime."

Though most lawyers well understand that if a client marches into their office with the proverbial "smoking gun" used in a homicide or the "bloody shirt" soaked with a victim's blood, they should arrange to have the evidence turned over to the police (this is usually done anonymously, through another lawyer hired for that very purpose), the tapes weren't quite that kind of animal.

Certainly, they revealed Bernardo as a violent sexual sadist and they revealed several serious crimes. But they were also so damning of Homolka—who from the get-go always portrayed herself as just another beaten and coerced victim of her husband—that it was certainly possible they could prove her to be a liar and perhaps even raise a legitimate doubt about which of the pair was the killer.

In fact, Murray's claim of how he had planned to use the tapes was supported by how Rosen actually did use them at Bernardo's trial—the very same way Murray imagined, to impeach and thoroughly discredit Homolka.

And there was no rule, either in the Canadian Bar Association's Code of Professional Conduct or the Law Society of Upper Canada's Rules of Professional Conduct, that told a lawyer what to do with physical evidence of a crime that fell short of the smoking gun.

However, to the families—and the Canadian public who venerated them and whose sympathies were so adroitly played throughout by Tim Danson—it seemed far simpler.

(Danson's handling of the entire file always brings to my mind a charity event I attended decades ago. It was to raise money for childhood cancer, as I recall, and after a poignant film and the usual pleas to the emotions, organizers finally brought their ace-in-the-hole, a bald little girl who was clearly frail, on stage. "This is Lucy," a woman breathed into the mike. "Lucy is seven." Long pause. Then, just in case anyone had missed the obvious, "Lucy has *cancer!*")

As Kristen's dad, Doug French, told *Maclean's* magazine at the time, "I haven't got much to say, other than we're pleased that they've [the two lawyers] finally been charged for what they've done."

In any case, at Cooper's direction, Murray duly reported to a St. Catharines' police station for photographing and fingerprinting.

It was only then that he learned he was also charged with possessing child pornography and making obscene material.

MacDonald was also charged with the child porn offence, though not with the obscenity count.

Murray was stunned, embarrassed, enraged: There are few charges more damaging, or which evoke more of a visceral public response, than child porn. As he once told me, with the obstruct justice charge, the state was questioning his professional judgment, and that he certainly could bear and understand. But with the porn and obscenity counts, it was as if the government was also saying, "Morally, you're bankrupt."

The obscenity charge was the worst, Murray said, because "people would think it was a commercial thing, that I was making copies [of the tapes] and selling them, marketing them. That's far worse than them thinking I had some prurient interest in watching them."

The Murrays—Ken, his wife, Sharon, and their two kids, Linzi and Callum, then respectively fifteen and eleven, and a menagerie of animals and birds—live on a lovely farm they call Ewetopia in the town of Sunderland, Ontario, about an hour northeast of Toronto.

The charges, of course, made front-page news.

Within a day, the boss of a local courier firm with whom Murray had done business for years announced he wouldn't be doing any more work for him.

The message was unmistakable: We can't afford to be affiliated with the likes of you.

Murray even tried to resign as the coach of Callum's ball team, afraid that "People were thinking, 'Do I want him coaching my team? Do I want him in the change rooms?'"

But the parents knew him and liked him and asked him to stay.

Besides, Murray said, half-kidding, the parents knew that as a coach, "You're never alone with the children" anyway.

It was, in fact, a classic case of what's known in the business as "overcharging." It means police charge someone either with multiple variations of essentially the same offence (a raft of weapons charges, for instance, in relation to a single gun used in a single offence) or toss in charges that the authorities suspect or know full well are unsupportable or will be dropped, but that will have the desired effect of irreparably soiling the accused's reputation.

Cops and prosecutors do it all the time—and depending on the case and where you live, it may be one or the other or both.

In British Columbia, Quebec and New Brunswick, prosecutors have "charge approval," as it's called. Charges can't be laid without their blessing. In the rest of the country, it's the police, in Murray's case the Ontario Provincial Police, who actually lay charges, with prosecutors left to sort the wheat from the chaff by deciding which charges are in the public interest, have "a realistic prospect of conviction" and should go forward.

But there's little doubt that with Murray, the cops and prosecutors were to all intents and purposes working hand-in-glove, speaking with one voice, just as the Niagara and Toronto forces had done at 720 Bay during the Homolka and Bernardo prosecutions.

Prosecutors and police have different roles, but as a recent Ontario Divisional Court decision nicely put it, the police "are the investigative arm of the state, with the responsibility for investigating crime and compiling evidence for charges prosecuted by the Attorney-General."

In fact, during the supposed three years of the OPP "investigation," no one from the force ever once spoke to Murray or asked for his notes or files.

As he put it furiously, "There never was any investigation."

He wasn't charged with the pornography offence because the authorities actually believed he held on to the tapes to watch and enjoy them, and he wasn't charged with making obscene material because they actually suspected he was frantically copying the tapes or, God forbid, selling them.

There wasn't a scintilla of evidence he had done anything improper with the tapes beyond the debatable act of hanging on to them for sixteen months and making a copy of them as any lawyer would with original evidence—not that anyone from the OPP ever asked him about it.

All charges against Carolyn MacDonald were dropped in May that year; the charges against Murray of possessing child porn and making obscene material were dropped a couple of months after that.

He had lived under that cloud for ten months.

As Murray said later, the obstruct justice charge, he always got, as it were. "The rest was a fuckover. Vindictive, small in the petty, little-man sense. They were shit-flinging."

He knew very well how it can work.

He'd been a prosecutor; in fact, at the time of the Emanuel Jaques case, the first trial I ever covered, Ken Murray was working as a Crown attorney in the downtown Toronto office, though he wasn't the one who handled the case.

There's a saying among prosecutors, he told me: "If you can't convict them, at least you can ruin their lives."

As Stephen Williams wrote of the charges against Murray, and this was after he himself had felt the sting of the state's wrath but not its full power, all but the obstruct justice count was ludicrous.

"His prosecution and the attendant publicity were nothing but a subterfuge and it had served its purpose. . . . In the public's mind, he was still the scumbag lawyer responsible for those terrible deals with that murderous bitch."

In February, the Law Society served Murray with professional misconduct complaints.

LSUC investigators, unlike their counterparts at the OPP, actually questioned him for three days and ordered him to hand over all his documents.

The Law Society put its hearing on hold pending the outcome of Murray's criminal charges.

The six-week trial started in the last week of March 2000 in courtroom No. 11 at the St. Catharines courthouse, one away from the room where seven years earlier, Karla Homolka had been arraigned and pleaded guilty.

The content of the notorious videotapes—ever radioactive, they were in the room, but sealed, of course—was central to Murray's defence and his contention that he was justified in hanging on to them as long as he did.

Could they really have helped him defend Bernardo, as Murray always claimed, or was he concealing them, as prosecutor Scott said, and intending to permanently suppress them? That was the issue.

The tapes were vital to Murray being able to defend himself. But they could never be played, heavens no.

No one had the stomach—not lawyers for the press, who could not have seen the tapes in any case, that issue having been argued and lost already at Bernardo's trial; not the prosecutors; not Cooper; and not Judge Gravely, who could have seen them— even to suggest the tapes should be unsealed.

And had anyone had the temerity to try, Tim Danson was there on guard in court, the families in tow.

He had no formal standing at this trial, but by God, now he didn't even need to seek it.

Gravely was acutely sensitive to the presence of Donna French and the Mahaffys in his court, and he did what judges always did when faced with these sad and haunted parents—he heard their lawyer.

In lieu of the tapes, what the court proposed to use was the police-produced, frame-by-frame transcript of what they showed and what words were spoken.

This exhibit also was sealed.

Also tendered as evidence were two transcribed interviews with Homolka, the first done by police, the second by Murray and MacDonald.

All the transcripts, naturally, contained sexually explicit descriptions and wretched details of what had happened to Leslie and Kristen. Danson argued that none of the explicit descriptions of the cruelties inflicted on the dead girls should be reported again or, if that was allowed, that the media should be prohibited from identifying Leslie and Kristen by name.

He proposed to ban the publication of parts of sixty-six pages.

(In the summer of 2013, Danson said that as he recalled it, mostly what he had been seeking to redact were places where Jane Doe's real name, for instance, appeared. That is not how I reported it at the time, for I covered Murray's trial, or how I remember it now. In any case, Danson was unapologetic: "I had obtained court orders [publication bans] and I wanted those court orders respected, about certain information that could and couldn't be disclosed." He admitted, however: "the joke is, I'm the one who maintained the integrity of the court order," by which he meant it was curious that an uninvolved third party to a trial should have had such power.)

The judge agreed that the descriptions should be cleansed.

He several times imposed temporary publication bans purely so that Danson could be contacted and come to court to make appropriate edits.

Gravely drew the line only at obliterating from the public record the names of the two murdered girls whose names in fact were so part of the public record they were already as familiar to many Canadian parents as those of their own kids.

The prosecutors from 720 Bay, Ian Scott and Howard Leibovich, routinely consulted the families and Danson. They supported every one of Danson's submissions, even on matters where prosecutors traditionally take no position.

The evidence had become the elephant in the room. It was a grotesque situation.

Once, there was the ludicrous spectacle of Murray, then in the witness box being questioned by Scott, both of them with copies of the hot potato exhibits in front of them—neither man daring to actually speak the words they were each silently reading.

Until Austin Cooper finally snapped—clearly deciding that, however unpleasant, Gravely had to know what Homolka had done and why his client may have thought it germane—Ken Murray was essentially hamstrung from vigorously defending himself out of courtesy to the sensibilities of the families, third parties who had absolutely no role to play in the trial.

I'd never seen anything like it.

At the end of a six-week trial, Murray was acquitted—"barely," as the University of Ottawa associate law professor Adam Dodek wrote in a 2008 paper on Canadian legal ethics.

Dodek noted that, for the legal profession, the twenty-first century had got off to a rather rocky start.

There was the Murray case, an ethical scandal at the University of Toronto Law School (two dozen students received sanctions ranging from reprimands to one-year suspensions for misrepresenting their grades to prospective employers) and no fewer than two prominent falls from grace—Howard Berge, the president of the Law Society of British Columbia, who quit in 2003 after pleading guilty to driving "without due care and attention" (he had consumed what the Law Society later called "a substantial amount of alcohol") and George Douglas Hunter, the treasurer of the Law Society of Upper Canada, who stepped down from his post and was later suspended for two months for "conflict of interest" during a lengthy affair with a family law client.

There were other, broader issues too, Dodek said.

The proliferation of class-action lawsuits—and some of the astonishing fees paid, such as for the settlements of the tainted blood scandal and residential school abuse claims—fed the public perception "that lawyers put their own interests ahead of those of their clients," Dodek wrote.

As well, access to justice, the phrase used to describe the ordinary citizen's ability to hire a lawyer and defend herself in court, was shrinking.

(For just a tiny glimpse, take the financial impact upon the Murrays. Though they managed to hang on to their farm and the renovated house out of which Murray runs his law office, the couple ran through their savings, cashed in life insurance policies and depleted their RSPs, which, for sole practitioners, are their only pensions. The bill for transcripts alone was $30,000; putting up Cooper and his junior at a hotel for almost two months cost close to $15,000.)

As legal aid funding in the provinces dried up and shut out thousands of Canadians who earn too much to qualify for assistance (in Ontario in 2007, that was $16,600 a year after taxes) but nowhere near enough to pay the going rate for a lawyer, so has the cost of a trial risen.

As Tracey Tyler reported in the *Toronto Star* in her excellent "access to justice" series in 2007, a bare-bones three-day civil proceeding, with no expert witnesses, then ran to about $60,000.

(Tyler, who was a terrific reporter—even and even-handed—and a lovely person, died of cancer in 2012 at the age of fifty.)

All in all, Dodek wrote, "For Canadian legal ethics, it has been an eventful and challenging decade." He dubbed 2006 and 2007 as the legal profession's *anni horribiles* from a legal ethics perspective.

It was in part to fix the sort of dilemma Ken Murray had faced with the tapes that six months after his acquittal in St. Catharines, the LSUC withdrew the charges of professional misconduct against him and instead appointed a big-name committee to study lawyers' ethical responsibilities and come up with a rule that would help them all know what to do.

It was an implicit acknowledgement that Murray had made his difficult decision in an ethical vacuum.

Gavin MacKenzie, who was then the head of the professional regulation committee of the LSUC, the body responsible for professional conduct and discipline, was asked to chair the new special committee "on Lawyers' Duties with Respect to Property Relevant to a Crime or Offence," as it was called in unwieldy lawyerly fashion.

MacKenzie is a leading light on ethical issues in the country, part of what Adam Dodek calls the new wave of legal ethics scholars.

MacKenzie's book, *Lawyers and Ethics: Professional Responsibility and Discipline*, was first published in 1993 and is credited by many, including Dodek, as having given Canadian legal scholarship a much-needed kick in the pants.

He also speaks, and writes, in remarkably plain English.

So he was the perfect guy to be heading this committee, and was joined by nine other leading practitioners, including senior Crown law officers and senior members of the defence bar.

They took their task seriously—reviewed the existing rules and standards in other countries (at the time, Alberta was the only Canadian province with such a rule) and the academic writing and case law, and met a dozen times.

By March 2001, the majority of the committee had agreed on a proposed rule, and proceeded to circulate it—as well as the alternative favoured by the two Crown representatives, Paul Lindsay, then the director of the Crown law office, criminal, at 720 Bay, and Tony Loparco, then the president of the Ontario Crown Attorneys' Association and now the head of Ontario's Special Investigations Unit, which investigates cases involving police-caused deaths or serious injury—to convocation, the regular meeting of the LSUC's board of directors, whose members are called benchers.

Briefly, the majority suggestion would have allowed lawyers to take or keep temporary possession of physical evidence of crime only in narrowly defined circumstances, chiefly if doing so was necessary to prevent the loss or destruction of the evidence or if the lawyer believed wrongful conviction could result if the evidence was disclosed before trial.

As James Lockyer, probably the best-known advocate in Canada for the wrongfully convicted, told *The Globe and Mail* at the time, "A very simple example would be where your client is charged with assault on someone, and he provides you with a tape-recorded conversation in which the complainant is a participant, and in which the complainant acknowledges he has made a false claim to the police."

In other words, disclose that tape-recording before trial, and the complainant then has time to adjust his false story and "tailor" his testimony to fit the new information.

That was not so very far from the way things had played out in the Homolka case, where she "recovered" her first memory of the first Jane Doe assault only after being shown a snippet of videotape by police.

While Homolka claimed she couldn't remember her full lascivious complicity in that attack, the disclosure of the tapes, however belated, still afforded her and her champions in the Crown law office plenty of time to prepare the "traumatic amnesia" explanation.

By contrast, the Crown-favoured rule would have left lawyers virtually no discretion, and forced them to immediately turn over to the authorities any property—including documents—"which may have evidentiary value" in a criminal or quasi-criminal investigation or proceeding.

The draft rule—and what's called "commentary," which is designed to put bones on the flesh of the rule—was published, and public submissions invited. As well, legal organizations and Ontario attorney general David Young were specifically asked for comment.

Young replied on May 28 with a five-page letter, laying out his "grave concerns" about the proposed rule and urging the committee to reconsider.

It did just that.

The draft was revised—changed in what MacKenzie called "substantive and structural" ways—further narrowing the circumstances under which a lawyer temporarily could keep physical evidence—now, it was only to prevent a wrongful conviction—and adding the requirement that the lawyer must first seek and get Law Society authorization to keep it at all.

It took more than a year, and as MacKenzie said in a July 2013 interview, "I'm not sure this rule we proposed is perfect.

"I think it can be criticized . . . but it would have addressed the Ken Murray problem, certainly. It would have obligated Murray to either turn over the tapes to law enforcement—not necessarily directly, he could have retained counsel and turned them over . . . or he could have come before a committee of the Law Society and tried to persuade" its members that keeping them was necessary "to prevent a wrongful conviction."

And, "I don't think there's any way he could have done that in this case," MacKenzie said. "[The tapes] were just so inculpatory of Bernardo. But you can imagine cases, and it's not hard to imagine cases, where you've got a Crown witness who's falsely implicating an accused person who will tailor their evidence if this physical evidence comes to light."

MacKenzie was "always troubled by how far the rule would go."

For instance, he said, videotapes, bloody shirts and smoking guns are one kettle of fish. "But if I get a document from a client that is evidence of a violation of the Securities Act or Competition Act, and there's no investigation going on, I'm not sure I have a duty to turn that over to the police, or the competition authorities or the securities authorities. You want to make sure the rule isn't overbroad."

Still, he said, the bottom line is, "I'm an advocate for there being a rule. I'm an advocate for this rule."

The rewritten rule, giving lawyers far less rope than the original version, was slated to be discussed at the May 23, 2002, convocation.

But as dusk follows dawn, two days before, a press release went out on the Canada Newswire, announcing that on May 22, Attorney General Young would "speak out against a proposed rule of conduct for Ontario lawyers that would allow them to suppress physical evidence of a crime."

Young, the release said, would be joined in the media studio at Queen's Park "by Deborah Mahaffy and Donna and Doug French."

And sure enough, the next morning, the day before the Law Society was to discuss the revamped rule, there was Young, flanked by the families.

He said—and while there could be honest disagreement about the rule, this was surely the sky-is-falling interpretation— that "even the proverbial smoking gun could be concealed from the authorities with the blessing of the Law Society if this rule is passed."

Young threatened to bring in legislation to override the rule.

Debbie Mahaffy told reporters the new rule would allow lawyers to "sabotage the Crown"; Donna French warned that "by concealing evidence," truth and justice would be ill-served.

The parents of the slain girls gave the press conference the "human face" the media, but particularly television, craves, and received wide coverage throughout southwestern Ontario.

For good measure, that day an opinion piece under Young's name also appeared in the *Toronto Star*. The last line read, "I hope the Law Society will reject this proposal today and adopt a more responsible approach to handling evidence in the future."

It all worked like a charm: Convocation shelved the rule with little discussion, saying further study was needed, and it died forever.

Though Gavin MacKenzie said "it wasn't because of anything the attorney general said," it sure looked that way.

And if ever there was a time when this particular Law Society needed this particular attorney general on side, it was now.

A fifteen-year war between Ontario lawyers and paralegals was on the verge of being settled. The LSUC was poised to tighten its grip on self-regulation by extending its turf to include the group of one thousand paralegals, despite earlier recommendations that the industry should indeed be regulated, but either by government or a body other than the LSUC.

In fact, as the paralegal report to convocation acknowledged, its proposal was developed "against the backdrop" of Peter Cory's study of May 2000.

The former Supreme Court judge, noting "the degree of antipathy displayed by members of legal organizations towards the work of paralegals," had recommended against the Law Society being the paralegal governing body.

Just weeks before convocation permanently shelved the "Ken Murray" rule, Kirk Makin wrote on the front page of the *Globe* about the coming deal that would see the LSUC accredit, license and discipline paralegals.

He quoted Vern Krishna, then the treasurer of the Law Society, positively burbling with excitement over the contribution of, guess who, none other than AG David Young.

"He is fully in the loop," Krishna said of the AG. "He has been very helpful, cooperative and encouraging."

The paralegal deal was presented at the April 25 convocation for "information."

In the July 2013 interview at MacKenzie's office at Davis LLP, where he is a partner, the Young press conference was one of the first things he mentioned.

"It detracted in that case from this being a deliberative process, a deliberative decision," he said. "It distorted it by the injection of this emotion."

It was quickly obvious, he said, "that there was a substantial feeling in convocation that now wasn't the time to debate," and that the decision "shouldn't be determined in that kind of an atmosphere."

The Canadian Bar Association, meanwhile, which was also overhauling its Code of Conduct, "ducked the Ken Murray problem," as Adam Dodek wrote in that 2009 piece.

As he neatly summed it up, "The Murray case thus ended in three negatives: no conviction against Murray, no disciplinary action by the LSUC, and no action by the LSUC to address the issue."

The CBA approach, MacKenzie said, was that "there's no need for a new rule, that this sort of event [i.e., a Ken Murray–type situation] happens once in a generation, if that frequently. . . . It's difficult if not impossible to try to come up with a rule that answers, that addresses in advance, every possible circumstance.

"So the best thing was, leave the rules as they are."

MacKenzie remembered no connection between the LSUC's need to keep Young onside on the paralegal issue and the way the proposed physical evidence rule he so publicly disliked was dropped like a hot potato. In fact, until I told him, he wasn't actually aware the two issues had come to convocation about the same time.

But, he said, "It's possible that some didn't want to alienate the attorney general for fear he would be less cooperative on paralegal regulation, but no one said that to me at the time or since."

Ken Murray remembered a meeting he and Carolyn MacDonald went to at the AG's office. This was early on, when they were still hoping they could get a deal for Bernardo.

But, Murray said, at 720 Bay they weren't much interested, either "in the case or what I had to say. They just wanted to prosecute.

"We could go over and over this, but the part that frustrates me the most—everybody wanted to stay away from resolving it. Everybody wanted to do it in a public forum, [have] a show trial."

He remembered how, after he turned over the tapes, he figured now "everybody had to know that the deal they had etched in stone was based on lies. In my ingenuousness with the justice system at the time, [I thought] maybe they'll say, 'You know what, we made a mistake. She [Homolka] lied to us.'

"But they kept protecting her."

It's his theory that "the grossness of the trial takes away from what they actually did in secret. [The evidence at trial] is so ugly, so horrific, nobody looks behind to say these guys cut the deal."

At least once a week in the halls of the busy courthouses where he makes his living, he encounters young lawyers, "obviously weaned" on his case in law school, who upon hearing his name ask if he's that Ken Murray.

"'That was your case?' they ask. '*R v Murray*?'"

Then they ask, "'Is there a rule? What do we do?' . . . and they [the Law Society] still haven't given any fucking advice about that," Murray said.

He is ingenuous no longer.

"I still think it's the best system we've got," he told me, "when it works. What screws it up is the politics."

No single person better embodies the terrible injustice that can result when the law is politicized than Stephen Williams.

When people think of wrongs in the justice system, naturally the names they remember are those who were wrongfully convicted and spent years in prison, often loudly proclaiming their innocence throughout, until something (like DNA) or someone (like James Lockyer or another lawyer) proves it true, the jail doors swing open and they stumble, permanently wounded, blinded by the light, into a world they may no longer know.

But there are wrongful prosecutions too—probably many more of them than convictions—and they can be just as ruinous.

As with wrongful convictions, wrongful prosecutions are rendered understandable—while still dreadful—if they occur unintentionally.

What happened to Williams, and his partner Marsha Boulton, was the furthest thing from accident or happenstance that I can imagine. Stephen Williams was deliberately persecuted by the state for the simple reason that he was the harshest critic of state conduct.

Over the span of seven years, he wrote two books on the Bernardo/Homolka case—*Invisible Darkness*, first published in 1996, and *Karla: A Pact with the Devil*, first published in French in 2002—which were devastatingly revealing of those who not only made the deal with Homolka but also stuck ferociously to the narrative they had woven about her and threw a blanket of secrecy over the whole kit and caboodle in order to protect their flanks.

Now, there were plenty of critics of the deal in those days—among them me, Kirk Makin at the *Globe,* and Rosie DiManno at the *Toronto Star.*

But we were all print journalists.

We could rant and rave in the pages of our newspapers every day of Bernardo's trial—and to varying degrees we did, Makin even winning a National Newspaper Award for his coverage—but there's a reason newsprint lines birdcages. It doesn't bloody last, and neither does whatever its impact may be, as all of us learn sooner or later. Print's clout, dubious always, is fleeting; the news cycle and, especially now, the public's attention span, see to that.

Enter Williams, who presented himself as a big-W writer (a lawyer representing him way back when once compared Williams to Truman Capote, a stretch at the time the lawyer said it, but perhaps no longer) with a slim c.v. of long magazine pieces.

But he proved himself to be a superb reporter.

For *Invisible Darkness*, he finagled access to the entire Crown brief in the Bernardo case.

I suspect on the basis of charm and genial good company, Williams was also handed the keys to the Karla kingdom by her treating psychiatrist, the late Dr. Hans Arndt, who was then dying of leukemia.

Introduced to Williams, Arndt decided to hand over to him two large attaché cases containing all of Homolka's school, medical and psychological records and various assessments done on her.

That book was a classic of the true-crime genre, if smarter than most.

(I am embarrassed that when it was first published, I gave it a mean review. I think now I was jealous, not only of Williams's several scoops within the book, but also of the fact that he acted as though he had invented the harsh view on Homolka. He hadn't, though he may have perfected it. In any case, I was unfair—it's an excellent book.)

After he was arrested for the first time in 1998, and charged with two counts of violating court orders, Williams was dragged back into the quagmire of Bernardo-Homolka in order to defend himself.

The late, legendary Eddie Greenspan, who ended up representing Williams in court on his acquittal, had told him, "You have to get everything you have in your possession out again, and we have to go through it with a fine-tooth comb, and you have to organize it—and you have to do it because you can't afford my juniors," Williams told me in a series of interviews in the fall–winter of 2012 and spring–summer of 2013.

"I had all the Crown disclosure, all the ninety binders," he said. "It was literally boxes, a small room full of boxes. . . . and we [he and Boulton] had to organize it in the fashion that a lawyer does. Well, in the process of doing that, I realized. . . . that Karla was going to get out, probably I thought at the time sooner rather than later. . . . And also, going through this stuff again, here's how I figured out what had really happened. The only way you can do this in a complicated criminal case is if you actually do have access to all the disclosure—all of it—and I did."

And in going through it all, again, he figured out that he had an even better book there.

This was Karla, and he was right.

It is even better, in part because he had access to more key voices, including that of Michael Code, the architect of Homolka's deal who had not yet been appointed to the bench and who met him for several long dinners, but also partly because Williams now had the wisdom of hindsight and could see things more clearly.

So he made another pitch and got another contract and he and Boulton were for a few days deliriously happy.

"The case was settled, we won, we've got some money, I've got a new project I know I can do," he said.

Then he woke up and realized he couldn't write the new book without Homolka herself and that, unfortunately, she probably loathed him because of what he'd written about her in *Invisible Darkness*. So he wrote to her, in prison, perhaps five times. There was no answer.

One day, as they were driving to the bank, Boulton was reading the obits and saw one for Dr. Arndt. Williams wrote to

Homolka one last time. "All I did was clip that and say he was a very nice man, you probably don't know this—he's gone."

Months later, by which point Williams had all but given up and was deeply depressed, a letter from her showed up in their mailbox.

Homolka had finally answered, thus beginning the strange and lengthy jailhouse correspondence that breathed life and the necessary dramatic tension into the second book.

He was off to the races.

Curiously, he has never really written about what happened to him in these years.

The first prosecution he didn't take terribly seriously, and by the time he was acquitted the second book was roiling about in his big head. And by the time the second prosecution was over, Williams was so flattened—financially and emotionally—he didn't have the resources, I think, to write about it, or much of anything else, either.

The best account of what happened to Williams and Boulton is found in a most unlikely place, the wonderful book Boulton wrote about the magnificent dog, Wally, who had got them through those awful years.

Wally was an English bull terrier, only the best sort of dog in the world. I have one too—Boulton introduced me to a superb breeder, and somehow I passed the heavy-duty screening interview—so I know. Mine is a big, strapping white one named O.B., for Other Boy, though over time he's come to be called Obie.

Even for people like Boulton and me, who have had dogs their whole lives and loved each unreservedly, there's nothing like a bully.

Her book, called *Wally's World*, was first published in 2006, and it's lovely: smart, thoughtful, funny. It's about the dog, of course, for even among bull terriers, Wally was a clown of a particular sort, so prone to pillow-humping, for instance, that

Boulton, feeling sorry for him when they were living for a time in an apartment in New York City, once bought him a cheap foam pillow and "allowed him half an hour of supervised humping" every day.

And the book is about Stephen, and about Stephen and her, too.

But dotted here and there throughout *Wally's World* are glimpses of what they went through at the hands of their government, and the loss of faith it engendered.

As she wrote in the book, ". . . it was one thing for the police to shut down a writer whose critical speech examined crimes of depravity and police ineptitude, but it was quite another to destroy the career of a middle-aged humorist-shepherd . . ."

The humorist-shepherd, of course, was her.

Unlike Williams, who before the Homolka case was but an aspiring author, Boulton was the real deal, with more than a half-dozen books under her belt, "country stories," as she modestly calls them, in which she refers to Williams as "Moose."

A winner of the Stephen Leacock Medal for humour, she was also a speaker much in demand, and a regular on CBC Radio, where since 1989 she'd been providing her "letters from the country" essays to various shows.

And at the time of Williams's second arrest, on the second set of charges, Boulton was three years into work on a new book, a historical novel based on a nineteenth-century Scottish Presbyterian cult in Cape Breton. If that sounds unlikely, in Boulton's hands I know it would have been great.

She lost everything—all that work—in the OPP's raid on the farm. She and Williams never did get their computers back, and what files Boulton belatedly had returned by the OPP mysteriously were corrupted and unreadable. But more important, by then, she'd lost her heart for the book.

"I was very excited about that," she said of the lost book in the summer of 2013. "I'd been to Cape Breton, and . . . I could see all of this stuff. I brought stuff back so that I had a library of research on that cult . . .

"But I'm a different person. I'm not sure I care about those characters any more, the Presbyterian cult. I've seen a much bigger cult, and how evil it can be."

It's not in Stephen Williams's nature to be shy or self-effacing, and after *Invisible Darkness* was published to considerable acclaim, he was neither.

As part of the publicity for the book, he appeared on all manner of TV shows and did all sorts of interviews. Notably, Williams allowed CBC's *The Fifth Estate* access to his archive of research and some of the interview clips from the Crown disclosure were part of the resulting show that aired in the spring of '97.

And in some of the interviews, he either led people to believe, or they assumed, that he'd seen the banned videotapes.

In fact, in a lengthy letter to *The Globe and Mail* on December 8, 1997, Williams wrote to correct the public record and a recently published column that had suggested he had used "fiction as an adhesive to glue together" the facts in *Invisible Darkness*.

"There is not one fictional word in my book, not even the parts where I put words and thoughts into Karla's mouth and mind, not even when I talk about the pimple on Leslie Mahaffy's face," Williams wrote.

Of course, he couldn't resist bragging just a little a bit, and fair enough: It was a hell of a good book and it was selling well.

Why, he said in the letter, he'd seen all the police interviews of Homolka, in jail and at her matrimonial home, and read the transcripts, and had handed the lot over to *The Fifth Estate*, which is how they produced their remarkable documentary.

It was that letter, in part, that led to a call he got near Christmas that year from *Sun* columnist Heather Bird. She wanted to talk about the book and the story, and Williams, in a weakened condition as he realized this gravy train of lovely attention was almost at an end, agreed.

Bird went away for Christmas, and so did Williams and Boulton. On January 4 or 5, she called him back and told him, he said, "'I'm going to write a column in tomorrow's paper and it's going to say you told me you'd seen the restricted videotapes.'

"Of course, I said, 'You stupid bitch, I didn't say anything remotely like that to you.'"

On January 6, 1998, Bird, who still maintains Williams told her he'd seen the tapes, wrote the column. "The deepest fears of the Mahaffy and French families may have been realized," it began. "Someone outside the authorized circle of people claims he has viewed the videotapes of Paul Bernardo raping their daughters."

A few paragraphs later came the key bit: "Lawyer Tim Danson, who represents both families, was aghast at the news and called for an immediate police investigation."

By January 11, Bird was reporting that the OPP had started an investigation, and within a week, there were demands from the usual quarters to expand it.

"Sometimes," Bird wrote on January 18, "when dealing with a controversial issue, a little perspective is required. And when it comes to the question of the police investigation around the Bernardo tapes, there's nothing like a conversation with Debbie Mahaffy to give you that perspective."

It was formulaic tabloid journalism, not that there's anything wrong with it, and I say that as one who practised the same dark art for a long time at the same newspaper and who has affected that sad-yet-wise tone myself too many times to count.

My only point is, you don't go to the lawyer or the mother of a murdered child for anything other than inflamed comment.

In a separate news story that same day, Bird quoted Tim Danson confirming that the two families had formally asked the OPP to broaden their probe of Williams to include his use of two court exhibit photographs (one of the cement blocks containing Leslie's dismembered body, the other of the crime scene where Kristen's body was found and which showed her clenched hand).

Using those two pictures may have been a lousy tactic. It may have been insensitive, with insensitivity already well on its way to becoming the cardinal Canadian sin. But the one thing it wasn't was illegal.

Williams took none of this seriously, not even after Clay Ruby, who was representing John Rosen and Tony Bryant—aware the OPP might want to speak to them as potential Williams sources, they did take it seriously—called and told him, "The police are investigating this, they're investigating it as a criminal matter: You need a lawyer."

Williams finally roused himself to ask York University law professor Alan Young, "an old hippie" in Williams's words, who agreed to represent him pro bono (the real pro bono), and at some point, the two went in for an OPP interview.

"I still didn't take it all that seriously," Williams said, "but I was nervous now about the police because having gone in and had this interview for a couple of hours, I then was aware they were really playing silly buggers."

On October 28, 1998, he was ordered to present himself for arrest at a Burlington, Ontario–area police station. This was some-what unusual, in that with most cases of this nature, the practice is for the police to deliver a summons to appear before a judge.

Young was in Vancouver and had to fly back.

"But what I did do," Williams said, "I called Kirk Makin that night, and I said 'Kirk, I'm being arrested in the morning, man' and he said, 'You're kidding' . . . so of course he wrote the story and it appeared at 5 a.m., whenever the paper drops."

When Williams got to the station, there was a huge crowd of media waiting for him. By now, he knew the press, and he knew they wouldn't have been so speedily roused to action.

"And I said, come on, you can't have followed Makin's piece in the *Globe* and come out here this fast, and they said oh, it wasn't Makin. The cops called a press conference for this morning, and we were supposed to see the Mahaffy and French families."

The one good thing, Williams said, is that, the cat being well out of the bag with Makin's front-page story, the press conference never happened.

He was charged with two counts of breaching a court order, the allegation being that he saw all or parts of the banned tapes contrary to Judge LeSage's order and that he couldn't have possibly written in such exquisite detail about what was on the tapes without seeing them.

In fact, he could have done, as could any of us who heard the tapes and in particular John Rosen's very descriptive cross-examination of Homolka. I've never seen the tapes but so familiar are they to me, from Rosen's cross, that I sometimes forget I haven't.

But finally, Williams was freaked out, at least a little. "I'd never been arrested before, I'd never been fingerprinted, any of that stuff. And I'd never been intimidated to that point."

He remembers seeing the letter—in the disclosure he later got—from Danson to Murray Segal, the long-serving government lawyer who was then the assistant deputy AG, criminal, or chief prosecutor for Ontario, and who was the fellow who prosecuted Homolka and sought all that secrecy.

Now, at the back of *Invisible Darkness*, Williams had a sort of true-crime staple, an update on the cast of characters. One paragraph read: "Two years later, Marion Boyd, the Attorney-General who sanctioned Karla's deal, was voted out of office. The assistant deputy minister, Michael Code, who had been instrumental in getting Karla her deal, quit. Murray Segal left his wife and three children, and moved in with Michal Fairburn."

It was a simple statement of the facts: Segal and Fairburn did take up with one another.

It must have seemed if not an entirely innocuous line, an inconsequential one. I've written many like it in my life. But it raised what lawyers often call the appearance of a potential conflict of interest—not of course that either Segal or Fairburn would ever have been so petty, but a sensitive fellow like Williams might see it that way.

In any case, his trial began at the Old City Hall courts in Toronto in September 1999 before Ontario Court judge David Fairgrieve.

Williams was still somewhat amused by it all, but Boulton, after glimpsing Fairgrieve at one point picking up Stephen's book as she inimitably put it "like he was holding a piece of soiled toilet tissue," knew, if Williams didn't, that "we were in trouble."

The trial dragged on, as they tend to do, and at some point, this after Young lost another motion, it at last sunk in with Williams that "I'm in deep shit, right?"

He phoned Eddie Greenspan, whom he knew socially from long dinners at Toronto's smartest restaurants with mutual friends.

Greenspan was a wonderful character, a prolific author and one of the biggest names in Canadian law, who also defended some of the biggest names, from former Nova Scotia premier Gerry Regan to my former boss and *National Post* founder Conrad Black.

(Greenspan died in Arizona on December 24, 2014. Though he was seventy and hardly in superb health or shape, his death came as a terrible shock. He was such a mensch, anyone who knew him imagined he would have to live forever, or at least I did anyway. As his daughter, and fellow lawyer, Juliana, told a packed house in a magnificent, and terrifically funny, eulogy, if only her dad had known he'd get such a turnout, he'd have faked his own death years before.)

Williams told Greenspan, "He is going to put me in jail. He said, 'Williams, don't be fucking ridiculous, he's not going to put you in jail. Who is it, anyway?' I said, David Fairgrieve." Greenspan replied, according to Williams, "Oh shit . . . I taught him. Not one of my triumphs."

Since Williams is a galoot, six-foot-four and huge, that didn't bode well for him.

Still doubting things were as gloomy as Williams said, Greenspan agreed to dispatch Marie Henein, then a young lawyer in his office, down to monitor the proceedings.

Henein went on, and quickly, to become one of the go-to criminal lawyers in the country; I've seen her in action several times, and she is a ferocious, even frightening, presence in court. She's also drop-dead gorgeous and wears terrific shoes. The only hint of weakness I've ever seen in her was when we once drove back together from some law conference in Quebec and both of us managed to misplace the Montreal airport.

But at that time she was just a decade out of law school and relatively junior, albeit a junior with fabulous shoes.

Henein duly sat in one day to see which way the wind was blowing and, as Williams put it, she "comes back and says [the judge is] going to put him in jail, and Eddie says, 'All right, I'll take the file.'"

That was the moment, Williams said, speaking for himself and Boulton, "The weight of the world was lifted from both our shoulders. We suddenly realized that I wasn't going to go to jail. We just knew that we were going to be all right."

Greenspan, according to Williams, in short order went to the prosecutor, Paul Taylor, and told him, "You haven't got a case and frankly, whatever you do, you know the videotapes are going to be brought into evidence."

Greenspan threatened to go all the way to the Supreme Court of Canada in order to make sure they were in court, Williams said, and told Taylor, "I'll win and then I'll beat your ass, because you haven't got a substantive case. You know it and I know it too, so what are you going to do?"

Taylor agreed not just to withdraw the charges, but also that Williams should be acquitted: The mere threat of the videotapes had worked their magic again.

On November 30, 2000, for the first and last time on behalf of this particular client, Eddie Greenspan actually appeared in court.

The place was packed with press, the joint jumping. "About thirty seconds after the judge sits down," Williams said, "Eddie strolls in . . . he always does this, I found out over the years, he walks like a penguin, right? Very slowly . . . he never goes any faster than he's going."

Williams was acquitted. Greenspan praised Taylor for doing the right thing, in the "highest traditions of the Crown." He offered sympathies to the families for their unspeakable loss and the nightmare they endured.

Then he said, "Stephen Williams is a writer. He wanted to capture that nightmare in a book. He wanted the world to know that Karla Homolka was evil personified, a metaphor for evil. That's what he wrote.

"Writing," said Eddie Greenspan, "can never be a crime in a free and democratic society. . . . At the centre of this case was the risk that for the very first time in our long and great history, a writer could face going to jail for the crime of merely writing.

"That is something one sees in Iraq, Iran or China. It is not something that we should ever tolerate in a free and democratic society."

Then they all went to the Rosedale pile of the poet and author Barry Callaghan, an old friend of both Williams and Boulton, for a big party.

It was over.

Boulton went back to working on the novel about the weird cult in Cape Breton, Williams to the new book about Homolka that he'd discovered that he had in him.

But it wasn't over.

To borrow from Winston Churchill, it was not the end. It wasn't even the beginning of the end. It was the end of the beginning.

Where *Invisible Darkness* had been an easy sell to publishers, the second book was tougher to pitch. Homolka was going through one of the valleys of public interest in her, and as Williams said, "She spent a lot of time out of the news" while she was in prison.

Still, he landed a contract, with General Publishing, but just as he was handing in the first draft of *Karla*, the company, part of the Jack Stoddart book empire, filed for creditor protection, and Williams had to scramble to physically retrieve his manuscript and then find another publisher.

He put out feelers to about ten top people. "Every one of them, without exception, turned it back and most without reading it. . . . There was some weird 'We heard enough about this case'" vibe in the air, he said. Besides, went this chorus, "It's prurient."

In the end, the book was first published in French in 2002 by a controversial Quebec entrepreneur named Pierre Turgeon, who then started a new company in Montreal, Cantos Publishing, to publish it in English early in 2003.

Indigo Books and Music, which at the time owned more than 250 bookstores nationwide (under the Indigo and Chapters names, but also Coles and SmithBooks) took 25,000 copies.

"And the first ten days, I don't know that it sold five copies," Williams said. "We were in a fucking panic. And then Danson pulled his stunt, and in three days, it sold out."

The stunt was of course yet another press conference, organized by the lawyer to denounce the book and its author and to beg bookstores not to carry it.

He was, as ever, accompanied by the families, in this instance Dan Mahaffy, who didn't speak, and Donna French, who did.

The chief objections once again centred on photographs in the book, in particular a clear close-up of cinder blocks containing Leslie Mahaffy's body parts (her sad, slim leg is visible), and one of Homolka with Jane Doe.

There was a small black bar over Jane's eyes, but the rest of her face was visible.

At the request of the Ontario government—that is, Attorney General David Young—Niagara Police had been on the case since the French publication of *Karla*, supposedly looking into whether Homolka had violated her plea bargain by co-operating with Williams through her letters.

But now, Danson was complaining that the picture of Jane Doe breached the publication ban protecting her identity.

Within weeks, Williams agreed that the offending photographs would be removed or altered from the second edition of the book, but pointed out, fairly I think, that the picture of Jane Doe was thirteen years old, and probably so dated she couldn't be identified in any case.

"I didn't set out to re-victimize the families," he told the Canadian Press in March of '03. "If these photos are going to make people grief-stricken and anguished, I'll take them out."

But earlier that same day, Niagara had asked the OPP to help in their investigation, and the OPP took the lead thereafter.

The so-called probe into whether Homolka had breached her deal disappeared in the investigation of that far more heinous criminal, Williams.

That winter, well before this hullaballoo, Williams had discovered software that allowed the user to build a website.

"My idea," he said, "was to put the entire Bernardo/Homolka archive on the Internet." He found a web guy to put up the site as a test. It was a dry run, in effect, to learn if the software actually worked and how the material appeared.

Naturally, being Stephen Williams, on April 28 he told the *Globe* all about it, including the fact that he intended to post excerpts of Bernardo and Homolka having sex, with Homolka wearing her then newly dead sister's clothes.

He was back as big news.

On April 30, Tim Danson told the paper that he and the families would use every legal means available to stop Williams from posting material on the web.

On the night of May 1, a Thursday, he and Boulton (and Wally) were in their room at the now-defunct Metropolitan, where for years they always stayed when in Toronto, largely because of the warm welcome given the dog.

"We're sitting in the room, Marsha looks at the website, she goes, 'Holy shit! There's a fucking victim's name, there it is right there.' Two or three other names. We were hysterical."

Williams began trying to track down his web guy to tell him to collapse the site.

He called Eddie Greenspan about 11 p.m.

"I said I fucked up. He said, 'What have you done?' And I said there are names of victims in one of the willsays [these are statements of what a witness will say] I put up on my experimental website.

"I said it's collapsed, I've taken it down.

"He said, 'No problem. You've done it on your own volition. It's an experiment. You recognized you made a mistake; you've taken it down; that's the right thing to do.'"

The site was up for only about eighteen hours. The mistake was clearly an honest one, as shown by Williams's quick corrective measures. But no matter: The OPP had found the site and copied it—every half hour, in fact, until Williams tracked down his web guy and he managed to take the site down.

The next day, Boulton was to read from her *Letters from the Country Omnibus* at the Tri-County Literacy Festival in Chatham, Ontario, a couple of hours west of Toronto. All the way there, Williams was talking to Greenspan.

Greenspan assured him he'd already written to the OPP commissioner, to the AG, to Murray Segal and to the fellow in charge of the OPP probe, telling them all he represented Williams, and if they wanted to interview his client or have him produced, he was the attorney of record.

With any criminal lawyer, this is standard stuff: You tell the people who count that you're happy to bring your guy in, just say when. It's both a gesture of good faith and a pre-emptive strike. But when the lawyer is as famous as Eddie Greenspan, I can't imagine prosecutors and cops just blithely ignoring it.

"We're now jacked up because of the site, and I'm really worried they're going to put me in jail, and [Greenspan] said, 'Williams, don't be fucking nuts. For Christ's sake, you're so fucking paranoid. They're never going to put you in jail for this shit.

"'It's just fucking breaches of publication bans. They don't put people in jail for that. Now stop hounding me!'"

Greenspan also told Williams to reassure Boulton. "Tell Marsha not to worry," he told him, adding, "Besides, if you do go to jail, she'll get used to it."

"That's not helpful," Williams replied, but actually, Greenspan managed to calm them both down, and despite themselves, they relaxed a little.

It was a lovely day, and they took the long way home, along the lake, stopping here and there, and didn't get back to Mount Forest and their farm until 9:30 Saturday night.

"Six [the next] morning," Williams said, "they're here, with [six] cops, all SWAT-team, guns-drawn, in full regalia."

"They came up with sirens blaring," Boulton said.

Later, they learned from their neighbours that the police had been there Friday night too.

Williams was cuffed.

Boulton put Wally on his leash, took him around and introduced him to the officers, saying, "This is Wally, he's a good dog; do not shoot him."

In any arrest situation, Williams said, police have one guy they call "the soother . . . they look for the guy who's the most calm, who actually does the arrest." It was the soother and another local fellow (Williams had played slo-pitch with him) who stayed behind to deal with Williams.

He's so big, they had to push him into the back of the squad car and he had to lie across the seats.

Williams was complaining all the while, telling them, "'I'm claustrophobic, this is bullshit.' I'm fucking chirping at them from the back seat." As soon as they were on the road, the cops pulled over and the fellow he played slo-pitch with undid his handcuffs, and they drove to the Mount Forest detachment.

"It's a Sunday morning," Williams said. "There's no one there. They let me sit in the office; they weren't going to put me in a cell."

They had a nice chat about Miles Davis, who'd been playing on the stereo at the farm; they let him call Boulton on his cell; they were friendly and pleasant.

"I said, 'What are you guys doing? What are we doing?'

"They said, 'Honestly, we don't know. We've been told to hold you.' I said, 'Who's telling you to do this?' They said, 'We don't know.'"

Boulton raced over to the detachment with all of Williams's meds—blood pressure pills; tranquilizers; pain killers for his bad knee—and an extra cellphone battery.

The soother and the slo-pitch cop let him go out and talk to her.

Williams got Greenspan on the phone and asked the cops if they'd talk to him, and one of them agreed. Greenspan asked what their instructions were; they didn't have any, the cop said. We don't know. Greenspan asked where they were taking Williams. The cop said they didn't know.

Williams took the phone back, and Greenspan said, "'I'll get to the fucking bottom of this; don't worry. I'll have you home for Sunday dinner at the worst.'"

An hour passed. Williams read the newspaper Boulton brought. "The soother comes and says, 'We're gonna move.'

"Okay, where we going?" Williams asked.

"'I don't know,'" the soother told him. "'I've been told to drive you around a bit.'"

Williams asked if there was any way to get a bigger car. "'We've got the Marquis,'" the soother told him. Williams was grateful, and thanked them.

"We get in this car, and we're driving sort of east, then sort of south, then west, basically going in zigzag directions," Williams said. They stopped at a McDonald's.

Finally, about 6 p.m., the cops dropped him off at the OPP detachment in Caledon, where two other cops, a man and a woman, from OPP headquarters in Orillia tried to interview him.

Greenspan, meanwhile, had been working the phones and found out finally the name of the person at the AG who was in charge of this circus—Michal Fairburn, the woman for whom, in Williams's inimitable words at the back of *Invisible Darkness*, Murray Segal had left his wife and three children.

Greenspan was apoplectic. He threw the phone against the wall and Todd White, then his partner, had to take over talking to Williams. Greenspan's wife, Suzy, later told Boulton she'd never seen him so angry.

"Eddie said to Michal Fairburn on the phone words to the effect of, 'How far are your mutual heads up each other's asses, you and fucking Segal? Do you think you can get away with this? You're putting a writer in fucking jail and you shouldn't be within a hundred miles of this fucking nonsense because you are a target in his books.'"

Greenspan wrote the AG, and faster than you could say "potential appearance of bias," Segal and Fairburn recused themselves from the file.

Since Segal was the senior official, it was him I would end up asking about all this.

After decades spent as a civil servant, he left the ministry in 2012 and went into private practice with Simcoe Law Chambers. He is now also Counsel to Henein Hutchison, Marie Henein's firm.

In those thirty-six years, except for the Homolka trial, I don't think I ever saw Segal in court.

And any requests for comment—and as Ontario's purported chief prosecutor or one of its senior law officials he was always a key player behind the scenes—from Segal or anyone else at that secretive ministry were and are funnelled through the PR arm and its spokesman Brendan Crawley.

Crawley is a pleasant guy, but often useless to a reporter seeking actual information, which is of course his real function—to deflect, defer, delay, deny. He is quite brilliant at it.

But as Segal had been in the background of so many cases and issues I've covered, I thought, when I heard he'd left the government, that I'd give it a whirl.

To my surprise, after a few days of mulling it over, he agreed to meet me at his then brand-new office. So on September 20, 2012, I showed up, and Segal, as promised, arrived shortly after with Timmy's for us both.

We chatted for about an hour, I think, some part of which was off the record so I turned off my recorder, and it was amicable enough. It was only when I transcribed the tape of our chat later that day that I realized that Segal, after years of practice, had said absolutely nothing that would have been remotely controversial.

Our conversation had touched on a number of subjects—from the *R v Elliott* case, which had seen Cosgrove resign from the bench, to the Homolka deal—and throughout, Segal was restrained, uber-cautious, entirely proper, completely anal.

I'd set out my usual ground rules off the top: I'd tape the interview and transcribe it, provide him with a copy and, if he had regrets about something he'd said, or wished he'd said it better, he could make changes. He was the boss of the interview, I said, and I meant it.

This is my book-writing practice.

I find it gives people comfort to have a record of what they have told me, and only infrequently, in dozens and dozens of interviews over the course of now three books, has anyone ever changed anything but occasional misspelled names.

And by this time in the work on this particular book I'd already interviewed a half-dozen lawyers and three judges, one of whom was then still sitting on the Ontario Superior Court, and not one had made a substantive change to their transcripts.

In fact, two of the judges—who were a hell of a lot more frank than Murray Segal—had added to the transcripts and expanded on what they'd said in person.

When Segal sent back his transcript—it ran to twenty-one pages—there were giant Xs across fourteen full pages and three half-pages, and editing changes everywhere else.

As an example of the latter, he'd originally told me he had left the ministry because "I thought I should try something a little different while I still have the juice."

He changed "juice" to "energy" in his edit, juice being what?—too sexy, I guess.

"Good to see you're still in constant touch with Crawley," I snapped back in an email, referring to the ministry spokesman.

"It's the ONLY explanation for some of what you've edited out. Jesus H."

So, when I realized I had some new questions about how he and Fairburn had handled the Williams prosecution, I was not optimistic. I emailed the questions to him, unwilling to go down to his office again for another chat in which he would say nothing and which he would then edit to less than zero.

Segal's reply was a curt, "Really Christie? Let me think about it."

After two days, I wrote him again. "Shall I put you down for a 'no comment' then?" He asked for more time.

My memory is foggy now—and emails have disappeared as, over the years I slogged on the book, laptops have come and gone—but at some point out of the blue, I received a note from a lawyer acting for Fairburn, urging caution upon me lest I might even suggest there had been anything improper, ever, about her conduct, which of course I wasn't doing.

Greenspan, the last time I saw him before his death, confirmed Williams's story about his initial rage and acknowledged that he had allowed himself to be talked out of doing anything formal about the matter. He asked me to keep the details private.

And Fairburn, who left the AG in 2013 to join the Stockwoods firm, was appointed the same year as a judge to the Ontario Superior Court.

Williams was questioned by the two OPP officers, though that is a loose description of what happened.

He told them, "You can talk all you fucking want," but he was waiting for his lawyer. One of them said, "Well, you were convicted the first time," to which Williams, ever-smooth, snapped, "You're as stupid as you look—I wasn't convicted, I was acquitted, you stupid fuck, and if you could read you would know that."

The cop pulled out a piece of paper and threw it at Williams; it was a "notice of action" that the AG was also suing him in civil court.

Fairburn had gone to court the day before—a Saturday!—with two of her colleagues from the civil side of the ministry and obtained an *ex parte* injunction from Superior Court judge James Spence.

Ex parte is Latin for "one side only." Neither Williams nor Greenspan, in other words, were in the judge's chambers when Spence ordered Williams to deliver all the Crown brief materials he had in the Bernardo-Homolka case and prohibited him from publishing or reproducing them.

Williams didn't have his phone any longer. He demanded to speak to Greenspan, and when he rang the office, he got Vanessa Christie, the new Marie Henein in Greenspan's firm and a doll in her own right.

"What the hell is going on?" Williams asked.

She told him they were trying to talk to the cops and prosecutors but, "We're not getting anywhere. You may have to stay [in jail] tonight."

Williams told his handlers he wasn't feeling well, and they called an ambulance. He suspected his blood pressure was skyrocketing. The "very attractive" female medic took it, and whispered it was completely normal.

Boulton knew very well what had happened: "He calmed down as soon as he saw an attractive female."

The medic offered to take him to hospital anyway, but warned he'd probably sit in a corridor all night. The cells were empty, but for him, and the cops had agreed to leave the door open—Williams is severely claustrophobic—and brought in a civilian to sit watch on him.

He spent the night on a concrete slab, with no blanket, but he had the pills and was able to induce a semi-stupor.

The next day, for his first appearance, he went to the far-flung Finch Avenue West courts—located at one end of a forlorn slice of low-rent strip mall and looking nothing like a courthouse—which just happened to be furthest from Greenspan's downtown office.

He was put in a crowded holding cell, but was befriended by a court officer, who recognized him as the writer and got him some orange juice. "She was just so nice," Williams said, "and if I called her, she would come, and [because of her] I was able to sort of weather this.

"They bring me up [from the cells] and there's Michal Fairburn in the court and of course this just made Eddie madder."

Fairburn was demanding bail.

Greenspan told the judge, "We have to be realistic here. First of all, I've never heard of a writer being arrested and thrown in jail in this country, Your Honour, and the idea that bail is being asked for is more than absurd."

The trusty Barry Callaghan acted as surety and put up a bond, and Greenspan drove Williams back downtown.

"As soon as we got in the car, I looked at him and said, 'They're never gonna put me in jail eh?'

"He said, 'Who said I've always been right? I've been wrong before.'"

Then Greenspan gave Williams his credit card, told him to go over to the Bistro (Bistro 990 on Bay Street, for a long time Williams's best-loved haunt and now site of another rising Toronto condo), and "'Have a nice lunch and whatever you want to drink, and in about three hours or so I'll send my driver and he'll take you back to the country.'

"That was enormously kind of him," Williams said. "I remember that day vividly. It was so kind that I had tears in my eyes."

If Tim Danson did one sort of pro bono, Eddie Greenspan did another—pro bono ne plus ultra, you could call it.

———

Greenspan and Christie went for the first pretrial conference with prosecutor Sarah Welch and assorted other officials.

"Eddie sits down, and he says, 'Look, this has all been very amusing, and you've had your fun. Let's just acknowledge you needed to teach us a lesson.'"

Then he said, "'We'll take a plea to a misdemeanour pub ban breach, and we'll all go home.'"

The prosecutors were chortling at this, and Welch said, "'We'll take two years less a day, and not a minute less.'"

"Eddie gets up," Williams continued, "and says, 'Thanks for your hospitality, Ms. Welch. This is the last conversation I will have with you until the trial starts.

"'You seem to have taken some sort of drug that has taken you to some other world than the one I inhabit.

"'Goodbye, and thank you.'"

Williams and Boulton were deep in the shit now.

He was charged criminally.

They—he and Boulton and their little company—were also being sued by the government for unspecified "punitive and exemplary damages."

And while he had Greenspan and Christie fighting the good fight for him on the criminal side—working for free, with Williams and Boulton paying just disbursements—he had to get himself a civil litigator too, just to fight the order to hand over his files.

Civil litigators are the lawyerly equivalent of Canadian super-model Linda Evangelista, who in her heyday once yawned that she didn't get out of bed for less than ten thousand dollars a day—except that litigators cost a lot more than that.

Greenspan referred him to someone who told him straight off, "This business of civil litigation is only for people who have twelve race horses in the barn" and said he would cut his fees in half as a favour to Eddie but would still have to ask Williams for sixty thousand dollars up front before he could even take a meeting.

Oh, and he couldn't take the file anyway, he said.

And, the lawyer told him, "It's more egregious still given that it's the AG after you—the government."

He gave Williams a list of others lawyers to try, and finally, he got someone. As he later put it, "In total, that month of May, I was relieved of $147,000 cash. Just that month."

That lawyer he describes as "the most arrogant, preening, eastern-seaboard, brogue-wearing dicksmack I've ever met in my life."

They lost the motion, Williams fired the fellow, and had to pack up all his Bernardo/Homolka boxes and deliver them to 361 University. He proceeded to go through two other civil litigators.

Then, on July 18, the OPP executed a search warrant on the farm—apparently, they were unconvinced Williams had handed over everything he had.

Again, there was a great whack of cops, and this time, they told Williams and Boulton they had to leave while their house was being searched.

In Toronto, Greenspan got on the phone to the officer in charge and tried to clarify a few things: He told him the farm belonged to Boulton and that the police weren't to touch her computers or files. He told them precisely where in the house her things were.

Williams and Boulton made arrangements for the animals to be fed (at that time, Boulton had twenty-five sheep, one horse, maybe fifteen chickens and the barn cattery) and drove to Toronto.

The police "go in and strip Marsha's office bare," Williams said. "They took everything they could get their hands on that looked like paper or files or discs or computers. . . . they took every computer in the house."

Williams and Boulton were now completely freaked out, because, he said, "this raid . . . says to me, this cross-purposing between criminal and civil" was going to crush them. And Greenspan was beside himself.

"It was the equivalent of being robbed when you've never been robbed before," Williams told me, "and having them shit on your carpets, take all your good stuff, all the things that matter to you—and then just vanish, after going through your underwear drawers.

"You're now afraid of them, very afraid."

Boulton also suspected—because the police had taken their two guns, a .22 rifle and a shotgun, and her firearms acquisition certificate for one of them, but not Williams's, because he had his FAC with him—that another shoe might be about to drop.

"I knew they could do something stupid," Boulton said, "because they weren't giving the guns back, and we were on a farm, and we're justified in having firearms. I take it very seriously, because I was scared to death of guns, for years. . . . they have this power.

"So I'd taken the hunter safety course and all that kind of stuff because I knew, if I was going to have a gun in the house, I had to know how to use it properly, how to store it, all that."

But sure enough, that fall, a fresh-faced constable came to the door with a summons and Williams and Boulton were off to be processed and charged with firearms offences.

"It's sobering to realize how they can fuck you," Boulton said.

But back in the summer of 2003, they couldn't summon the heart or will to go home.

"We were afraid," Williams said.

A kindly pal picked up the tab for three months at the Metropolitan, where only Boulton was on the record, all calls were screened and anyone phoning the front desk asking for Williams would be told he wasn't there.

Then the same friend offered up his place in Quebec, and they went there for a week.

Then Boulton called up another friend, who had a flat in Greenwich Village in New York; as it happened he was working that fall in Los Angeles and told them to make his apartment theirs.

It was there, during that stay, that Boulton took pity on Wally, bought the cheap pillow (he missed the nice ones at the Metropolitan) and allowed him some supervised humping every day.

But at last the goodwill ran out, "because we ran out of everything," as Williams said, and they came home. "There was no choice; we had to go back to the farm."

It was October 2003. Shortly after they got back, an OPP officer came to the door to arrest them on firearms charges. Off to the detachment in Mount Forest they went, to be fingerprinted.

As Boulton was sitting outside on the steps, waiting for Williams to be processed, she got a call from a CP reporter, asking about the new charges. Boulton asked how the reporter knew about the gun charges since they'd just been arrested. But that's not why the reporter was calling: "I've got a press release here from the OPP," he said. "You've got like ninety-eight more charges."

The government had charged Williams with a further ninety-five counts of disobeying court orders and publication bans, twenty-eight of them related to his first book, the subject of the first unsuccessful prosecution and now almost seven years in print.

At that news, Boulton went to see her mother, "to warn her, that there was probably going to be something in the newspaper and she might hear about it at the lunch table.

"And she said, 'I'm so glad that your father isn't alive to know that this is happening.' And I thought, I'm not glad that my father isn't alive because this is happening. It just sunk in to me how even your mother can find something appalling.

"But you find with all people," Boulton said, "any time you're charged with something like that, people assume you're guilty of it."

Nine months later, the gun charges were withdrawn.

It was only much, much later, in 2004, after Boulton couldn't get her gun registered and couldn't understand why, that she did a Freedom of Information search.

The AG fought her hard, and when the Information and Privacy Commissioner ruled in Boulton's favour, ordering the community safety ministry to disclose some documents, the AG took it to the Ontario Divisional Court.

In March 2009, that court dismissed the attorney general's applications, and Boulton learned the OPP had filed false information about her at the gun registry in Ottawa, saying she had been arrested before and was prohibited from possessing firearms.

Williams and Boulton weren't entirely alone throughout all this: They had Greenspan and Vanessa Christie; they had their good friends, and at least in the beginning, they weren't without supporters.

The Canadian Journalists for Free Expression (which prepared a 2003 report on the "highly unusual dual criminal-civil prosecution" and concluded it was "fatally tainted by the appearance of a conflict of interest and self-justification" by the very AG office "that Williams criticized in his books"), the Writers Union and PEN Canada "all tried in their way," Boulton said.

"What moved me was getting cheques to the defence fund from poets," she said. "It was the ten- and twenty-five-dollar cheques, where people were showing they supported the notion that no writer in this country should be arrested for writing."

But that sentiment effectively dried up, she said, "when Stephen was charged the second time. Words *website*, and *video*, and people go, 'Yech.'"

For about three years, neither one of them could work—that is, write—and they had absolutely no income. Yet they were paying their civil lawyers and trying to keep body and soul together. They came close to having to sell the farm, and struggled for months even to pay hydro.

Williams won't even discuss what they spent. "I don't know that's really even relevant," he said, "because regardless of the hundreds of thousands of dollars that we had to pay, it was much less than would have befallen anybody else because of Eddie's beneficence and his connections.

"And it wasn't the point, because the second time, neither one of us could work. . . . Writers like us, you get a rhythm going, it's like a baseball pitcher—an interruption has a debilitating effect, and the longer it goes on, the more debilitating it gets.

"How do we know that [the novel] wouldn't have been Marsha's breakout book? It was a very interesting book; it could have done, and we had the New York connections then. You can say it took her three years to write it, but the real way to account for something like this is, 'What could they have done, what would they have done, had they been left alone?'"

Boulton made good use of her time at Greenspan's office.

As Crown disclosure came in, much of it redacted, she figured out a system of erasing the covering ink. It worked only with original documents that had been blacked out. As Williams said, because "the cops were too fucking lazy" to make copies and sent mostly originals, Boulton was able to render much of it readable.

The result, Williams said, showed that the civil and criminal sides of the AG were colluding, and "we were certainly going to embarrass them."

Whether it was to avoid that possibility, or simply because at 720 Bay, they figured Williams had been punished enough, one day in early January 2005, Sarah Welch dropped by Eddie Greenspan's office.

Suddenly, the woman who two years earlier had sworn she wouldn't take anything less than two years less a day in jail for Williams was looking for a plea.

On January 14, he was in a North York courtroom, pleading guilty to a single count of breaching a court order by publishing the names of some of the sexual assault victims on his short-lived, experimental website that had only ever been viewed by police officers and a few reporters.

He was given a suspended sentence and three years probation—and a criminal record. But given the lottery he and Greenspan would have been playing had they gone with ninety-seven charges before judge and jury, it was as good a deal as there was.

In exchange, the government agreed to withdraw its ruinous civil suit.

But to hear Welch carry on—I was there—you would have thought Williams had done far, far worse.

Welch told Judge Derek Hogg that Williams had no respect for "the rule of law," and read aloud a victim impact statement from one of the victims.

"'At least Bernardo was honest in his rape,'" Welch read, quoting what the woman had written. "'He made no pretence that it was anything but. Williams lacks that class. He is nothing less than an exploiting bastard.'"

I was gobsmacked.

Bernardo is a convicted killer, multiple rapist, and dangerous offender; Williams is a rumpled writer who merely wrote about that offender and his wife.

"How did we get here, to the point where vicious killers and gentle writers are indistinguishable one from the other by rape victims, the agents of government and, I suspect, by a goodly segment of the population?" I wrote that day in the *Globe*. "To the point where the best and most effective weapon in the prosecutorial arsenal has come to be the pain or psychic suffering of a victim of crime or the relatives of a victim of crime?"

Boulton was in court, of course.

"I'm sitting there and I realize they're bringing in victims and they're sitting them right behind me," she said. "Bringing in people who had already been through enough?"

As reporter Shannon Kari, then writing for the now-defunct Canwest News Service, proved, the AG ministry itself may have violated two of the same pub bans under which Williams was prosecuted—because the Ontario Court of Appeal website disclosed identifying information about one of the victims.

As well, other books published about the case included the names of women who had been stalked by Bernardo—their identities were also protected.

Even the online version of *The Canadian Encyclopedia* of the day contained banned information.

Yet only Williams was ever prosecuted, the state cloaking its shameful treatment of its staunchest critic in the robes of the unassailable victim.

As Greenspan snapped that day in court, "This is a case of administrative vengeance. . . . We have left the world of sanity for the world of hysteria."

He called the day of Williams's arrest "one of the darkest days for freedom of expression in this country's history."

It was, finally, over.

Boulton's work for CBC Radio had disappeared overnight with Williams's second arrest, no explanation offered.

"Just because you stand too close to someone who is under siege," she said. "Stephen was truly under siege. I was just being pestered, and I wasn't going to back down from standing beside him at all."

Her speaking engagements mostly dried up too.

She sold her sheep as she was finishing the manuscript for *Wally's World* "because we needed to eat." And if the book helped her pull herself out of the gloom, she notes, "I don't have the same sense of humour that I had, I just don't. I have a much darker sense of humour.

"I realize the world is just not all sheep gambolling in a field, and Palomino horses rushing at me, and lambs sucking on bottles, all of that.

"That was gorgeous," she told me. "But I'm not going to have that again, I don't think."

As for Williams, who is terribly proud and desperately afraid of being pitied, he said, "It's very possible [the government] didn't care if, in the end, they won or lost, because they knew that the process alone was going to ruin us, financially, and most people assume if you're ruined financially you're ruined psychologically, and it will ruin your life in every way.

"And I must say, the financial consequences are devastating, and the psychological consequences have been very difficult to deal with, not in the sense that I'm psychologically negated by it, but we both had a very difficult time trying to get back to write."

"Would you do it again?" I asked Boulton once.

"As long as I could live in America afterwards," she said. She wasn't smiling.

A few months after Williams pleaded guilty, in July 2005, Homolka was released from prison having served every last day of her twelve-year sentence—one of a very few inmates who stay in jail until what's called "warrant expiry."

But for a few blips—the latest in 2012 when former broadcast journalist Paula Todd tracked her down to the Caribbean island of Guadeloupe, where she was living with her three kids and husband—Homolka has largely managed to remain out of public view.

Todd wrote an e-book about it all, called *Finding Karla*.

Homolka is married to Thierry Bordelais, brother of the lawyer who represented her while she was imprisoned, Sylvie Bordelais.

I remember Bordelais well; I covered Homolka's last hearing in Joliette, Quebec. I recall Bordelais as a devout advocate for her client, a real believer in Homolka's victimhood. When I first learned her brother had married Homolka, I remember thinking: You think she's so swell? Fine, then you have her in the bosom of your family; you have her at your table for Christmas dinner every year.

The notorious tapes, of course, had long since disappeared.

They were destroyed, along with much of the other evidence from the Bernardo trial, in December 2001 at a secret burning ceremony.

The only reason the public or anyone outside the circle ever learned of it was because the Frenches and Mahaffys, decent folks that they are, wanted to tell Canadians, who had for so long supported them financially and otherwise, that they had found a measure of peace.

On April 2, 1996, Danson had gone to court and convinced Judge Patrick Gravely that once these exhibits "are no longer required for the due administration of justice," they should be returned to the AG "for destruction."

The AG was represented in court that day by John Pearson and Lori Sterling, but, as Gravely noted in his judgment, there was no respondent to Danson's motion. Or, as the judge said, "Here there is no contradictor" and "the Attorney General . . . supports the objective of the applicants that there be no future public access to either the visual or audio components of the videotapes."

The only place the prosecutors departed from Danson's position was that the AG didn't see a need for Charter interference with the legislation, which Danson was also seeking. He wanted the Criminal Code amended to give automatic status to all victims in criminal trials and there, at least, he failed.

But Gravely ordered that fifty-two exhibits—which he listed by the numbers they had had at trial—be destroyed.

All that was preserved of the tapes' existence—the only evidence there ever were tapes—was the written document with the transcript of what was said on the videos on one side and the frame-by-frame description of what was on them on the other.

"We did preserve that," Tim Danson said. "And that's a very searing document. . . . but it's still not the imagery."

As ever, he was in charge of gathering up all the material to be destroyed—the hope chest to which Kristen French had been tethered in her final hours; the circular saw Bernardo used to dismember Leslie Mahaffy; autopsy and crime scene photographs.

"It is kind of extraordinary that I'm doing this," he told me in 2013, a bit disbelieving still, but terribly pleased.

The destruction happened at a still-unidentified facility.

"We were all there," Danson said.

"The Green Ribbon [task force] guys, all the prosecutors, the families, Jane Doe, and [the evidence is] being tossed in and it's going up in smoke, and it's interesting—to incinerate a steel circular saw, that's a lot of heat.

"And all I can say, and this is maybe some kind of metaphysical expression, but, as it was going up, and I'm really watching the families, and it was as if the evil was being purged, and they were finally set free. . . ."

What Bernardo wanted to accomplish, what Ken Murray was once criminally accused of trying to help him manage, the Ontario government succeeded in doing.

The state—which refused to prosecute Karla Homolka when it had the chance, which seized every opportunity to crush

Stephen Williams and make Ken Murray pay, and which played footsie with the families whose interests so aligned with its own and provided such brilliant cover—had now destroyed the videos that were so damaging to the decisions it had made.

There really was nothing to see here anymore. Move along, people.

R v GHOMESHI, ETC.

"We are what we always were in Salem, but now the little crazy children are jangling the keys of the kingdom, and common vengeance writes the law!"

—FROM ARTHUR MILLER'S *THE CRUCIBLE*

WHEN ON FEBRUARY 11, 2016, lawyers in the Jian Ghomeshi sexual assault trial finished their closing submissions, Ontario Court judge Bill Horkins said that he was taking some time to render his decision.

Once one of the biggest names at the CBC, Ghomeshi was pleading not guilty to four counts of sex assault and one of choking with intent to overcome resistance, with a separate trial on another charge, a sexual assault that allegedly occurred at the network's Front Street West Toronto headquarters, slated for that June.

That case was resolved a month early with a peace bond. In exchange for a promise to "keep the peace and be of good behaviour" and an apology to the complainant, writer and former *Q* colleague Kathryn Borel, prosecutors withdrew the charge, leaving Ghomeshi without a criminal record.

The trial had been brief, pointed, and for the three female complainants, little short of disastrous.

Yet there was Horkins saying, as though the weighty nature of the task before him was terribly obvious, "It won't come as any surprise to counsel that I'm going to reserve judgment on this matter." He added that he'd come back with his decision on the next scheduled return date for the case—forty-two days later.

Now, there was a time not so long ago when there sat in the province of Ontario a judge or two, probably never more than that, who not only would have had the self-confidence to render an immediate decision from the bench, but also might have had the stones to tell Ghomeshi's lawyers, Marie Henein and Danielle Robitaille, that they needn't bother with a closing address at all, thanks very much.

For instance, when Robitaille, who handled the first part of the defence submission, got to her feet, Eugene Ewaschuk (until recently a judge of the Ontario Superior Court) or the late Dave Humphrey (of the same court) might have said, "Sit down, Ms. Robitaille," looked over to prosecutor Mike Callaghan, who had already made his sad final arguments, and chirped, "Got anything else, Mr. Callaghan?"

And when Callaghan, whose entire case had been knocked out from under him by his own duplicitous complainants, inevitably replied that he didn't, Ewaschuk or Humphrey may well have acquitted the fallen CBC star on the spot.

What either judge might have said would have gone something like this: "This was an interesting trial in which three women testified.

"They all recounted aberrant and frightening aggression by the accused. The similarity in their accounts makes me think what they described might have happened, but that's not the issue before me or the test to be applied.

"As witnesses at a criminal trial, each was to varying degrees and for different reasons untrustworthy. Each makes me unsure of their evidence.

"To find the accused guilty, I must be much more certain than I am that the Crown has established the elements of the offences charged beyond a reasonable doubt.

"I am not.

"Mr. Ghomeshi, you're found not guilty."

It goes without saying that Ewaschuk, possessed of a ferocious intellect, and Humphrey, canny and intuitive, were smart judges.

But what was really remarkable about them was that, as a veteran lawyer put it, they didn't care if they got invited to the right cocktail parties. (This lawyer says Ewaschuk wouldn't have gone if invited, and Humphrey was such delicious company, he would have been asked despite anything he did or said in court.) They just didn't give a flying fig about being in the club of the special, and thus felt no need to please anyone else or be well regarded.

(In a delightful story in *Learned Friends*, a book about fifty of Ontario's top advocates, author Jack Batten begins the bit on Humphrey by recounting his one-line closing address to the jury in a rape trial. "Members of the jury," he said, "if this case is rape, then I'm a monkey's uncle and, though the resemblance may be amazing, I ain't." The jury promptly acquitted his guy.)

In short, Ewaschuk and Humphrey were thoroughly unconventional members of one of the most conventional groups of Canadians there is—the bench.

So why would Horkins, and most other judges, take six weeks to come to a decision in a case that had acquittal written all over it?

My naked fear on hearing his intention to reserve was that it was a need to equivocate, to write a judgment that would be as pleasing as possible to all reading it, particularly those who persisted—against all the evidence and despite the genuinely spectacular crash-and-burn of Ghomeshi's accusers—in seeing them as victims (of abuse, of violence, of the patriarchy, ultimately of the justice system) and the trial itself as a critical test of the system's ability to deal with sexual assault cases.

But on March 24, to my delight, Horkins proved me wrong.

If he knew full well what was his role in this political show trial—to "validate" the complainants, to denounce sexual assault in all its forms, to mouth the right platitudes even as he acquitted Ghomeshi—he had the courage to do little more than pay lip service to it.

Judges in the criminal courts love to imagine they're above the fray, immune to the currents that pull the culture and the rest of us one way or the other. Horkins's decision, spare and cool as the best judgments are, showed he was fully aware of those pressures but strong enough not to yield to them.

The Ghomeshi prosecution was born in the late fall/early winter of 2014. That was the period that saw the first calling out of Bill Cosby as a rapist by a stand-up comic, the publication by *Rolling Stone* of a (now discredited) nine-thousand-word story about a 2012 gang rape of a University of Virginia freshman, the expulsion of Liberal MPs Scott Andrews and Massimo Pacetti from Parliament Hill with reputations shredded on the strength of vague allegations of "personal misconduct" from two NDP MPs, and a Twitter feeding frenzy, all of it sparking a much-admired, still-ongoing "national conversation" about sexual assault, harassment and the purported barriers to reporting it.

In the beginning, the story floridly unfolded in the pages of the *Toronto Star*—mostly through the work of the paper's excellent lead investigations reporter Kevin Donovan—which first published allegations against Ghomeshi by what were then three anonymous women.

A fourth, who had worked alongside Ghomeshi at Q, the pop culture/interview program he created and hosted on CBC Radio, alleged he had told her he wanted to "hate fuck" her and had once grabbed her ass and dry-humped her from behind in front of a mutual colleague.

She later identified herself publicly as Kathryn Borel.

The paper had been working for six months on the story, originally brought to them by independent journalist (and now Canadaland media critic) Jesse Brown. In an October 26, 2014, editorial that appeared with the news story, one of those why-we-published pieces notable for their piety, *Star* editor Michael Cooke explained, "The reason *The Star* did not publish a story at that time was because there was no proof the women's allegations of non-consensual abusive sex were true or false."

"They were so explosive that to print them would have been irresponsible, and would have fallen far short of the *Star*'s standards of accuracy and fairness."

Well, actually there was *still* no proof the women's allegations were true or false, and the *Star*'s purported standards remained as distant as before.

But earlier that evening, Ghomeshi himself had taken to Facebook to explain why he'd been fired from the CBC just hours before.

In the post, he blamed his dismissal on "the risk of my private sex life being made public as a result of a campaign of false allegations pursued by a jilted ex girlfriend and a freelance writer [Brown] . . ."

Ghomeshi admitted to liking "rough sex" and "adventurous forms of sex that included role-play, dominance and submission," but added, "I only participate in sexual practices that are mutually agreed upon, consensual and exciting for both partners."

If it was an astonishing bit of self-outing even in the age of too much information, nothing in it offered a lick of substance to the allegations of coercion and violence that the *Star* had been pursuing for so long but had heretofore deemed unworthy of printing.

But the Facebook post did change the air considerably: Ghomeshi, for his own reasons, was now talking openly about his sexual practices, and that appeared to render publishing the allegations irresistible and defensible both.

(It was reminiscent of how the same paper, years earlier, had been hanging on to the story of the then mayor, Rob Ford's, notorious crack video. The video had been viewed by two of its own reporters—Donovan and Robyn Doolittle, the latter now of *The Globe and Mail*—but the *Star* finally published the story only after it got word that someone else, in that case a reporter for the U.S. gossip site Gawker, had also seen it and beaten them to the punch.)

In any case, within days, there were nine women who had come forward to the *Star*, among them *Trailer Park Boys* actor and Royal Canadian Air Force captain Lucy DeCoutere, who was the first to publicly identify herself and who later became a complainant in the main court case.

Author and former lawyer Reva Seth was the second, writing in the *Huffington Post* that she too had been violently attacked by Ghomeshi.

They knew each other only casually, Seth said, and had been seeing each other occasionally in a low-key sort of way, when, at his house one Sunday night in the summer of 2002 they were kissing and the attack happened, she wrote on October 30, 2014.

Seth said she was inspired to go public by DeCoutere, whose allegations were similar (both women said Ghomeshi choked them, and both described a sudden Jekyll-to-Hyde change in him) and who called for other women to come forward.

October 30 was, it turns out, a momentous day in the Ghomeshi story. That day, former *Toronto Star* journalist Antonia Zerbisias got a Facebook message from Sue Montgomery, a court reporter for the *Montreal Gazette* who has since left the paper and who tried unsuccessfully in 2015 to win the NDP nomination in the city's Notre-Dame-de-Grace/Westmount riding.

As Montgomery later told *Chatelaine* magazine, she was angry "because people were blaming Ghomeshi's alleged victims for not going to the police, for not giving their names." She suggested to Zerbisias, "Why don't we start a list of all the women who have been raped but never reported it, and I'll go first."

Actually, Zerbisias, herself a day away from taking early retirement from the *Star*—went first. Using the hashtags #ibelievelucy and #ibelievewomen, she tweeted, "And yes, I've been raped (more than once) and never reported it. #BeenRapedNeverReported."

The next day, Montgomery tweeted, "He was my grandfather. I was 3–9 yo. Cops wanted to know why I waited so long to report it. #BeenRapedNeverReported" and a minute later, "He was senior flight attendant. I was summer student flight attendant. Learned later there had been many victims. #BeenRapedNeverReported."

The hashtag went viral, blew up completely: Within days, it was viewed by almost eight million people online, translated into French and other languages, and flung like a boomerang around the world. I was in Montreal all that fall and winter, for the trial of Luka Magnotta, and the papers there were full of it.

There were other developments: The *Star* got its hands on an internal CBC memo which said that on October 23, "CBC saw, for the first time, graphic evidence that Jian had caused physical injury to a woman"; the network appointed employment lawyer Janice Rubin to conduct an independent investigation, and the *Star* reported that now there was even a man named Jim Hounslow, a former student at York University when Ghomeshi was president of the student union there in the early nineties, who was claiming Ghomeshi had once grabbed his genitals.

The "graphic evidence" referred to in the CBC memo never publicly surfaced, certainly not at Ghomeshi's criminal trial; Rubin wrote a fifty-six-page report which concluded that over Ghomeshi's dozen years in various incarnations at CBC, "We found no evidence of a formal complaint made against Mr. Ghomeshi under the CBC's policies," but which nonetheless slammed management for ignoring informal evidence of Ghomeshi's flagrant breaching of the corporation's "behaviour standard," and Hounslow was but a short-lived distraction for the press.

However, Hounslow handled the alleged assault in a way that may stand as an example of one effective way to respond to abusive conduct.

Now the e-learning specialist at the Canadian Museum for Human Rights in Winnipeg, Houslow worked for Ghomeshi in those days. He was his communications coordinator, and they were waiting for an elevator after a meeting in a pub when, Hounslow claimed, Ghomeshi started fondling him through his jeans.

He said he grabbed Ghomeshi's arm, pulled it behind his back and pushed him hard against the elevator doors and told him never to do that again.

(I have found meeting force with force to be effective, though I don't suggest it's the only acceptable recourse. When I was a teenager, at a movie with a couple of friends, a man who'd taken the seat beside me put his hand on my leg and began moving it under my skirt. I elbowed him hard in the gut, and once he got his wind back, he moved far away from me, out of my sight and reach if not out of the theatre.)

The next day, Hounslow said, Ghomeshi accused him of being "macho, violent and homophobic," and said he'd just been fooling around. Hounslow replied that what he'd done was sexual harassment "and that shut him up."

As with most of the others claiming they'd been assaulted by Ghomeshi, Hounslow didn't formally complain about the incident. In fact, only the writer and former Q staffer Borel, who in December 2014 identified herself in a column in the British paper The Guardian as the woman Ghomeshi once threatened to "hate fuck," ever complained in a quasi-contemporaneous way, by which I mean about two years after the fact.

As she wrote, she was but a few months into her new job as a producer at Q in 2007 when she let out a big yawn at a staff meeting and Ghomeshi told her, "I want to hate fuck you, to wake you up."

As she put it in The Guardian, "I was 27 years old. I made sure never to yawn in front of him again."

She said he would also massage her back uninvited, and that he once grabbed her ass and also emotionally abused her, playing "psychological games that undermined my intelligence, security and sense of self."

By the time a friend convinced her to go to the union in 2010, Borel said, she was binge-drinking on the weekends and missing work, and had gained twenty-five pounds.

She met Timothy Neesam, an elected rep of the Canadian Media Guild, who, she said, basically gave her two options: start a union arbitration or file a formal grievance. Neither appealed to Borel.

"Confronting Ghomeshi directly seemed like a nightmare," she wrote. "His star was rising fast. He was inextricable to the brand of the show. I worked behind the scenes and could be replaced at a moment's notice."

Soon after, Borel took a leave of absence, went to Los Angeles where she decided to build a new career, and resigned from Q.

She came forward in 2014 after her friend Jesse Brown leaned on her.

Brown was then working on the first iteration of the Ghomeshi story (the one I believe he took to the *Star*) and had interviewed two other women who said they'd been assaulted by him.

"I wasn't keen to be called a slut and a liar and a fabulist," Borel wrote, but eventually she gave Brown permission to write about her anonymously and then in December wrote *The Guardian* piece.

The thing is, though the permutations of social media make it impossible to say this with 100 percent certainty, it doesn't seem that anyone serious (that is, a non-troll) ever called Borel any of those things; in the modern lexicon, she wasn't "slut-shamed."

And despite what Sue Montgomery described as the *force majeure* that led her to start #BeenRapedNeverReported, neither were any of the Ghomeshi accusers roundly criticized for not reporting to police—except once by me, and I'm not sure what I wrote could be construed as criticism.

In an October 27 column that year, I noted that none of the

purported victims had either gone to police or put their names (at that time DeCoutere had not yet had the publication ban on her identity lifted) to what I described as "life-smashing accusations," which surely is an accurate description of publicly made allegations of coercive and violent behaviour and sex assault. My fundamental point was only that when women decide to "report" crime, surely it should not be to a newspaper.

In a similar vein, neither were the two anonymous complainants or DeCoutere at Ghomeshi's trial subjected to prurient questions in cross-examination. In other words, the changes made long ago to sexual assault laws in Canada—including so-called "rape shield provisions" in the Criminal Code that restrict the admissibility of a complainant's prior sexual history—weren't even tested.

None of the three was asked by Henein, who conducted all the cross-examinations, a single question about previous boyfriends, past sexual experiences or sexual preferences.

None was questioned about her use of alcohol or drugs in general or on the night in question.

None was grilled, let alone asked, about what she was wearing when she was allegedly attacked.

In other words, not even the spectre of the three bad old assumptions about sexual assault—that the unchaste woman can't be trusted, that late disclosure discredits a woman and that failure to fight back suggests consent—was raised.

There was never a hint of a whiff of any of it—that the women had been inviting sexual violence by what they did or how they conducted themselves—from Henein.

(She did file an application under .271 of the Criminal Code, seeking permission to question the third complainant about one aspect of her sexual conduct—but this came only after the woman made an eleventh-hour disclosure about it to police on the eve of her appearance in the witness box.

The woman admitted that despite her insistence to police and the press that after the alleged attack on her she had seen Ghomeshi only in public and always had kept her distance from him, she'd actually taken him home to her bed one night and given him a hand job, whereupon in the time-honoured fashion of men the planet over, he fell asleep for a time and then left. Prosecutor Callaghan, telling the court the disclosure had "significant probative value," reasonably consented to this application.)

Neither did anything happen in court to the Ghomeshi three that remotely resembled what Seth, who though she no longer practises did train as a lawyer, had confidently predicted in her *HuffPo* piece would happen to her had she engaged the police: "I was well aware that I, as a woman who had had a drink or two, shared a joint, gone to his house willingly and had a sexual past, would be eviscerated."

And that's the thing: These women weren't eviscerated.

Rather, they self-eviscerated, self-destructed, did themselves in, each more spectacularly than the last.

With the first complainant, for instance, Ghomeshi was charged with two counts of sexual assault, the first of which allegedly occurred in his car in December 2002, the other at the Riverdale house where he lived in January 2003.

The woman, Linda Redgrave, had the ban on her identity lifted in the late spring of 2016. As the least potentially compromised of the three—because she'd not participated in online chatter about Ghomeshi and the case as the other two did—she was considered by prosecutors as the best of the lot.

And she was certainly the most sympathetic—a suburban mom who was separated from her husband at the time and who wasn't one of the culturati, the cool kids, as Ghomeshi, DeCoutere and the third complainant were.

Redgrave was working as a server at a CBC Christmas party when she met Ghomeshi: They flirted madly, he kept asking for more hors d'oeuvres as a pretext of bringing her near him, and before the night ended, he invited her to a taping of *Play*, the artsy-fartsy show he was then hosting on CBC TV's news channel.

She was interested in him, and she thought he was interested back.

A couple of days later, she drove in from her far-flung suburb for the taping. Afterwards, they went for a drink (they were joined by another former CBC rising star, Evan Solomon, and veteran journalist Carole MacNeil, and in one of her greatest lines, the woman said with what was no doubt whopping under-statement, "I was doing a lot of listening to them speak"). Then he offered to drive her to her car, even though it was just across the street from the CBC building.

It's the sort of thing you do when the sparks are flying with someone and you're not quite ready to call it a night.

"We go to the parking lot and I notice that his car is a bright yellow Volkswagen Beetle," she testified, "and he's not driving a Hummer, he's not driving a sports car, he's driving a car that reminds me of a 1960s Disney movie.

"So I'm thinking he's humble, he's sweet, he's charismatic, he's intelligent, he's—opens door and he drives a Disney car. So I'm feeling very safe at the moment when I'm with him."

(The popular need to "feel safe" I find astonishing. I've worked with men, often wildly outnumbered by them, all my life, and God knows have been around the block more often than I care to say, but I can honestly never remember ever fretting or think-ing about my purported safety. It marks me as an old broad as surely as my wattle.)

She clearly found the car tremendously endearing, and she anchored her story of what allegedly happened next to the bright yellow Beetle.

There they were, facing each other in the Disney car, flirting and kissing, when suddenly, "he reaches around behind my head and he grabs my hair really, really hard and he pulls my head back and holds it there for two, three seconds, enough where, in my mind, I'm saying, 'Ow, ow, ow' and I've been thinking, 'What have I gotten myself into,' and then he stops."

He said something, she said, like "Do you like it like that?" or "Do you like this?" and then it was over, "he was right back to the sweet, charming, nice guy" again.

It was unsettling, but mostly confusing, Redgrave said, and she wondered if maybe he didn't know his own strength, and decided "this is something that in the future we would just have to sort out." (That hopeful, misplaced trust, that she thought there might be a future for them, broke my heart a little.)

In any case, she came downtown to see him again at *Play*, the second time in a snowstorm with one of her girlfriends. After-wards, they dropped the girlfriend off at the subway and the woman went back to Ghomeshi's house, where he put on some music and made them drinks, and she practised a couple of yoga moves, hoping to be enticing.

Then, she said, he came up behind her, grabbed her by the hair again but harder than the first time, and punched her hard in the head multiple times, such that her ears rang and she thought she was going to faint.

She started crying, she said, and Ghomeshi told her coolly that she'd better go, and called her a cab. "He threw me out like trash," she said.

Now, her evidence was not without difficulties.

For starters, Redgrave seemed to consider memory as a sort of tidal pool you sit in, whereupon memories rise up and wash over you, some enduring, some not.

For instance, she acknowledged she'd told police, without ever correcting it, of at least one false memory of her head smashing into the car window, and repeatedly said that she had "to sit with" her memories a while before she knew if they were true or not.

She was also all over the map about whether she'd been wearing hair extensions that night or not—absolutely sure in one instant that she had been, every bit as confident in the next that she had not. This was not insignificant in a case of hair-pulling so extreme that you might imagine the extensions would have ended up in the puller's hand.

And after the second alleged assault, as emerged only in cross-examination, she admitted sending Ghomeshi a come-hither picture of her in a string bikini—and only then did she explain that it was just bait to try to get him to call her so she could ask him why he hit her.

As Horkins drily noted in his decision, ". . . this spontaneous explanation of a plan to bait Mr. Ghomeshi is completely inconsistent with her earlier stance that she wanted nothing to do with him and that she was traumatized by the mere thought of him."

But the biggest problem with her testimony was that it appeared Ghomeshi didn't get that much-described VW Beetle until seven months after she claimed to have sat in it only to have her hair viciously pulled.

Though there was no independent evidence before the judge on what cars Ghomeshi drove or owned back in the day—it would have been a walk in the park for police to get that information from the provincial transportation ministry, but they didn't—in July 2003, he and DeCoutere exchanged emails in which they discussed his brand-new car and DeCoutere suggested he call it "Citrouille," French for pumpkin. And the third complainant, who rode in the car with Ghomeshi that July, described it as "an orange convertible Beetle."

Still, compared to DeCoutere, Redgrave's reliability and credibility were, if hardly intact—the Beetle was so central to her recollection of the first alleged assault, if Ghomeshi didn't have such a car then, and it seems he didn't, how could it not raise real doubts about the assault itself?—only moderately dented.

DeCoutere imploded, as I wrote one day, as surely as if she were wearing a suicide vest, and as she did, so too did the allegations relating to her against Ghomeshi—one count of sexual assault and the choking-to-overcome-resistance offence.

She alleged that at his house after a date on July 4, 2003, Ghomeshi pushed her hard up against a wall, took her by the throat, leaving her unable to breathe for a few seconds, and then slapped her hard across the face three times.

It's difficult to know where to begin, so gaping and plentiful were the holes in DeCoutere's evidence and the chasm that emerged between her public persona and how she behaved when she imagined she was in private.

First was the fact that in less than a year, from October 29, 2014 to September 23, 2015, she and the third complainant exchanged more than five thousand messages about the case and about Ghomeshi.

The messages were produced as the result of what's called a third-party records application, made by Henein and heard in October 2015. The defence was seeking only the communications among the complainants or with other witnesses, nothing confidential like private therapeutic records.

Witnesses, especially complainant-witnesses, aren't supposed to talk to each other about the case, lest, even innocently, they taint what are supposed to be their independent recollections of events.

Though I don't recall Henein actually using the word "collusion" at trial, the sheer volume of communications between the two women certainly raised the possibility and gave the appearance of it. And Horkins, in a section of his judgment entitled "Possible Collusion," remarked upon the "extreme dedication to bringing down Mr. Ghomeshi" shown by the two.

He said that while anger and animus may be legitimate feelings for abuse victims, "it also raises the need for the court to proceed with caution."

The two gleefully shared news about the case and tracked Ghomeshi's court appearances; they also had a publicist in common and, until prosecutors suggested the third complainant should have her own counsel, were represented by the same lawyer, Gillian Hnatiw.

(The third woman ultimately retained a different lawyer, Dawne Way, for the third-party records application. The first complainant was represented throughout, also pro bono, by Jake Jesin.)

Prosecutors were also concerned about something attributed to DeCoutere in a June 17, 2015, piece in *Toronto Life* by Leah McLaren about Ghomeshi.

"The actor Lucy DeCoutere . . . became a point person for others who wanted to tell their story but couldn't bring themselves to do it publicly," McLaren wrote. "The way she described it to me, she co-ordinated a covert network of women who have spent the last seven months sharing their assault stories with each other." DeCoutere admitted in court that the Crown had called her about it, but denied ever saying she had a covert network.

The tenor of some of the messages between DeCoutere and the third complainant stands in stark contrast to how DeCoutere portrayed herself in the media and even in court in her examination-in-chief by prosecutor Corie Langdon, where she cast herself in the most noble light imaginable.

For instance, in explaining why she stayed at Ghomeshi's house and then saw him several more times that weekend—this, remember, after he'd allegedly choked her and slapped her hard— DeCoutere told Langdon, "I felt sorry for him because he thought this was an appropriate thing to do," and said that afterwards, she didn't tell people about what had happened in part "because I wanted to protect him . . ."

And, the following year, 2004, at a TV industry conference in Banff, DeCoutere testified, the only reason she spent time with Ghomeshi was because she was worried that he wouldn't know anyone and would be alone, or as she put it once, "God forbid he'd be by himself."

Yet even as she was publicly painting herself in press interviews as high-minded and magnificently empathetic, she was contemporaneously messaging friends, telling one on October 26, 2014, "I want him [Ghomeshi] fucking decimated" and "He's walked the line so long, he's had so many women afraid of him or at least creeped out for a very long time, all the while becoming more famous and successful," and on November 13 that year, "The guy's a shit show, time to flush."

It wasn't a one-way road. Complainant No. 3 was also writing to DeCoutere, saying for instance on November 5, "It's time to sink the prick. . . . I'll do whatever I can to put this predator where he belongs."

But most critical is how DeCoutere spun the nature of her post-assault relationship with Ghomeshi to the police.

After he purportedly attacked her, she said, because she's a people pleaser and tries to normalize weird situations, she spent much of that weekend with him, as she'd promised she would, and yes, she may have seen him in the months and years later, and sure, she and her *Trailer Park Boys* co-star and friend Sarah Dunsmore may have gone on Q once in 2008, and she and Ghomeshi may have communicated occasionally—but all that, DeCoutere said, was just making nice with someone who moved in the same small slice of the world she did. It was just smart business.

The one sure thing she knew, DeCoutere insisted, was that after the alleged assault, she didn't want to have a romance with him, and that thereafter their relationship was purely professional.

Yet there was her lawyer, Hnatiw, on the evening of Tuesday, February 2, 2016—the trial was underway, DeCoutere next up in the batting order—calling the prosecutors, and asking, hypothetically, if there were some other interactions between her client and Ghomeshi, would the Crown like to know about them?

The Crown did indeed want to know.

Callaghan asked for court to take the Wednesday off—his head must have been near to bursting into flames—and on Thursday, just before she walked into the witness box for the first time, DeCoutere gave police a second statement in which she disclosed a number of things she'd never mentioned to anyone before.

For instance, it was through this last-minute disclosure that the police and prosecutors learned that after the choking, she and Ghomeshi sat on his couch and made out for a while; that she kissed him goodbye; that the next day, they walked in Riverdale Park and smooched a bit; that after the weekend in Toronto, she returned home to Halifax, where she was then living, and sent Ghomeshi flowers; that the following year, she sought him out in Banff at the same TV conference where they had met in 2003; etc.

Given the details DeCoutere did tell police about in her first statement—the sort of cheese Ghomeshi wanted to order at dinner (DeCoutere wasn't eating cheese at the time), how he arranged his shirts by colour, lighter to darker, the eerily perfect temperature in his house—it seemed odd she would only belatedly reveal so much kissing.

But so what?

As DeCoutere said frequently, perhaps she really didn't understand the importance of giving the police that kind of information. Perhaps it genuinely was more memorable to her that the temperature in Ghomeshi's house was not too cold and not too warm than that they snogged in a park and she saw him again and again and again over the next two days.

But what she *wouldn't* forget, or misremember, is how she'd felt about him. There's always an ember in the human heart of a torch that once burned there.

As Henein put it once, during a protracted exchange with DeCoutere about what she remembered and what she didn't,

"You wouldn't be wrong on how you felt, right? . . . Can we rely on your recollection of your feeling . . . ?"

"Absolutely," said DeCoutere.

And how she felt about Ghomeshi, Henein pointed out a little later, was just as DeCoutere told the police: ". . . you didn't really have any dealings with him afterwards, except professionally. That you didn't engage with him. And that you weren't friends with him. That there were no romantic feelings afterwards.

"Those were your words."

"Oh, there were no romantic feelings afterwards, I guarantee you that," DeCoutere said.

"Do you?" Henein asked. "Under oath you're going to guarantee me that?"

"Oh, God yes," said DeCoutere.

But what became excruciatingly obvious over the next hour or so, through a devastating series of about two dozen email messages Henein presented to DeCoutere, was that while she may not have had a romance or affair with Ghomeshi, it was not for lack of trying.

These messages spanned a time period from the very day after the alleged choking-and-smacking on Friday, July 4, 2003, through 2004 and beyond.

What is undeniable is that Lucy DeCoutere was absolutely nuts for Jian Ghomeshi.

As she emailed him on July 5, just hours after he supposedly assaulted her and just hours before she saw him again, "Jian, getting to know you is literally changing my mind—in a good way I think. You challenge me and point to stuff that has not been pulled out in a very long time. I can tell you about that sometime and everything about our friendship so far will make sense.

"You kicked my ass last night and that makes me want to fuck your brains out. Tonight."

Not all were so blunt, but the collective tone of the messages is that of a woman in hot pursuit; it's unmistakable, and unsettlingly familiar to anyone who has been crazy about someone and in the first throes of that madness.

On July 17, 2003, she wrote him a lengthy note that began with her description of a scene from *Six Feet Under*, the HBO series then on the air, featuring the matriarch and her beau.

"They are in a hardware store considering what kind of screwdriver they should get—more specifically cordless or not.

"Somewhere amidst the deliberations, she turns to him and says, 'I don't want to do this by myself anymore,' and they get married ten minutes later. . . . I think you are magic and would love to see you," she said.

And what she realized, DeCoutere told him, is that in the love letter she'd sent him the week before, which he clearly hadn't yet received or acknowledged, "I was really asking if you would like to go to Crappy Tire to help me pick out an electric rake.

"And I'm thinking now that maybe you would not because I really pissed you off . . . somehow. . . . So can you help me out with this? Do you want to hang out again?"

And that love letter, written July 9, an old-fashioned handwritten letter, began with an ode to the pleasures of such letters over instant communication.

"And for me," DeCoutere wrote, "if I had given my time to be with someone, I don't want to have my cell phone make me or rather put me at someone else's disposal. And letters are keepers. Once delivered, you may re-read this, tuck it under your pillow, burn it, whatever, whatever."

Alas for her, Ghomeshi didn't burn it; the six-page original became an exhibit.

Amusingly, the fact that he hung on to it was greeted in some quarters as further evidence of his creepiness, and far more important than the fact that DeCoutere wrote it and never told a soul about it.

"Why Did Jian Ghomeshi Keep Lucy DeCoutere's Letter?" asked a headline over a Jesse Brown piece on the Canadaland site two days after the revelation in court. That piece came with what was by then, among progressive bloggers, Tweeters and some media, the de rigueur "trigger warning," telling swoon-prone readers, "Some parts of the article below describe instances of violence."

Such warnings were all the rage in certain quarters during the trial, but I suspect their day is almost done, and properly so. As my friend Skeeter Jones says, if Holocaust survivors don't need trigger warnings every time Auschwitz or Nazis are mentioned in news stories, no one should.

The death knell may have been sounded by the impeccably credentialed #BeenRapedNeverReported co-founder Antonia Zerbisias, who wrote in a February 18, 2016, column in the alternative Toronto weekly *NOW* magazine, "Enough with the 'trigger warnings.' They have become epically ridiculous."

Another feminist fetish is describing alleged victims as "survivors."

Indeed, the 2015 *Use the Right Words* guide produced by femifesto, a Toronto-based collective, urges journalists not to "default" to the "victim" descriptor and to ask each person which word she prefers, and notes prissily, "Many people may prefer the term 'survivor' because it conveys agency and resilience."

That it may do, but it's also a statement of fact—e.g., that such a person has survived a sexual assault—and thus antithetical to the presumption of innocence which is supposed to be the golden thread of the justice system.

In any case, DeCoutere's letter was little short of a confession.

In it, she said that although she'd told Ghomeshi (and the court) that she was coming to the city that weekend for work and had a busy calendar, in fact, "I had no reason to come to Toronto except to hang with you."

She said that although she found his remark, over that first dinner, about wanting just to lie with her and hold her, awkward at the time, she'd actually loved it: "I mean, really, what on Earth could be better than lying with you, listening to music and having peace. Nothing. But put to me like that then? I really could not deal."

Nothing may better illustrate the fundamental outrageousness of DeCoutere's deceptive conduct.

This was the same remark, the very same anecdote, that in 2014, during her media blitz, she offered up in some of her nineteen interviews as a telling delicious tidbit about Ghomeshi's general ghastliness, describing the line as "creepy" and "cheesy."

(I concur with DeCoutere's latter-day characterization. A friend of mine was once involved with a fellow, a lawyer by the way, who early on in the relationship told her, "I love you more than life itself." It probably doesn't need saying that no suitor has ever said anything remotely like that to me. But I would have run for the hills had one done so.)

Yet what DeCoutere wrote at the time was this: "I loved spending time with you this weekend. You are hilarious. And I really loved seeing you become progressively more relaxed [with] me. . . . I appreciate your advice [about] Trailer Park Boys. The songs you write . . . that I've heard . . . are really beautiful . . .

"Jian. You're great. And I want to know you more, have more fun easy times with you because it is so very rare . . .

"I am sad we didn't spend the night together.

"I could have been more open [with] you in person rather than [with] pen and paper. I find disclosure in cafes tricky.

"I love your hands. Lucy."

In the language of the courts, this was the first contemporaneous, and wholly voluntary, statement DeCoutere ever gave after the alleged choking-and-slapping.

However Ghomeshi responded, or didn't, DeCoutere kept up her online courtship of him for the following year.

As the annual Banff conference approached, she emailed him several times, once asking, "How busy are you going to be in Banff? I want to play with you" and offering options of ". . . go for a hike? Pims on the Terrace? Chance encounter in the broom closet?"

And when he replied that he'd love to hang out but his time in Banff was going to be "absolutely bonkers," DeCoutere emailed again a couple of weeks later, "maybe dinner or perhaps I could tap you on the shoulder for breakfast?" and attached a cute picture of herself, faux-fellating a beer bottle.

Months later, now with the Gemini Awards on the horizon, she wrote to him again, telling him, "I'd love to see you. Gonna be around?" and then again, "Do you know yet if you're gonna be at the Geminis?"

Ghomeshi usually replied, always friendly and polite, but rarely seeming to match either her flirtatiousness or eagerness to get together.

And where DeCoutere was forever talking about the pressing demands of her crazy schedule (but always promising she could fit him in), Ghomeshi seemed to be genuinely up to his ears in work.

In the cruel parlance of the 2009 movie of the same name, it appeared that he just wasn't that into her.

Now, DeCoutere had convoluted explanations for each and every email, picture and overture.

She said she was "trying to flatten" a negative experience, the alleged choking, by drowning it with positive ones; she was trying to "friend" Ghomeshi; she was just using sexual innuendo "to be hilarious" because she has a salacious sense of humour; she was merely trying to control how and when she would see him because they were in the same small entertainment industry and surely they would run into one another anyway.

Better to pretend she wanted to fuck his brains out, she was saying, than risk an awkward encounter at a party.

None of it rang true. After a dozen or so years, a person can certainly lose details and dates, soften up or gloss over some memories, but do you ever forget how you felt about someone? Are you able to change a narrative from you loving X more to X being the one who chased you? Do you ever erase how it hurts to realize you couldn't make someone adore you as you adored him?

I remember every male I have ever crushed on since grade one (starting with the late Herbie Scott, whom I mercilessly tossed about in square dancing), which is not to say all women do the same.

But certainly, every significant crush and its essential truth stays with the heart—in my case, for instance, that the first husband probably loved me more than I did him; that I may have loved the second more than he did me; that the serious college boyfriend disengaged over a hurtful weekend on a sailboat; that the guy who invited me to come along on a business trip to Miami studiously ignored me the whole weekend; etc.

Now, the third complainant's collapse was less dramatic, and she was nowhere near as feisty as DeCoutere and was quick to agree whenever Henein suggested that she'd lied or deliberately misled the police.

But finally, in this sex assault trial that to this point had had no sex, No. 3 at last provided some, the hand job she described in her eleventh-hour statement to police.

And what was crystal clear by trial's end was that this wasn't a case where a nasty defence lawyer ran roughshod over a bunch of vulnerable women.

Rather, the opposite was true: Henein's approach was unfailingly mature, modern and matter-of-fact. She treated the complainants as the adults they were at the time of their alleged attacks by Ghomeshi (No. 1 was forty-one, DeCoutere thirty-three, and No. 3 thirty-two) and that they remain.

And for all the nonsense written about abuse victims behaving in unusual ways, about the "trauma bond" that can form between compliant women and battering men, none of these women *had* a prior relationship with Ghomeshi.

No. 1 was on her first "date" with him when the first alleged assault happened, and on the third when the second occurred.

DeCoutere was on her first date with Ghomeshi when he allegedly choked and slapped her.

No. 3 and Ghomeshi were also on a first date when, after her performance one night, they headed off to a park bench to snog, and she purportedly found his hands on her neck and then over her mouth.

The only relationships they had with him, in other words, began after the alleged assaults. They weren't partners. They weren't spouses. They were barely going out. As the writer Georgie Binks said in an email to me, "After a three-hour date, women don't develop Stockholm Syndrome."

In any case, Henein was neither giggly nor leering when she asked them about the consensual kissing with Ghomeshi that preceded the alleged assaults, or when questioning the third woman about the hand job.

Henein is crisp and cerebral by nature, not a yeller, and these qualities serve her well in court, where her questioning is invariably straightforward, calm and respectful. She's a quintessential grown-up.

(For the record, I've seen her at work through two major sex assault trials before the Ghomeshi case—in 1998 in Halifax, where Henein and the late Eddie Greenspan successfully defended the former Nova Scotia premier Gerald Regan on multiple counts of historic sexual assault, and a decade later in court in Napanee, Ontario, where she secured an acquittal for former minor league hockey coach David Frost on four counts of sexual exploitation of former players.)

But by far, the most important development on that critical Thursday, October 30—the day #BeenRapedNeverReported was born, the day that the CBC announced it was hiring an investigator to probe its own role in the Ghomeshi accusations, etc.—was that Bill Blair, then the Toronto police chief and now a Liberal MP, held an impromptu press conference at headquarters.

Asked by reporters why there was no investigation into the Ghomeshi case, Blair replied, "We need a complainant," and then offered his encouragement, generally and not just in this case, for any alleged victims of sexual assault to come forward.

He added, "Our first priority is their safety and their recovery."

It was an astounding remark from the head of an agency whose primary function is to investigate allegations of crime, not comfort those reporting it.

It also played a key role in encouraging the woman who became the first complainant in the court case to come forward, just two days later.

As she testified at trial, "So when I went to the police, it was because Bill Blair gave a press conference and he was encouraging people to speak up and said that we will listen to anybody, that there was no statute of limitations, and prior to that, I thought I had no recourse, no one would listen."

And the same day this woman went to the cops, a Saturday, Inspector Joanna Beaven-Desjardins, the unit commander of Toronto's sex crimes unit, held a press briefing to announce that three women had now come forward with allegations against Ghomeshi and that an investigation was underway.

She said that when she became aware on October 30 that nine victims (there was none of that bothersome "alleged" business with her) had been talking to the press, she'd assigned investigators to contact the media outlets and ask them to contact the women on behalf of the police.

(Presumably, it had also come to Beaven-Desjardins's attention that her chief had been beating the bushes for complainants just forty-eight hours earlier.)

By reaching out to victims proactively, she said, police would be prepared to make a "seamless" transition to the investigation stage.

In a Q&A afterwards, speaking in general terms about her unit, Beaven-Desjardins said repeatedly, "We believe victims when they come in, 100 percent. We are behind them 100 percent" and "We believe them right from the onset. There's never a doubt about believing them" and "It's all about the victims and moving them forward."

Alarmingly, that attitude appeared to permeate the detective office, where it endured throughout the complainants' interviews, all of which were uber-respectful, delicately done, minimally probing—almost apologetic in tone, says someone who has seen all three of the videos.

Redgrave's interview was over and done with in less than an hour (the other two lasted about forty minutes each), minus time eaten up with all the standard police cautions. Like the others, she was interviewed just once.

From the few excerpts of DeCoutere's interview played at trial, it's clear that she was exceedingly comfortable, or as she put it in a press release she issued after the interview, that she "felt heard and validated."

But with the third complainant, who made the late-in-the-game disclosure about the hand job, court heard that the re-interview—the constant late-breaking news, Henein told Horkins that day, "makes me feel like I'm in the Twilight Zone"—lasted, as Henein said, "a grand total of nine minutes."

This, bear in mind, was an interview on February 4, 2016,

taking place as DeCoutere was finishing up in the stand. As usual, for this was by now the norm, it was prompted by a text to prosecutors the night before from Hnatiw, the lawyer representing both DeCoutere and the third woman, saying she wanted to tell them something else.

If, in fairness, the police didn't know what it was the woman had to tell them until she began speaking, they sure knew as soon as she opened her mouth that it was important, despite what she said about it being "the little thing I didn't say."

It was dynamite.

The woman was disclosing that directly contrary to what she'd repeatedly told the detectives and the media before—"I felt unsafe around him" and "I always kept my distance, you know"—one night, after the alleged assault, they had dinner and drinks and oh yes, she took Ghomeshi home with her and masturbated him.

Detective Ali Ansari interviewed her. The officer in charge (OIC, it's called) of the case, Kim Hancock, was in the courtroom, watching DeCoutere's testimony blow up. But, Hancock later told Henein and Robitaille, she gave Ansari specific instructions to conduct the re-interview at headquarters without audio or video running. And that's just what Ansari did.

Videoing interviews, which allow a judge or jury to also see the subject's demeanour and body language (and that of the police), is universally considered best practice. It's why, for instance, the detectives recorded the initial statements given by the three women.

But they didn't do that with this bombshell new disclosure, in what Toronto Police spokesman Mark Pugash later told me in an email was a mistake.

"Videotaping is our policy in conducting interviews and is the best-practice rule," he wrote after the verdict.

When Henein and Robitaille learned it hadn't been done, they asked Hancock why Ansari hadn't thrown the complainant on video once he learned the stunning nature of the disclosure.

Hancock replied, "We would not re-victimize the victim."

"Re-victimize?" Robitaille snorted. "She was describing a consensual hand job!"

Now of course, all purported victims of crime, any crime, should be treated decently and politely, but what was obvious from Hancock's remark is that the culture of #ibelievewomen wasn't confined to Twitter or the court of public opinion, but was now embedded in the very unit responsible for investigating sex crimes.

(It's a bit rich that Hancock should be such a devotee of the #ibelieve dogma. In 2007, already with the sex crimes unit, she was charged with three counts of assault in connection with a domestic dispute. As the charges were later withdrawn, arguably her colleagues had been too quick to believe her partner, the primary alleged victim in the incident. Hancock later launched a complaint with the Ontario Human Rights Commission, alleging her case was handled differently from that of "heterosexual officers." She also faces internal disciplinary charges. Both the complaint at the commission and the internal charges were still ongoing at the time of writing.)

But in what world does questioning a sexual assault complainant, on camera, about her late disclosure of significant, relevant evidence qualify in any way as "re-victimizing" her?

It wasn't that the woman had forgotten about the incident. She had merely chosen not to tell anyone about it.

She admitted, in cross-examination, that she lied about it in her first statement, when she told police that after the alleged assault, "When he [Ghomeshi] calls me, I say, 'Well, let's keep it in public'"—that she deliberately meant to leave the police with the inaccurate impression that because she felt unsafe with Ghomeshi, she'd only see him in a public space, in a crowd.

It was embarrassing to discuss, the woman said, and besides, the detectives never really asked her about "consensual sexual stuff."

And finally, she was reduced to saying that masturbating Ghomeshi "wasn't sex. It wasn't, it wasn't sex" and that when she told the police, "I never had sex with him," what she meant by sex—*a la* former U.S. president Bill Clinton in his encounter with Monica Lewinsky, wherein he famously received oral sex in the Oval Office—was intercourse.

(Here, I defer as ever to my oft-quoted friend Tracy Nesdoly, whose entirely reasonable question on this subject is, "What's the point of being the president of the most powerful nation on Earth if you can't get a blow job in the Oval Office?")

As Henein said in her closing argument, "The extraordinary fact about this case is that all three complainants withheld information from the police and from the Crown and, in my submission, most importantly from the court in the course of their testimony.

"And they didn't do it because, as we have heard in many, many cases, and judges routinely accept these sorts of explanations, 'I forgot' or 'I wasn't really focusing on that irrelevant aspect.'"

Rather, Henein said, they did so "only when there was a concern that they would be contradicted by objective evidence. Because until that moment became apparent, the truth was not going to be told.

"And that is more than deeply troubling, that the truth or portions of it are to emerge only when these complainants knew that they may be confronted with objective evidence, their own words."

It was their collective willingness to lie about the conduct, under oath, that was "more troubling than the conduct itself. "The oath or promise to tell the truth means something," Henein said.

"And in cases where a conviction for a crime requires this honourable court to rely on the words of a witness when there is nothing else, then their disregard for the obligation to tell the truth is meaningful. . . . The oath is spelled out in real simple language: tell the truth, the whole truth, and nothing but the truth."

The judge, Henein said, was left "to rely on the word of a person who will decide for themselves what is and what is not relevant, who will only tell you half-truths and who will withhold information. That is a witness that cannot be relied [upon] beyond a reasonable doubt.

"This courtroom," she said, and now she was mad, "should not be a game of chicken."

In a furious indirect but unmistakable shot at the #ibelievewomen culture, Henein snapped, "In our courts, witnesses are not presumed to be truthful because of who they are.

"A witness is not believed just because he or she is a police officer or an expert, and we've been reminded of those lessons over and over again. . . . Courts don't play favourites with one kind of a witness or another. No witness enjoys a presumption of truthfulness; nor should any witness be subjected to a presumption of untruthfulness."

In other words, having breasts doesn't—or shouldn't—get you a pass.

As for the sex crimes boss, this wasn't her first dance at the victim-coddling party.

Just days before the Ghomeshi trial began, lawyer Brian Greenspan—Eddie's look-alike brother—told reporters a shocking story.

In October 2015, Beaven-Desjardins held a press conference to reveal that two Brazilian soccer players who'd recently been in Toronto for the Pan-Am Games were wanted on sex assault charges.

Standing in front of large pictures of the two men—Andrey Da Silva Ventura and Lucas Domingues Piazon—the inspector described how they had assaulted a sleeping woman in her bed just a few hours after Piazon had scored the bronze-medal-winning goal over Panama.

But according to Greenspan, by the time of the press conference police had already been told by senior Crown prosecutors in no uncertain terms that they had no case against Piazon.

In Ontario, as in most provinces, charges are laid by police and pursued by the Crown, who must decide if there is what's called a reasonable prospect of conviction before proceeding further. This is not only in the name of fairness for an accused, but also in the greater public interest—charges that don't stand a hope in hell won't eat up valuable court resources.

But sometimes, police in Ontario do consult the Crown before they lay a charge, and that's what they'd done here.

Yet despite getting an "unequivocal" thumbs down on the Piazon charge from three prosecutors, and knowing that if a charge were laid it inevitably would be dropped, Greenspan said police "defiantly" held the press conference anyway, its only apparent purpose being to smear the young player.

There'd been a hint of something fishy at the presser.

Beaven-Desjardins said that while Ventura was wanted on a Canada-wide warrant, which meant he could be extradited, Piazon was sought only on an Ontario warrant, which is not enough to trigger extradition.

Asked about the difference between the two warrants, Desjardins sloughed the responsibility off to the Crown's office. "That's up to the Crown attorney to decide, on Canada-wide warrants," she said, telling the inquiring reporter, "You'll have to ask the Crown."

But that isn't so. Beaven-Desjardins was being at best misleading.

Because the Crown is responsible for paying the cost of what's called the "return" of a suspect, a prosecutor must sign off on a Canada-wide warrant.

But that isn't true of Ontario-only warrants; police can, without the okay of the Crown, appear before a judge or justice of the peace to get such a warrant signed.

As Greenspan said, "The reality is that, at that time, police already knew that the charges would not be proceeded with. Because the decision had already been made by senior Crown prosecutors that there was no reasonable prospect of conviction, there would be no extradition."

So the cops went with the warrant they knew they could get on their own.

The charge against Piazon was withdrawn only on January 26, the day of Greenspan's statement to the press, despite repeated pleas by one of the prosecutors that the police bring the information to court ASAP so it could be dropped quickly.

Instead, the twenty-one-year-old Piazon, who is signed with the famous Chelsea FC but is on loan to the Reading club, was left to twist in the wind of the damning worldwide publicity for about three months.

Interestingly, Greenspan also pointed out that "the investigating officers were accepting and compliant with" the Crown decision, but were overruled by the brass. "It was senior members of the unit" who chose to disregard the Crown advice, he said.

In response to such a serious complaint from such a big-time lawyer, Toronto Police chief Mark Saunders ordered an investigation by the force's professional standards unit.

This review wasn't completed at the time of writing, but it conceivably could expand to include a look at the Ghomeshi case, as well as the fact that at least two members of the unit, including Hancock, had formally complained about Beaven-Desjardins before this, alleging "tyrannical" behaviour.

But the results of the investigation won't be made public, and even if the name at the top of the unit is changed—as indeed it did in May 2016, when Inspector Pauline Gray took over—that alone may not address the scope of the problem.

Three detectives were involved in the Ghomeshi investigation: Hancock as the OIC; Ansari, a veteran of the force; and

Lisa Ferris. There was at least another pair—one was Detective Steve McIlwain—assigned to and overruled in the Piazon case.

Since there are usually twenty detectives, give or take, in the section that investigates general allegations of sexual assault (other sections handle child exploitation or human trafficking, etc.), that means that at least a quarter of the staff were directly exposed to Beaven-Desjardins's adherence to the #ibelievewomen creed.

It's not rocket science, this balancing of sympathetic treatment of alleged victims with the need to conduct a vigorous investigation. Says one long-time detective with a large municipal force in Southwestern Ontario, "It's easy. You don't have to make the person feel victimized.

"You say, 'Look, part of my job is to prepare you for these questions from defence counsel, and we have to know what the answers are. We're here to find the truth.'"

He has taught detectives at all levels and run hundreds of sex assault investigations himself, and says that while he was flabbergasted to learn how institutionalized the #ibelievewomen culture was at Toronto Police, he says that at all forces, "the pressure is there, from police college on" through the regular meetings many sex assault sections have with women's groups and their advocates.

In fact, Jake Jesin, who represented the first Ghomeshi complainant, says police should spend some time telling alleged victims about the process—that, for instance, the videoed interview will be provided to the defence; that they will be challenged and must expect it; that they should take their time and be as descriptive as possible.

"I think the Ghomeshi investigation was a very normal, a typical, investigation," Jesin said shortly before the verdict.

This was not a compliment.

"Most often," Jesin said, "the 'investigation' is the taking of a complainant's statement and then simply laying a charge."

None of it is a confined-to-Canada problem, either, but rather an issue bedevilling other first world democracies too. In fact, just as the Ghomeshi trial was wrapping up, the top cop in the United Kingdom, Sir Bernard Hogan-Howe, commissioner of London's Metropolitan Police Service (or New Scotland Yard, as it's also known), wrote a piece in *The Guardian*.

In it, he referred to a sweeping 2015 review, conducted by Dame Elish Angiolini, a Scottish lawyer, former solicitor general and former prosecutor, into how the Met approached rape investigations.

She traced how the policy had changed from 2002 to 2014, moving from a notional acceptance of allegations from victims "in the first instance as being truthful" to a flat-out recommendation in 2014 that "The presumption that a victim should always be believed should be institutionalized" in British police forces.

That came from the November 2014 report of Her Majesty's Inspectorate of Constabulary, or HMIC, the independent body (it reports only to Parliament) that examines and publicly reports on police operations.

Though this particular report was about how police record crime (or don't, which in the U.K. is called "no-crime-ing" an incident), it focused on how rape is categorized by officers and sometimes wrongly written off with a "no crime" report because police disbelieve victims.

Recommendation 11 called for forces to ensure that "the presumption that the victim should always be believed is institutionalized."

Though the report was silent on how just far "institutionalized belief" should be maintained—that is, beyond the simple recording-of-a-crime stage—it was enough, Dame Elish said, "to support the current perception amongst many officers that the policy of belief applies throughout the life of the investigation."

It's far more appropriate, she said, for police to remain professional, be respectful of complainants and maintain an open mind.

As well, she pointed out, the always-believing practice often results in getting less-than-stellar witness statements. Many of these, she said, are lacking in critical detail—why the complainant acted as she did; how she felt; why she did or didn't do something.

And the low quality of the statements she examined "may suggest that officers are apprehensive about closer questioning of the witness in case such questioning is misconstrued as disbelief or cynicism."

Police, she said, need to put themselves in the position of a juror (or judge) "who will want to know much more than a basic factual narrative of what took place.

"The juror would expect the trial lawyers to drill down into the evidence to elicit how and whether the witness can explain contradictory, odd or unexplained matters that appear in the interview or elsewhere in the evidence."

And if such inconsistencies aren't explored with the complainant, Dame Elish said, she is likely to "feel ambushed with such questions in the adversarial context of cross-examination at the trial."

And she pointed out, and here she could have been predicting how the Ghomeshi trial unfolded, "The consequences of any resultant inhibition on the part of the officers are some bland and basic statements that provide rich pickings for subsequent cross-examination at trial."

As Dame Elish questioned whether it's appropriate (let alone possible) to order a police officer to believe, so did the Met boss express his view—immediately and predictably denounced as retrograde—that perhaps it's time to "be clear about the principle of impartiality at the heart of criminal justice."

While the first officers who take a victim's complaint "should proceed on the basis that the allegation is truthful," Hogan-Howe said from that point on "a good investigator would test the accuracy of the allegations and the evidence with an open mind, supporting the complainant through the process" yet making it clear "that officers do not believe unconditionally what anyone tells them."

This, he wrote, is particularly true with historical allegations, which may be decades old, and particularly with suspects who are public figures.

He was referring to Operation Midland, a Met probe to examine allegations, made by a single purported victim known only as "Nick," that he and other children were abused, some murdered, between 1975 and 1984 as part of a VIP pedophile ring linked to Parliament.

Nine high-profile men—including a former British prime minister, the late Edward Heath; former Conservative MP Harvey Proctor; former Conservative home secretary Lord Leon Brittan; and D-Day veteran and former chief of the defence staff Lord Edwin Bramall—were publicly identified in the media as suspects in the case, though none had been charged by the time the sixteen-month-long investigation was shut down in March 2016.

As the Met commissioner wrote, "Those investigated are innocent until proven guilty, but reputations may be tarnished before we have been able to reach a conclusion."

This was surely putting it at its mildest.

Lord Bramall, for instance, was among those who lived almost a year with the darkest of clouds—the allegation that he was a pedophile—over his head. He feared he wouldn't live long enough to see his name cleared.

He was ninety-two when, in January 2016, police told him they were dropping their investigation into him.

Ten months before, to much press attention, his home (with those of the other suspects) had been raided by twenty officers. His wife died that July, before he was cleared.

He was furious that he'd been smeared as a result of "bizarre and outrageous and grotesque" statements made by a lone complainant. "I knew there was not one grain of truth in them," he said. "I was mystified the police could believe them."

He wasn't even told what the specific allegations against him were (rape and indecent assault against "Nick") until two weeks after the much-publicized search of his home.

That's a common feature of the modern sexual assault or harassment accusation, especially the one made anonymously or via the media: Absent a transparent investigation, the man in question may not know precisely what he's accused of doing, let alone be able to challenge or counter the narrative.

Consider the case of Patrick Witt, who while he was a twenty-two-year-old undergraduate at Yale, had an informal complaint filed against him by his ex-girlfriend with the then brand new University-Wide Committee on Sexual Misconduct.

In a piece he wrote in the *Boston Globe* in 2014 while a first-year student at Harvard Law School, where a similar policy had just been adopted, Witt said, "I would say more about what the accusation itself entailed if indeed I had such information. Under the informal complaint process, specific accusations are not disclosed to the accused, no fact-finding takes place, and no record is taken of the alleged misconduct."

Witt described how he had been summoned to a sort of mediation, at which he wasn't allowed to have a lawyer, was warned to stay away from the former girlfriend he already hadn't seen in weeks and was told there was an "expectation of confidentiality" from him so as to prevent any "retaliation" against his accuser.

He demanded fact-finding be done, so he could clear his name, and was told, "There's nothing to clear your name of." He asked that a formal complaint be lodged, a process that involves an actual investigation, but was told he couldn't initiate it—only his accuser could.

As things happened, that same day the woman launched her complaint, the news broke that Witt had been selected as a finalist for the prestigious Rhodes Scholarship. Because he was also Yale's starting quarterback, with his Rhodes interview set for the same day as the big final Harvard–Yale game of 2011, the story got lots of national attention: Which tremendous opportunity would the golden boy choose? How could he manage both?

A few days later, Witt got a call from the Rhodes Trust, informing him they'd received an anonymous tip that he'd been accused by a fellow student of sexual misconduct. The next call was from his summer employer, who got the same tip, and who rescinded his offer of full-time employment upon graduation.

"Months later, long after I had already withdrawn my Rhodes candidacy, the *New York Times* somehow also learned of the 'confidential' complaint made against me," Witt wrote in the *Globe*.

At the time the lengthy *Times* article was published in late January 2012—it was purportedly about the fact that Witt didn't choose the big game over his shot at a Rhodes as other stories had suggested but that the choice had been made for him by the allegation against him—Witt was one of top college quarterbacks in the United States.

In fact, he was getting ready for the National Football League Combine, an annual, invitation-only showcase for the best college players in the country. Predicted to be a likely NFL draft pick, he went undrafted and completely untouched by any NFL team.

Witt wrote his piece in the *Globe* after twenty-eight members of the Harvard law faculty protested the university's adoption of the new and expansive sexual harassment policy.

"If considered only in the abstract, many might wonder how a policy with such a laudable aim could draw any serious objections," Witt wrote. "And I might well have been among them— were it not for the fact that such a policy nearly ruined my life."

As he put it, "The complaint lodged against me caused me and my family immense grief, and as a simple Google search of my name reveals, its malignant effects have not abated.

"It cost me my reputation and credibility, the opportunity to become a Rhodes Scholar, the full-time job offer I had worked so hard to attain, and the opportunity to achieve my childhood dream of playing in the NFL," he said.

"I have had to address it with every prospective employer whom I've contacted, with every girl I've dated since, and even with Harvard Law School during my admissions interview.

Witt ended the piece with this: ". . . the reader might note that I have yet to even address the question of whether I was innocent of the accusation.

"I was.

"But it does not come up at any point above for the same reason that it never came up in any of the actions taken against me—because by the nature of the proceedings that follow from these new policies, it simply does not matter."

(The *Times*'s "public editor" months later wrote a piece examining the original story, which had had no named sources, and concluded in part that perhaps "when something as serious as a person's reputation is at stake, it's not enough to rely on anonymous sourcing, effectively saying 'trust us.'")

The names of public figures, whether athletes or parliamentarians or celebrities, *will* emerge, either because at a certain stage the police release them (when formal charges are laid, it's the usual practice in both Canada and the U.K. to release names, but "wanted" persons are sometimes identified too) or because journalists will find out on their own.

As Hogan-Howe explained it, "During an investigation, we have to track down witnesses and are obliged to provide complainants with information, so journalists will, in all probability, find out the names of public figures who are suspects."

It's his view that "the time is right for suspects facing allegations of sexual offences to be offered anonymity prior to any charge." He would only allow police to name suspects in a sexual assault case after an application to a court so that a judge can assess the public interest. "The media could argue their case if they wished to name someone, as happens in other areas of the law."

As antithetical as this is to a reporter, I am on the cusp of agreeing with him, only because we in my business now so often lead the lynch mob, without accepting any responsibility for the consequences.

As Hogan-Howe pointed out, the evidentiary standard at the beginning of an investigation (when only an allegation is required) and at the time of arrest (when police must have reasonable grounds to believe an offence has occurred) is considerably lower than the "reasonable prospect of conviction" standard prosecutors use to determine if a charge will go forward.

In real-world terms, however, such distinctions are academic, even precious. The well-known person suspected of sexual misconduct is usually accused first (and sometimes only ever) in the press and/or on social media, then smartly tried on Twitter and in the unforgiving court of public opinion.

Their number may not yet be legion, but recent examples abound where such allegations were either made only in the press or social media, or where the stories that first appeared one place or another in fact drove the criminal investigation.

Consider what happened to John Furlong, the former boss of the 2010 Vancouver Olympics.

If Patrick Witt was once a golden boy at Yale, so was Furlong once a golden man in this country, greatly admired after the success of the Olympics and widely seen as one of those warming success stories Canadians so enjoy, a charming Irish immigrant who'd risen high in his beloved adopted country.

By the time in 2015 that a British Columbia Supreme Court judge dismissed a defamation lawsuit against him—Furlong had had the temerity to defend himself and was sued by the reporter he'd labelled as reckless—he'd fallen about as far as it's possible to fall.

As the *Vancouver Sun* and Postmedia sports columnist Cam Cole wrote that autumn, "once the word 'abuse' appeared in front-page stories alongside John Furlong's name, the public face of the 2010 Vancouver Olympics couldn't win."

In September 2012, as Furlong's post-Olympic life as an inspirational public speaker was flowering (he was sixty-two then and as he once put it, this was his pension plan), the independent journalist and activist Laura Robinson wrote two stories about him.

One appeared in the popular Vancouver weekly *Georgia Straight*, alleging he had physically and emotionally abused Aboriginal children while he was a young teacher at a parochial school in Burns Lake, B.C. The other was in the *Anishinabek News*, a weekly published by the Ontario Union of Indians, and said that a former student had gone to the RCMP to report she'd been sexually abused by Furlong.

Many more mainstream media reports, of course, immediately followed, and as Furlong told Cole, he was soon so mortified he began doing his regular exercise routine at 4 a.m. or after 10 at night, "when it was dark," so no one would see him.

Furlong said he'd had a "huge Rolodex, and a lot of people in my corner. And the corner just emptied out."

This was a case where the reporter had a heavy hand in guiding the alleged victims.

Robinson had been deeply suspicious of Furlong since she read and reviewed *Patriot Hearts*, the behind-the-scenes story of the Vancouver Olympics he co-wrote with *Globe and Mail* columnist Gary Mason.

Published a year after the Games, the book didn't mention that Furlong first came to Canada as a young gym teacher and taught at a couple of schools in northern British Columbia as a member of the Frontier Apostles.

The Apostles were founded by Bishop Fergus O'Grady, the top Catholic in northern B.C., and was a sort of peace corps—thousands of young people from Ireland, Western Europe, the U.S., Philippines and Japan came to more than a dozen O'Grady-built schools in the remote north to volunteer their time for twenty-five dollars a month plus room and board.

Robinson believed the omission meant that Furlong had been hiding his past work as a missionary so as, she alleged, not to hinder the bridges and good relationships he wanted to build (and indeed had built) at the Games with Aboriginal organizations.

But Furlong testified that these were fundamentally uneventful years for him, and that it wasn't until he was well back in Ireland that he and his family made the far more momentous decision to emigrate to Canada.

And if he'd been hiding his history with the Immaculata Elementary School in Burns Lake, a small far-flung community 225 kilometres west of Prince George, and later at Prince George College, Furlong had done a piss-poor job of it.

In a 1976 interview with the *Prince George Citizen*, for instance, he'd spoken openly about having first come to Canada in 1969 and worked at Burns Lake. And as the CEO of VANOC, the Vancouver organizing committee, he insisted over objections from his colleagues that the Olympic Torch relay go to Burns Lake.

According to B.C. Supreme Court judge Catherine Wedge—whose September 18, 2015, tossing of Robinson's defamation suit provides a crisp summary of the entire case—by 2012, Robinson was convinced by former students she'd interviewed and incidents she'd been told about that Furlong liked to "beat the kids," as indeed she cheerfully wrote to the CEO of the Canadian

Newspaper Association, where Furlong had delivered the key-
note address in April of the previous year.

One of those incidents was a purported meeting between
a woman named Deb Hogan (her name appears that way in
the judgment, but the correct spelling is actually Hoggan), who
told Robinson that a student and Furlong had met at her house
shortly before the Olympics.

According to Hoggan, in the course of the meeting, the student alleged that Furlong had beaten her; Furlong denied it.

Robinson wrote to the publishers of *Patriot Hearts*, saying,
"My research now leads me to ask Mr. Furlong for his version of
these events" and actually asking the are-you-still-beating-your-
wife question, "Is he still denying the beating took place?

"I know for sure the meeting took place," Robinson wrote,
"so very much need his version of what happened."

She asked for her inquiry to be forwarded to Furlong. It
landed on the desk of Marvin Storrow, then Furlong's personal
solicitor, who replied that his client denied wrongdoing of any
kind and warned that anyone who wrote anything defamatory
about him did so at her own risk.

But at the defamation trial, Furlong testified that in 2009, he
was approached by Hoggan's husband, Gary Youngman, then a
First Nations lawyer working for VANOC. Youngman said he'd
met with a young woman who alleged she'd been strapped by
Furlong; Furlong replied that if a former student said she'd had a
bad experience with him, he wanted to meet her.

The meeting took place at Youngman and Hoggan's home,
where Furlong said flatly he'd never strapped anyone and that
only the school principal could do that and he'd never seen it
happen in any case. According to him, he and the student shook
hands when he left.

But at some point in the meeting, Furlong testified, Youngman
raised the Truth and Reconciliation Commission, which spent

five years examining residential school abuse, and then said that for five thousand dollars, the former student's complaint "could probably go away."

Furlong was so shaken by Youngman's words that he called the police officer responsible for Olympic security and reported the threat and its context. The officer told him to report the incident formally to Vancouver Police, which he did.

As the judge noted, "Correspondence sent and received at that time confirms that Mr. Furlong reported the matter to police."

But by now, Robinson believed she was on to something big, and in April 2012, she emailed the lawyer Storrow and said, "There have been so many alleged abuse incidents committed by Mr. Furlong against former students it would be impossible to have forgotten about the abuse. . . . I would appreciate straight answers to my original questions."

She then arranged to travel to Burns Lake. Before she went, she posted an ad-for-victims in the Burns Lake post office and the Babine Lake band office.

"Did you attend Immaculata school or Prince George College?" the notice began.

"A journalist who is investigating abuse at both schools will be at the Burns Lake band office on Saturday April 21 from noon until 6 p.m. Lunch provided. Please come and tell your story in confidence or leave your contact info and she will contact you.

"She is interested in students who attended between 1969 and 1976 and had John Furlong as a phys ed teacher or had relatives who had him.

"He was a tall man from Ireland and a Frontier Apostle."

The announcement ended with a quote: "No legacy is so rich as Honesty.—William Shakespeare."

On April 21, 2012, about thirty-five people had gathered to wait at the band office; Robinson's train was late, so they had an hour to discuss the subject at hand.

Most, as Robinson testified, had nothing at all to say about Furlong, and wanted to speak generally about their experiences as First Nation youngsters in a school system that in many cases traumatized them. But seven individuals alleged they'd been physically abused by Furlong or been the target of racist epithets; an eighth said she'd been sexually abused by him.

Robinson wrote down what the former students said and had them initial what she'd written. She then began pitching what she told an editor at the *Georgia Straight* was "obviously a massive, massive story." The editor told her the paper was interested, but only if she obtained sworn declarations from the eight accusers.

Robinson then drafted the documents, returned to Burns Lake and hired a lawyer to prepare the declarations and swear them.

In the days and weeks afterwards, she also pitched the story to the *Toronto Star* (which declined) and the CBC (where someone presciently told Robinson she was part of the story rather than just the journalist who found it, and assigned its own reporter).

She also emailed officials at the Canadian Olympic Committee (COC), Vancouver mayor Gregor Robertson and Dick Pound at the International Olympic Committee, sometimes attaching some of the sworn declarations and asking, in effect, why the hell these people hadn't done their "due diligence" or what they were going to do about Furlong now.

The person who had alleged sexual abuse was Beverly Mary Abraham, and on May 8, 2012, Robinson emailed her, asking "if you (and others) plan on proceeding with civil action against Furlong. Since there is no statute of limitations on sexual abuse, will you move forward on criminal charges?"

Abraham replied that she was ready and willing, but Robinson heard nothing more from her for several weeks—a concern for Robinson, because, as Judge Wedge wrote, "she was hoping to publish the story on Mr. Furlong to coincide with the 2012 Summer Olympics in London. . . ."

On July 5, Robinson wrote to Abraham again, asking if she had yet gone to the RCMP and posing a set of leading questions ("Do I have your right age? . . . if you went to kindergarten at age 5 in 1963, you would have been 11 in the spring of 1969. . . . I don't know if I have the correct dates though") and wondering if Abraham knew of any other girls, dead or alive, who'd been sexually abused by Furlong.

On July 10, she told her editor at the *Straight* that Abraham was going to the RCMP in two days, and sure enough she did.

Robinson wrote her story about the sexual allegation, sent it off to the *Straight*, then tried again at the *Star*, telling the then editor, Colin MacKenzie (my former boss when we were both at *The Globe and Mail*), "I believe the complainant, watched as she broke down more than once while she told me what he did. . . ."

MacKenzie said he'd take a look at her piece, but soon replied that, "Squeamishness on high means we're not going to run."

Robinson also shopped the story, with the allegation of sexual abuse, to *The New York Times*, the *Irish Independent*, *The Guardian* and *Sports Illustrated*; none was interested in publishing.

On September 27, the *Georgia Straight* published, online and in hard copy, its story, minus the sexual abuse allegation; later in the day, the *Anishinabek News* posted a short piece about the sexual allegation.

That morning, Robinson emailed out a link to the *Straight* piece and an alert that the *Anishinabek News* would soon publish the story of "allegations of child sexual abuse" to 180 friends and colleagues, many of them journalists.

Furlong had been forewarned that the *Straight* story was coming, and as it gathered steam internationally, he decided he'd better quickly put his categorical denial of the allegations on the record.

Just before his press conference, he learned that the allegation of sexual abuse had also been made against him.

He read a prepared statement, denying any wrongdoing what-soever, said he believed the RCMP would discredit the sexual complaint "because it JUST didn't happen," and said Robinson had showed "a shocking lack of diligence," that his character had been "recklessly challenged" and that it was "beyond all belief" that the *Straight* didn't place a single call to him.

It's those words Robinson said were defamatory of her repu-tation.

In the next month, Robinson emailed the CEO at Own the Podium (a non-profit sports outfit, where Furlong was and is the chair, that works with national sports organizations) and the COC, claiming "there is a great deal of confirmation that Mr. Furlong was violent and a racist" and asking if Furlong had ever been violent toward his first wife or former fiancée.

On November 27, 2012, Furlong filed a defamation claim against Robinson.

She filed a Response to Civil Claim, made new allegations against him of rape and domestic violence on his first wife and another partner, and was "undeterred," as Judge Wedge said, when members of Furlong's family, including the allegedly beaten first wife, completely denied the allegations involving her.

"The public should be deeply concerned at the power of a single journalist whose words can smash into a family like a wrecking ball," the family statement read.

Robinson's reaction was to post her Response to Civil Claim, in its lurid and untested detail, on her website. Its contents, the judge said, "were widely reported in the media."

By June 2013, Robinson was emailing the Response to both a Native newswire service that was advertising a Whitecaps Football Club event (Furlong was and remains the club's executive chair) and a First Nation that was being honoured by the Whitecaps; and that fall, she sent a series of emails, with her Response, to each individual director of several other organizations with which Furlong was associated, including Own the Podium and Canadian Tire (where he was and is a director).

Also that fall, at an October international sports ethics conference in Denmark, she presented a paper called "Truth, Lies and History: John Furlong and Canadian Sport's Moral Vacuum."

In it, she recounted her discovery that Furlong had taught at Immaculata, linked him to the residential school scandal, and said there were "dozens of former students" accusing him of "physical, psychological and racial abuse."

The paper also described the sexual abuse allegation of Abraham and two civil lawsuits from former students of Furlong, Grace Jessie West and Daniel Morice. All three were among those who gave statements to Robinson in Burns Lake. (Robinson, in the paper, also said Furlong was sued for sexual assault by a fourth student, Audrey George. "In fact," Judge Wedge wrote, "no such civil suit was ever filed.")

Abraham's complaint was investigated by Corporal Quinton Mackie, who testified at the defamation trial that Abraham told him it was Robinson's coming to Burns Lake that sparked her to come forward.

Mackie interviewed Abraham several times, as well as her mother (through an interpreter) and a brother and sister, as well as others Abraham told him would provide corroborating details; they did not.

"He was also of the view that [Abraham's] description of the events contained many troubling inconsistencies," Judge Wedge wrote. "Among other information, names and dates changed with each interview."

Ultimately, Mackie told Furlong's lawyer on April 12, 2013, that "the RCMP have concluded their investigation and have found nothing to substantiate the complaint."

But just as he was about to close the file, Mackie was advised that his bosses had directed there be a file review by an independent investigative team of Alberta RCMP. According to the judge, the review uncovered nothing new about the Abraham complaint, or anything else, that required further investigation.

Finally, on December 5, 2013, the RCMP investigation was really over.

There were three civil suits filed that year against Furlong—one by Abraham and one each by Grace Jessie West and Daniel Morice.

West alleged that Furlong was her gym teacher at Immaculata in the school year 1969–1970, and that he physically and sexually abused her there. Furlong brought an application to dismiss the claim on the basis that West wasn't a student at the school in either year.

According to B.C. Supreme Court judge Miriam Gropper, who heard the application, at West's examination for discovery in April 2014, she at one point listed the various schools she attended. Immaculata wasn't one of them.

At another point, West couldn't recall the name of the school she alleged she attended when Furlong taught her. She also said she attended Immaculata from 1964 to 1977 and then said she was there for only one year, when she was six years old and in kindergarten.

"The evidence adduced . . . established that Ms. West attended St. Joseph's School in Smithers, B.C. from 1966 to 1970," Judge Gropper wrote. The school register for Immaculata at no time showed West there, and Gropper concluded she didn't ever attend Immaculata and specifically not in the 1969–1970 school year.

West dropped her claim, by which point her lawyer had withdrawn from the file, in December 2014. Abraham also consented to the dismissal of her civil suit.

Morice had had the same lawyer as the other two, who also withdrew from his file.

Thereafter, Morice left abusive and obscene messages about Furlong on his lawyer's voicemail, and even threatened him with physical harm. It also emerged that Morice had received $120,822 from Ottawa (part of the Indian Residential Schools Settlement Agreement, the largest class action agreement in Canadian history) in compensation for similar abuse allegedly committed by another man at a residential school in a different town during the same time period when he claimed that Furlong had been abusing him.

Oops.

B.C. Supreme Court judge Elliott Myers dismissed Morice's claim and awarded special costs to Furlong as a result of Morice's "egregious, reprehensible" conduct.

Furlong dropped his suit against Robinson, too exhausted, he said, for any more of it, and besides, he considered himself effectively cleared.

But Robinson persisted with hers, and Judge Wedge's seventy-eight-page decision was the result of that.

She found that Robinson's "reportage" was dubious. Instead of being scrupulously careful about the gathering of statements from purported victims, as a good investigator would be, she "initiated the investigation and set its parameters, solicited the statements after telegraphing the purpose of her investigation, and then published the contents of the statements in her articles for her own purposes."

Further, the judge said, the tone of Robinson's stories "cannot be fairly characterized as a simple reporting of what others told her." Anyone so attacked was entitled to vigorously defend himself, Wedge said.

She also found that Robinson's dissemination of her Response to Civil Claim "was an improper use of the court's process."

"She attached the Response to dozens of emails she sent to organizations with which Mr. Furlong was associated and posted it on her website." Why did she do that?

"A reasonable inference is that Ms. Robinson included these

new allegations because the contents of her Response are privileged as part of the litigation record and could not give rise to a defamation claim," the judge said.

She found that Robinson had encouraged Abraham to file a complaint with the RCMP, and said pointedly, of Robinson's call to the RCMP to confirm Abraham had filed, "One must ask why Ms. Robinson felt she needed independent verification of the fact that Ms. Abraham had filed the complaint when she saw no such need for verification of the facts underlying Ms. Abraham's sexual abuse allegation before publishing her story."

Her conclusions: Robinson's stories weren't just reporting the allegations of others, as her lawyer argued. "Rather, the publications constitute an attack by Ms. Robinson on Mr. Furlong's character, conduct and credibility," and she wasn't just a reporter, but an activist.

Perhaps the most important finding the judge made was this: Of the multiple declarations Robinson obtained, she said, only those of Abraham, West and Morice "were even minimally tested in a way that we, as a society, believe our system of justice requires when a citizen faces such serious and devastating allegations. All three proved to be unreliable."

Referring to Robinson's habit of emailing the organizations where Furlong was on the board, Wedge noted that she "repeatedly asked why Mr. Furlong had not been asked to step aside from those organizations until the allegations of abuse had been resolved.

"Again, the obvious question is by what process the allegations could possibly be resolved," Wedge said.

"Who, or what entity, would determine the truth or falsity of the allegations when complaints were not brought to the police and civil claims (other than the three that foundered) were not filed?"

And there's the rub: How *can* someone publicly accused of sexual misconduct or assault, but never charged criminally, defend himself?

Furlong was lucky, in a very narrow way, in that he had the means, or generous friends with the means (in his 2015 interview with Cam Cole, he said "some people helped" with his enormous legal costs), to battle it out for three years in the civil courts, and ultimately, he was well served by the truth-seeking process there.

But it didn't restore his reputation. It didn't undo the damage done.

It certainly didn't stop some—and Robinson, even as an independent journalist not on the payroll of a major media organization and thus responsible for her own legal bills, nonetheless had powerful supporters of her own—from continuing to believe that where there's smoke, there's fire.

But it was something, and it was a start on Furlong's long march back.

Yet what of those who are accused only in the press, or on social media?

Can it really be true that the ones who are criminally charged, or sued civilly, are the fortunate ones because at least they have a forum, an entity in Judge Wedge's words, in which they are able to fight back?

I fear it is.

Apart from living my life—which early on taught me that men and women are pretty much equally prone to telling the truth, or not, and that neither sex has the patent on good behaviour—Jamie Nelson provided my first formal close-up with a woman who falsely cried rape.

On August 23, 2001, I was at the Ontario Court of Appeal for a very brief proceeding.

Prosecutor Scott Hutchinson was joining with Nelson's lawyer, Todd Ducharme (now an Ontario Superior Court judge) in asking that Nelson's earlier convictions for sexual assault, assault, forcible confinement and uttering death threats be quashed, and acquittals entered on the record.

The panel of three judges agreed and said that new evidence showed "the trial proceedings [against Nelson] resulted in a miscarriage of justice."

Nelson wasn't even asked to get to his feet.

He sued his accuser, the Ottawa police and the Crown attorney for malicious prosecution but predictably, three years later, ran out of both money and steam and dropped the suit.

Nelson spent 1,047 days of his life in federal prison; lost his business (he was a chef) and nearly his life (in 1996, while awaiting trial and having been denied bail, he tried to hang himself, saved only by his cellmate); and while serving his time, saw his youngest son be first abandoned by his mother, then taken into care of a children's aid society, and finally adopted.

There was no state misconduct in his wrongful conviction. There was no botched police investigation, except for the bias inherent in the believe-survivors mantra, by then apparently establishing roots in the Ottawa force, as in others. What there was, was only a single lying woman.

She was Cathy Fordham, a friend of Nelson's common-law wife, with whom he was then engaged in an ongoing custody-and-access battle over their son.

The alleged rape, Fordham said, had occurred in the early morning of February 28, 1996.

Though she went to hospital hours later, she complained only of assault, said she'd been beaten days before by an ex-lover, and described bite marks that doctors and nurses couldn't find. Only nine days later, while seeing her own doctor, did she mention the alleged rape.

And her first formal complaint to police wasn't until April 28 of that year—just long enough later that Nelson had no specific memory of the alleged night.

It was a classic he said/she said case. Nelson said he didn't rape her; Fordham said he did, and Ontario Court judge Hugh Fraser, while pronouncing Fordham's evidence "not perfect" on November 1, 1996, convicted Nelson.

Flash forward to 1998.

Ottawa Police began receiving complaints from parolees about the "general administrator"—this was Fordham—of a halfway house for parolees called the Vanier Community Support Group.

By May 1999, Sergeant Keith Patrick was reporting to the Ottawa Crown that there were allegations that Fordham had made "sexual advances" toward the residents of the house, that she was actually "having sex with two or three of the males," that she allowed drug use and sometimes used drugs herself, and that she was an emotional volcano and chronic liar who manipulated the vulnerable men under her control, their limited freedom being in part dependent upon what she told their parole officers.

At a meeting with Nelson and his original trial lawyer, Ken Hall, police gave them a computer printout of "hits" of Fordham's various contacts with the force—there were fifty-five of these, seven of which involved claims of sexual assault.

By 2001, Fordham had been convicted of public mischief in connection with a false allegation of assault, placed under a peace bond in connection with another false allegation, and deemed by one judge to be an inventive and theatrical witness.

Later, she was convicted of making a false police complaint and threatening to kill a former boyfriend, and was sentenced to six months in jail.

Her rich track record was part of the "fresh evidence" application agreed to by prosecutor Hutchinson and defence lawyer Ducharme, which led to Nelson's acquittal at the appeal court.

"This is a cautionary tale for anyone who suggests that people who make allegations of sexual assault must be telling the truth because why else would they go through the process," Ducharme said after the brief formalities.

But in 1996, as I wrote five years later in a piece about Nelson's acquittal, "Advocates for sexual assault centres were in full flight; police forces across the country were getting the message that women did not lie about this sort of thing and that they should treat such allegations as gospel.

"Jamie Nelson was ripe for the plucking.

"He was plucked; the tie went to the girl."

That conceit—that surely no woman would put herself through the ordeal of having to testify in a public courtroom about such an intimate matter if the crime didn't happen—was the fuel that saw sexual assault become a crime apart from other offences.

It wasn't for another couple of years that I ran into a similar sort of case—and by that I mean not that there are dishonest women everywhere falsely accusing men of sexual assault but that the presumption of male guilt was gaining a foothold—this one a complaint of sexual abuse that was being heard at the College of Physicians and Surgeons of Ontario.

I went because I was invited to come by the complainant.

On Sunday, November 30, 2003, I got a lengthy email from her.

"I would really like you to cover the hearing," she wrote.

"Only 2 percent of women who have been abused come forward to complain to the College. . . . I feel if more women knew how to report, and trusted the process, they would complain. . . . If you or someone from The Globe came to the hearing, I would be very co-operative with sharing documents, such as my medical charge, his letter of response to my letter of complaint, and so forth."

I have no idea now, if ever I did, where the woman got the 2 percent figure; the usual one used in Canada is that there is only a 5 percent reporting rate for sexual assault and that most assailants aren't ever held to account.

Numbers like these have come to utterly dominate the public discussion of sexual assault and abuse. It's by now widely accepted not only that sexual assault is woefully under-reported, which is true, but also that it has a ridiculously low conviction rate, which isn't.

Figuring out the true prevalence of sexual assault is tricky, partly because Statistics Canada obtains its stats from two sources—the first is police-reported data and the second is what's called the General Social Survey or GSS, which consists of self-reported data from alleged victims themselves.

In any case, by the first measure, in 2014, there were about 20,700 sexual assaults reported to the police, most of them classified as Level 1, the Criminal Code definition of sexual activity that ranges from kissing to intercourse and that results in minor physical injury or none at all. (A Level 2 sexual assault involves a weapon or the threat of a weapon or any threat of bodily harm or incidents where there are multiple assailants. Level 3 is aggravated sexual assault and means the victim is left wounded, maimed or disfigured.)

By the second measure—the GSS survey is conducted only at five-year intervals and the most recent available one is from 2014—there were 633,000 incidents of sexual assault in Canada.

The GSS data, StatsCan says, "suggest that the majority (83%) of sexual assaults experienced by Canadians aged 15 years and older are not brought to the attention of police."

That would seem to say that 17 percent of sexual assaults are reported to police, but apparently not. Much of the 17 percent, StatsCan says, probably falls under the "don't know/refused to answer" category, rather than the "not reported" category.

In any case, the number most widely reported, if not beloved, is the 5 percent one.

As for why so many women—most victims of sexual assault, or about 70 percent, are women—don't report to police, the main reason, according to victims themselves (this from a January 2015 brief from the Sex Information and Education Council of Canada) is that fully 58 percent of them felt it was not important enough or that they dealt with it another way.

That conforms with what the three Ghomeshi accusers all said about one of the main reasons they didn't go to police at the time—as No. 3 put it once, "I wasn't sure that there was anything to go on."

In a much-cited 2012 analysis by University of Ottawa criminology professor Holly Jones, who used the 2004 data, of an estimated 460,000 sexual assaults committed against women every year, only 15,200 formal complaints are made to police, and of these, 2,824 are prosecuted in court, with just more than half resulting in guilty verdicts.

The end result, which *Maclean's* magazine decried in a November 2014 editorial as "pathetic conviction rates," is that for every 1,000 sexual assaults, 997 assailants purportedly go free. But, as the editorial noted, albeit much later on, citing a review done in England by Baroness Vivien Stern, if the figures are calculated in the usual manner, the real conviction rate in Canada is about 54 percent.

As Stern found in her 2010 independent review of how rape complaints are handled by English and Welsh authorities, the conviction rate for rape is calculated differently (as sexual assault is in Canada) than it is for any other sort of crime. With other crimes, she said, the term "conviction rate" describes the percentage of all those cases brought to court that end in conviction.

With rape (and with sexual assault in Canada), the term is used in a different way and "describes the percentage of all the cases recorded by the police as a rape that end up with someone being convicted of rape."

And that, she said, mixes apples with oranges, conviction rates with the process of attrition—attrition being what happens when an initially reported rape doesn't proceed to court for a variety of reasons.

English studies, Stern said, consistently show that of every hundred rapes reported, fifteen either aren't recorded as crimes or are retracted or withdrawn very quickly by the complainant. Of the remaining eighty-five, about twenty are withdrawn later by the victim, twenty-three are not proceeded with because the evidence is deemed too weak, and fourteen are dropped for other reasons.

Thus in about twenty-six cases, a suspect is charged with rape—a figure reduced to nineteen when the decision is made to go ahead with a prosecution. Of the nineteen, about twelve result in a conviction for rape or a related offence.

Calculated in the usual manner, Stern said, the real conviction rate for rape in the U.K. is 58 percent, and, she noted, "juries actually convict more often than they acquit in rape cases."

Stern was obviously frustrated at the way the "6 percent conviction rate" figure widely used in Britain "has been able to dominate the public discourse on rape, without explanation, analysis and context . . ."

She pronounced it "extremely unhelpful" and detrimental to "public understanding and other important outcomes for victims." She recommended an overhaul of national crime data "that enables comparisons to be made of the outcomes for various offences and makes clear what conclusions can and cannot be drawn . . ."

In any case, I haven't a clue where the woman who wrote to me got her 2 percent number. But she sounded otherwise literate and rational, and so in early December, off I went to the hearing.

The story that unfolded over the next weeks and months was considerably more nuanced and less one-sided than the woman had presented it to me.

R v GHOMESHI, ETC

Dr. Alan Abelsohn was a general practitioner who did a little counselling on the side, as many GPs do, but who was woefully ill-equipped to help a ruinously difficult patient like her.

The woman was a "borderline," short for someone diagnosed with a borderline personality disorder, one of the trickiest psychiatric disorders there is to treat and one that is usually accompanied by personal and social chaos. Predominantly women, borderlines in other times were called hysterics, in large part because of the insatiable neediness and chronic manipulation that define the illness.

Now, what happened between Abelsohn and the woman was utterly bizarre, with her grabbing the therapeutic reins and him allowing her to dictate the course of her own treatment until it got so weird that on a half-dozen occasions, with his consent, she was masturbating on the floor of his office.

Abelsohn was ultimately found guilty of incompetence and misconduct involving sexual abuse of the woman and was suspended from practice for a year and indefinitely prohibited from conducting the sort of one-on-one therapy that got him into so much trouble.

Clearly, he'd been in way over his head, and shouldn't have been doing that kind of therapy, and had lost control of the sessions, though it's worth remembering that the very organization that prosecuted him for screwing up, the College of Physicians and Surgeons of Ontario, still allows family physicians like him to do counselling.

And the woman was undoubtedly mentally ill, if also unimaginably scary.

She stalked Abelsohn, once to a conference in Ottawa; sent an anonymous email about him to the college (she used a damp facecloth to seal the envelope so she wouldn't leave DNA), and gave his girlfriend a list of women with whom she claimed he'd been intimate.

But what was really troubling about the case was that the college paid out ten thousand dollars for counselling for the woman seven months before the hearing to determine Abelsohn's guilt or innocence even began.

In other words, she was presumed from the start to be a truth-teller and a victim; Abelsohn, of course, was presumed to be guilty.

As I wrote in one of my last pieces on the hearing, and here I confess to feeling prescient: "All over Canada, in quasi-judicial proceedings like this one, at similar inquiries held by the self-regulating professions, at labour dispute tribunals, in family court and even to some degree in the criminal courts, the same general presumptions exist: Women are in need of protection from men; women rarely lie (Why would she make it up?' is always the implicit question, as though women are not subject to the normal unpleasant human characteristics of viciousness, get-even bitterness, or even the raw exercise of power for its own satisfying sake), while men lie and are predatory."

And, of course, her name was protected throughout.

Not so the poor doctor.

In April 2015, I conducted a completely ridiculous experiment: I covered part of the gang sex assault trial of two Ontario physicians without using their names.

They were charged with administering a drug with intent to stupefy, sexual assault and gang sexual assault in connection with a February 12, 2011, attack upon a woman one of them knew from medical school.

That doctor was also charged with intent to stupefy and sexual assault in connection with another attack in 2003 upon a different woman, who came forward after the pair's arrest on the 2011 charges got significant press attention.

It was a useless exercise, in which Postmedia kindly indulged me, because other media covered the trial, as they had covered the charges, and weren't bound by my decision, and anyone with half a wit could have put two and two together.

What offended me was that the previous fall I'd covered a trial—I can't now remember which one—in which virtually everyone but the accused men were guaranteed anonymity.

And similarly, in this case, Ontario Superior Court judge Julie Thorburn agreed to prosecutor Cara Sweeny's request for publication bans upon the names of the two complainants.

Fair enough: I find the law condescending, but it is, after all, the law that if a complainant in a sexual assault case wants a publication ban, she gets one. But Sweeny had also sought, and been granted, a pub ban on the name of a woman who was testifying as a "similar fact" witness.

Neither man was charged with any offence in relation to her, and indeed, she didn't claim that any sex assault had occurred.

But in December 2008, she testified, she met the doctor I'll call Dr. K. on the Plenty of Fish website. (Note to women: If there's one hookup site with an unfortunate track record, it's this one. The child rapist and murderer Michael Rafferty and Canada's youngest convicted serial killer, Cody Legebokoff, were both regulars on Plenty of Fish.)

After a few texts, they arranged a date, which included a drink at Dr. K's condo, then an outing to a club. The last thing the woman, then twenty-nine, remembered was being on the dance floor, lights flashing, and after, she told the judge, "It's all black for me."

The next morning, she awoke feeling like she was "nailed to the bed, like I was paralyzed."

She'd had lots to drink on other occasions and on this one, she said, but this was no ordinary hangover, and she even told her mother about what had happened. "I didn't know what to do, if he had touched me or not, if I was drugged or not. . . . I decided to talk it through."

After she read of the doctors' arrest, she said, "I thought I should at least tell my story."

The woman was just being a good citizen, and she was an agreeable and endearingly frank witness.

When she read about the arrest of the doctors, and the Toronto force issued its standard appeal for "more victims" to come forward—police always do this, and if it may be warranted now and then, it's reprehensible as a general practice—she contacted the force in the western Canadian city where she was then living and gave a statement.

But as it turned out, her lack of memory was virtually complete, and she was far less firm about everything in the witness stand than her police statement suggested.

Why should she have been given a publication ban on her name? She was just a witness. Even she didn't claim she was a victim.

It meant that except for police and expert witnesses such as biologists and the like, only the two accused men were ever identified publicly. The names of the alleged victims and the witness, all adults about the same age as the men, are forever secret.

On September 25, 2014, the doctors were acquitted of all charges (though they may still face disciplinary proceedings at the college).

But that's the thing: If the names of the famous are bound to emerge, even if they aren't charged, the names of their accusers usually won't, at least if they seek to remain anonymous.

My experiment did prove something to me, and that was that it's possible to cover such a trial—in all the usual detail—without naming the accused person.

And it is astonishing, given how newspapers and other media routinely contest publication bans in the courts—hiring lawyers who invariably argue that only with publicity and transparency, meaning media stories, does proper scrutiny follow—that they effectively grant them themselves with alacrity.

Probably nothing illustrates this inequity—and hypocrisy—better than the Scott Andrews/Massimo Pacetti story.

I was in Hamilton, Ontario, on October 28, 2014, for the funeral of Corporal Nathan Cirillo, a member of the Argylls and Sutherland Highlanders, a wonderful reserve regiment I got to know in the years after my book on Canadian soldiers in Afghanistan, *Fifteen Days*, was published in 2007.

In 2006, I worked as an embedded reporter (for *The Globe and Mail*) four times with troops serving in Kandahar. The experience remains the most significant of my life, and I struck up enduring friendships with a few of the soldiers I met there, and others I met back at home. The Argylls were one of the latter.

It didn't hurt that they're based in Hamilton, a rough-edged city I adore because it's not yet completely gentrified—okay, because it's hardly gentrified at all—and that I already knew the regiment because once, in 2004, with other militia units, the chronically underfunded Argylls had actually run out of money for bullets and I'd done a story about it.

But it was after I got back from Kandahar that I really got to know the regiment, finagling invites to a half-dozen Robbie Burns Suppers at the armoury and even a rare dining-in—or, as it should be called, a drinking-in—with Argyll officers.

I never met Cirillo, but on the day he was shot in the back while standing guard over the Tomb of the Unknown Soldier in Ottawa, I began receiving increasingly alarmed emails from the Argylls' then commanding officer, Lawrence Hatfield, who was at first just trying to find out if it was one of his soldiers who'd just been killed.

It was Cirillo, a gorgeous young man, and at twenty-four, a proud and keenly engaged father to five-year-old Marcus.

So all of that, and to write about the funeral, is why I went.

As it happens, shortly before the service began, I was standing just outside the doors to the church when the then Liberal leader, Justin Trudeau, the New Democratic Party leader, Tom Mulcair, and a gaggle of MPs arrived.

Christine Moore may well have been among those who walked past me. She was certainly there.

As a former reservist for three years herself, she would have felt right at home.

Moore is the MP for Abitibi-Témiscamingue, a big slice of northwestern Quebec that just happens to incorporate my hometown of Rouyn-Noranda, where Moore has her main constituency office.

Though she had run unsuccessfully at the federal level twice before, she was elected in the 2011 election as part of the "Orange wave" of young NDP MPs in the province.

But Moore wasn't one of the untested flukes: A nurse by profession, she was a serious candidate, well known in the riding, and she quickly proved herself a capable or better performer in Ottawa.

Like Ruth Ellen Brosseau, who epitomized the surprise of the NDP's success in Quebec—in that she didn't campaign, hadn't been to the riding, and mid-election was on holiday, thus earning herself the nickname of "Vegas" for the city where she'd been vacationing—Moore was re-elected in 2015.

In any case, the parliamentarians had travelled together from Hamilton airport to and from the funeral on a bus.

The Ghomeshi allegations, of course, had just broken and were much in the collective air, with women all over the country coming forward to share their unreported-to-police stories about having been sexually assaulted or harassed.

On one of those bus rides, Moore spotted Trudeau, sitting alone. She decided to grab the seat beside him and the chance to tell him that one of his MPs, Scott Andrews, who represented the district of Avalon on the east coast of Newfoundland, had allegedly (my word) behaved inappropriately with one of her colleagues.

Then thirty-nine, Andrews, as the *Vice* writer Drew Brown put it in a savagely funny 2015 election piece, "grew up inside the Liberal party . . . living and breathing the thick fog of provincial Liberalism as long as he's been alive." He was a former Young Liberal president, a former executive director of the provincial party, and since 2008 had represented Avalon.

Moore named as Andrews' purported target another rookie NDP MP.

Just twenty-seven when elected, the woman was now thirty.

Moore's disclosure lit what proved to be a bonfire.

In fairness to the Liberal leader, as my *Post* colleague John Ivison wrote at the time, "having heard the allegations, Mr. Trudeau could not un-hear them" and had to do something. He immediately directed Liberal whip Judy Foote to tell NDP whip Nycole Turmel about the allegation, and on October 30, the two met Moore and the other woman to discuss the Andrews complaint.

It was in that meeting that Moore first brought up her own more serious accusation about a second Liberal MP, Massimo Pacetti. Pacetti, then fifty-two, was the veteran MP for Saint-Léonard–Saint-Michel in Montreal, first elected in a 2002 by-election and re-elected three times thereafter.

On November 5, Trudeau temporarily suspended both men, "pending the outcome of an investigation," for what he described only as "serious personal misconduct."

The problem is, there *was* no real investigation, and what there was—a secret review by a lawyer—was never made public.

But a lot did become public.

In a March 22, 2016, email interview, Moore said that in the days after the meeting with the whips, journalists began calling her with "information that I only said in the meeting with the Liberal whip. . . . I knew that the Liberals [were] leaking information. . . . If I do not [go] public that day, the day after, the information will have been published anyway."

So starting on November 25, Moore gave a series of interviews—with the *Huffington Post*, the *Toronto Star*, *The Globe and Mail*, the *National Post*, QMI, CBC and Global—and gave details of her encounter, one night in March 2014, with Pacetti.

In none of the resulting stories was she named; in the television interviews she was in shadow and unrecognizable.

What happened, Moore said, went like this:

She and Pacetti played in a sports league and often afterwards people would go for drinks. He invited her to his hotel room for a nightcap at about 2 a.m., but hotel rooms, as she explained, have a different connotation for out-of-town MPs, for whom they are de facto homes.

Soon after they got there, she said, he made it clear he wanted more than friendship by sitting on the bed and patting it for her to join him.

She excused herself to go to the loo, thought over what to do and decided she'd leave, but claimed that as she passed by him, "He grabbed me and I froze after that." She'd been sexually assaulted as a teen, she said, and felt paralyzed by the similarity.

". . . and then we had sex with no explicit consent from me," Moore told *The Globe*. She provided a condom, and after intercourse, she dressed and left the hotel.

Helpfully, other unnamed sources provided the press with alleged details about the complaint against Andrews. They'd allegedly been at a social event on the Hill; Andrews, Pacetti and the other woman then went to Pacetti's office for some wine; Pacetti left, and Andrews allegedly followed her home, forced his way through her door, pushed her against a wall and ground his pelvis against her.

When she ordered him to leave, he did, but afterwards, the sources told the Canadian Press, Andrews harassed her and thereafter called her a "cockteaser."

Both Andrews and Pacetti denied any wrongdoing. But they also wanted to hang on to their jobs, so signed strict confidentiality undertakings that preclude them still from publicly defending themselves or speaking about the case. (Neither responded to repeated requests for interviews.) And they did so in the hope that this was their best shot at keeping their suspensions temporary.

From the Liberals, the hot potato was passed to the then Speaker, Andrew Scheer, who referred the matter to the Board of Internal Economy, and in the end, on December 5, the Liberals hired Cynthia Petersen, an Ottawa labour lawyer with a speciality in workplace human rights law and the discrimination and harassment counsel for the Law Society of Upper Canada, to "conduct an independent, fair and confidential investigation" into the allegations that "will result in the production of a confidential report."

And that's exactly what happened.

Petersen produced a report, the contents of which no one outside a select circle of Liberals has seen, and the fairness and thoroughness of which cannot possibly be judged.

And on March 15, 2015, with Trudeau planning to tell Andrews and Pacetti they were permanently expelled from caucus, the news leaked before he could do so and the men instead learned of their fate from the media.

Pacetti quickly announced he wouldn't run again in the October 19, 2015, election; Andrews, who said he was "astounded" to get the news in the press, still hadn't even seen Petersen's report, and said he'd take some time to think.

In the end, he ran as an independent seven months later and finished about sixteen thousand votes behind Liberal Ken McDonald. At forty-one, his near quarter century in politics was over.

Neither Andrews nor Pacetti ever faced a single criminal charge or a single formal complaint (the House of Commons didn't even have a code of conduct, and thus a process or a forum for dealing with sexual harassment, until June that year). Both men faced ruinous accusations made in public by women who remained in the shadows.

Though most on Parliament Hill knew who the NDP MPs were, in all the media coverage, only two publications ever identified Moore by name.

Frank magazine was the first (the mag actually named the wrong MP as the second woman on the first go-round, then corrected it in the next). The second was *The Black Rod*, an excellent blog written by unidentified citizen journalists in Winnipeg.

In our brief email exchange in March 2016, Moore didn't even raise the possibility of confidentiality with me, nor did I offer her anonymity. She confirmed that in her earlier "press tour," as *The Black Rod* called it, she'd "asked for confidentiality and it was a condition for the interview."

She said she regretted how what she told Trudeau on the funeral bus "was managed. I was thinking the harassing [of the other woman] will stop and [she] will be able to work more easily. Instead of that . . . it was more stressful." Her intention, she said, was never to ruin the Liberal MPs' lives.

"If the Liberals had asked [Andrews] to take a behavioural therapy and say sorry it would have been enough for me. It was Mr. Trudeau's decision to go public with that and that made the two men have their lives shredded."

How is it fair that Andrews and Pacetti—Pacetti, after all, was basically accused of sexual assault—should be convicted after a trial conducted by one of the accusers and a friendly and carefully selected press?

That's what happens in a #ibelievewomen world.

It's increasingly obvious that this is the modern world. The attitude is not confined to feminists or social activists or progressive media publications or police forces.

First of all, right smack in the middle of the first wave of the Ghomeshi scandal, as Marie Henein and her client were waiting for the judicial pretrial later that month, Ontario premier Kathleen Wynne took to a podium at the downtown Toronto YMCA to give a speech.

What she was announcing was a forty-one-million-dollar, three-year initiative—what governments like to call an "action plan"—to combat sexual assault and violence.

"Many women in the province do not feel safe," she said. "And I have a problem with that."

An accompanying thirty-five-page document, with the same name as the theme of the public education campaign—"It's Never Okay"—included a section on the justice system.

"Some sexual assault survivors say that going through the justice system as a complainant can be almost as traumatic as the sexual assault itself," it read.

"The often lengthy and public nature of a trial, reliving the event to provide testimony, methods of questioning and cross-examination: these can all cause extreme distress, and often don't feel fair to survivors."

The paper promised sweeping changes—including better training for prosecutors via "an enhanced prosecution model"—and the following March, while Horkins was off considering his decision in the Ghomeshi case, Ontario attorney general Madeleine Meilleur made good on some of it. She announced what was hailed as a Canadian first—Ontario was launching a $2.8 million pilot program in three cities to give survivors of sexual assault access to free legal services, four hours per from a list of approved lawyers.

And on March 8, the bill—its short title is "Sexual Violence and Harassment Action Plan (Supporting Survivors and Challenging Sexual Violence and Harassment)"—received royal assent and became law.

It's now in the law in Ontario—as conveyed in the very title of Bill 132—that a person who says she (or he) was sexually assaulted is a survivor.

The bill amends six existing acts; eliminates the time limitations on using the civil courts and the Criminal Injuries Compensation Board so that, as Tracy MacCharles, the minister responsible for women's issues, put it more than once in the Legislature, "survivors can bring their . . . claims forward whenever they choose to do so"; and mandates every university and college in the province to have a stand-alone policy to combat sexual violence.

Lest anyone doubt how the first Ghomeshi case propelled the government to action (though in fairness, the premier's mandate letter to MacCharles, which predated the scandal by about a month, gave her marching orders to continue the work against sexual violence), a search of his last name gets 110 hits on the government's site official Hansard and committee transcripts.

Everyone really *was* talking about the case, even the lawmakers, who are also hoping to influence the lawyers.

A troubling provision of the sweeping sexual violence action plan has a bit devoted to getting "better outcomes for survivors through the justice system."

It hits a lovely Big Sister note with a pledge to call on "law schools to ensure all Ontario lawyers uphold their professional responsibilities as well as Canada's rape shield laws. . . . [W]e expect perpetrators of sexual violence to be held to account."

Asked to clarify just what that means, Brendon Crawley, spokesman for the Ontario AG, said, "We are in communication with the Dean of Law Schools and working with the Law Society of Upper Canada" to develop and deliver professional legal education to inform "members of the bar regarding the impact of sexual violence on victims."

Another spokesperson, Judy Phillips, later fleshed it out. Ministry officials, she said in an April 5, 2016, email, were working with the former and current chairs of the Council of Canadian Law Deans Camille Cameron and Ian Scott, and with Law Society treasurer Janet Minor.

At the same time, there's a vocal minority of lawyers and law professors banging the drum for ethical constraints to be placed on defence counsel in sex assault cases.

This is the now well-known anti-"whacking" movement, whacking being what Ottawa lawyer Michael Edelson once urged a group of lawyers to do with sexual assault complainants.

The leading lights of this movement are University of Windsor law professor David Tanovich and Schulich School of Law (at Dalhousie University) assistant professor Elaine Craig.

Craig wrote "The Ethical Obligations of Defence Counsel in Sexual Assault Cases" in the Winter 2014 edition of the *Osgoode Hall Law Journal*.

Tanovich wrote "'Whack' No More: Infusing Equality into the Ethics of Defence Lawyering in Sexual Assault Cases," published in September 2015 in the *Ottawa Law Review*.

(Craig's piece, ironically, is built upon a 2004 case known as *R v A.A. et al*, A.A. being one of four young men who sexually assaulted a fifteen-year-old girl. Craig is sharply critical of the four defence lawyers, whom she names, for their tactics. The four were all convicted by Ontario Court judge David Cole, an adjunct professor at the University of Toronto Law School and a man with a reputation for solidly progressive decisions. He found that the victim "stood up very well under rigorous—but by no means unfair—cross-examination.")

In any case, the two pieces nicely bookend the start and progress of the Ghomeshi case through the courts.

What was surprising is that the professors joined forces to write, while the trial itself was ongoing, a piece for *The Globe and Mail*. It was published on February 10, 2016, the day before Henein and Robitaille and Callaghan made their closing arguments.

Headlined "Whacking the complainant: A real and current systemic problem," the article began with the proposition that all sexual assault trials "harm complainants," even when conducted ethically and within the bounds of law.

I'm not sure it's even correct that all complainants are harmed—for some I've seen, men and women both, testifying and facing down the person who assaulted and abused them is liberating and empowering—but even if it were, such harm is not peculiar to sexual assault cases.

The writers went on: "Throughout the very public trial of Jian Ghomeshi, the term whacking—which refers to tactics that seek to exploit the stereotypes and vulnerabilities inherent in sexual assault cases to secure a favourable outcome—has been prevalent."

They then listed eight examples of recent cases that purportedly show illustrations of what whacking is.

None arose from the Ghomeshi case. None had any bearing or connection to the Ghomeshi case. Nothing like any of the examples had happened during the Ghomeshi trial, and Henein had engaged in none of the verboten conduct, or even come close.

At the end, Craig and Tanovich called for "an explicit no-whacking" provision in lawyers' ethical codes, for prosecutors to fill out a form at the end of every sexual assault trial about "the nature of the defence" (the ratting-out of the defence bar), and for greater law society oversight.

And the stunning thing about Jian Ghomeshi's trial and acquittal, which saw the case against him unravel so quickly, is that outside the courthouse, a good chunk of the world carried on post-verdict pretty much as if none of it had ever happened.

Despite their general and widely reported discrediting, Lucy DeCoutere and complainants No. 1 and No. 3 were still being hailed in some quarters as plucky heroines for having come forward. DeCoutere and No. 1 even continued to give interviews. Lawyers and law professors who weren't in court were telling the world that defence lawyers, who were by implication like Henein, needed to be reined in. And the complainants were clinging ferociously to their victim/survivor status.

Weeks after the trial ended but before the verdict, DeCoutere told *Chatelaine*'s Sarah Boesveld that she felt "shamed" and "eviscerated" by Henein and said, "I don't think you need to interrogate somebody in such a fashion that it takes them weeks to recover from a reasonably brief chat."

If DeCoutere needed weeks to recover from her cross-examination, she needs, in the immortal words of my favourite Argylls slogan, to "Harden the fuck up."

And she was still deciding for herself, thanks very much, what the courts should or should not be hearing—the very behaviour that had got her in so much difficulty.

Of her post-attack conduct, virtually all of which she'd failed to disclose to police and prosecutors, she said, "I wasn't even thinking about after because I didn't think it mattered—because it shouldn't matter."

On verdict day, women marched in at least two Canadian cities, Toronto and Ottawa, in support of their sisters, chanting, "We believe survivors." On social media and in the mainstream press, people who had never come within a hair's breadth of the courtroom or heard an iota of the testimony confidently railed against the decision and the rebirth of old "rape myths."

Inspector Joan McKenna, head of criminal investigations for the Ottawa force, tweeted a picture of six unidentified women, one holding a #WeBelieveSurvivors sign with a line that read "We believe survivors of Sexual assault," along with #WeBelieve, #selfcare@OttawaPolice and #EndTheStigma.

McKenna's tweet was duly retweeted by Ottawa chief Charles Bordeleau.

If there is anything more heartwarming than the thought of senior police officials firmly lining up behind survivors on the day of an acquittal, it's that politicians did the same.

NDP leader Tom Mulcair (the messages are written at NDP HQ but under his name) tweeted the day of the verdict, "Today and every day, #IBelieveSurvivors"—in both official languages of course.

He attached a personal statement linked to the tweet, in which he spoke of encountering "the culture of dismissive victim-blaming" during his years at Quebec's professions board, said "there is also no doubt that the fear of not being believed may prevent a survivor of sexual assault from coming forward," and concluded, "And most importantly, I believe survivors."

Mulcair is a lawyer by training, and once worked in Quebec's justice ministry.

A couple of weeks later, when in late March Marie Henein made a rare public appearance on CBC's *The National*, where she was interviewed by Peter Mansbridge about hashtag justice and took a pretty naked shot at Mulcair for the tweet, he promptly tweeted, "I believe strongly in the presumption of innocence and the right to a strong defence but I also believe survivors."

Well, no: It's akin to saying you believe in both Darwinism and creationism. If you believe in the presumption of innocence, you can't honestly also believe survivors, because to do so defeats that presumption. It's an elusive fiction anyway, one that lives only in a very few heads.

On the day the Ghomeshi trial began, the publicity had been

so enormous, the number of accusers so great, the woman-as-truth-teller meme so prevalent, that there probably wasn't one ordinary person in the courtroom who didn't already believe that Jian Ghomeshi was really guilty.

I was one of the skeptics, ready to be otherwise convinced, but I believed it too.

I didn't even realize it until at some point during DeCoutere's lunatic testimony I suddenly thought, "What if this incident never happened?" which was followed by, "My God, what if he didn't do this?" which was followed by, "Shame on me."

Henein and Robitaille were Ghomeshi's advocates.

Only Bill Horkins, who had no dog in the race, saw and never lost sight of the presumption of innocence, wrapped as the lawyers say like an invisible cloak around Jian Ghomeshi's shoulders as it is around all of our shoulders.

It's the saving grace of the imperfect system and the flawed human beings who work within it.

Early in April 2016, another *Trailer Park Boys* star made front-page news. It was Mike Smith, the Nova Scotia actor who played the bespectacled character Bubbles.

He was arrested in Hollywood and charged with misdemeanour domestic battery, according to the Los Angeles Police Department, in connection with an incident at the historic Roosevelt Hotel, where he allegedly pinned a female friend, Georgia Ling, against a bathroom wall in the midst of an argument.

That was late one Friday. On the Saturday, *Trailer Park Boys* released a statement saying, "The other members [of the cast] and all staff stand behind Mike and look forward to the matter being resolved favourably."

In an account given with the statement, Smith acknowledged "a loud and heated dispute" with Ling, but said, "At no time did I assault her. I am not guilty of the misdemeanour charged against me."

In her own account of the events, Ling, the purported victim, said she was capable of calling the police herself and didn't, because "at no point did I feel I was in danger," but that third parties, not present in the room, had misinterpreted things and done so.

Hours later, Lucy DeCoutere tweeted, "I have resigned from Trailer Park Boys" and then, "If I find out that somebody is abusive, I cut them out of my life. It's very easy."

Really? I was gobsmacked she could say this, or much about anything else for that matter, and still be quoted. You really can't make this stuff up.

She had Bubbles, her old buddy, tried and convicted in a New York minute and in that minute, like the little crazy children Arthur Miller wrote about, she proved the very worth of the justice system.

EPILOGUE

KINDLY, MY EDITOR put it a couple of dozen ways.

The book needed, he said, "a summing up," a "snapshot" of my current thinking, "a final pronouncement," etc., etc.

I didn't know how to break it to him that I've either spent too much time in the company of lawyers (and thus can no longer see things normally, without saying "on the one hand this," and in the next breath "but on the other hand that") or I've managed to spend four years of my life thinking about the justice system without coming to any big conclusions.

My objections aren't the usual ones, I don't think.

I don't believe sentences are too light, except for sexual offences committed against children, especially by trusted family members or others in positions of trust. No one is more damaged more permanently by crime than children who are sexually abused.

I don't want to see more people in prison.

Jail in my view pretty much should be reserved for those who have committed serious violent offences.

I don't think government needs to make prison more cruel than it inherently is; you lose your liberty, you don't need to be also denied library books, decent jam for your toast or the ability to smoke a cigarette.

But the system is opaque from top to bottom.

Judge-picking is mostly mysterious, with judges answerable only to themselves. Lawyers are clubby. The public isn't terribly welcome in Canadian courtrooms, merely allowed. Jurors are treated with naked condescension and sometimes deceived. The alchemy of sentencing is confusing, and if those in my business do a poor job of explaining the alchemy of sentencing, at least we try from time to time. Why can't judges themselves explain that the ten-year sentence doesn't mean a decade behind bars, but rather the chance for day parole after a sixth and full parole after a third?

No one ever understands the absolutely frightening power of the state until it is brought against her.

At least in America, they're up front about it: I remember when David Radler, the prosecution's key witness against Conrad Black at his fraud trial in Chicago, described some of the early meetings he had as he was working out his plea deal. Sometimes, there were several representatives each from the U.S. Attorney's Office, the FBI, the U.S. Postal Service, the U.S. Securities and Exchange Commission, and the federal Internal Revenue Service.

Radler could actually see what he was up against and the message was unmistakable: You mess with us, these are the ways we will crush you. The Canadian accused should be so lucky.

By the way, at Black's trial, exhibits were electronically filed on a website available to press and public; transcripts were similarly available, free online, a day later. That was almost a decade ago.

How is it that in many courthouses across Canada, access to such things is late or non-existent, and expensive, and must always be accompanied by the requisite bowing and scraping?

Why, after decades of the bench talking about permitting cameras in court, hasn't it happened?

The last case I was able to include in the book was the trial of Jian Ghomeshi.

It was held in courtroom No. 125 at the Old City Hall courts in downtown Toronto, easily the most glamorous courthouse in the city by dint of its architecture, if also one of the grittiest.

There, prisoners in jumpsuits and handcuffs, accused people seeking bail, distraught relatives and families, and lawyers and judges walk the same halls, sometimes side by side, which is only right, and a testament to the genuinely egalitarian beast that a modern justice system should strive to be.

I love the place, and am so glad it was there that I rediscovered what I so admire about the rule of law—that it is the antithesis of vengeance. This alone is reason enough to keep the system and make it better.

I was also reminded that there are those who do good work in the trenches every day.

Well, in between various recesses and lunch breaks, that is.

I fell a little back in love with the justice system at that trial, and I'm grateful.

ACKNOWLEDGEMENTS

IT WAS ONE day in April 2015, during the Mike Duffy trial, that I apparently lost my mind entirely, whether because of Duffy's habit of never paying for a thing, or his lawyer, Don Bayne's, general unctuousness (not to mention his party trick of whirling about, pointing at his client and crying, "This man is on criminal trial for his liberty!"), or just because I'd had it that day with the widespread habit among lawyers of overpraising one another.

I wrote to Kirsten Smith, the librarian-cum-researcher who helped so much with this book, and said, "Hey, any chance you can get a Latin translation of 'Let no cock go unsucked'? Seriously."

Most courts in Canada favour Latin or French mottos, usually *"Justicia"* (Justice) or *"Honi soit qui mal y pense"* (loosely, "Evil to him who thinks evil").

I imagined my motto better described what often happens there. In my dreams, I pictured it on a fancy coat of arms.

That was April 14.

Latin professors the land over turned Smith down. One decried the vulgarity of the phrase as "not contributing to public discourse."

"Sir," I imagined myself saying with great dignity, "I'm a journalist; I'm not supposed to contribute to that."

But on May 4—if it takes Kirsten Smith twenty days, it's a monstrous task—she emerged triumphant. She'd found the wondrous Alban Walsh, of Newfoundland it goes without saying, and with a few notes of explanation (involving "the rare form future imperative that is used only for legal/court documents") he came up with "Omnia membri fellanto!", literally meaning, "All cocks shall be sucked!"

With, I hope, that same generosity of spirit, I have many to thank, first among them of course Smith, who was, for so long, tireless and good-humoured in her work for me, and Walsh, for his genius.

Over the course of serving my life sentence, I've been lucky enough to have worked with and been inspired by marvellous colleagues (Rosie DiManno and Sam Pazzano; court artists Marianne Boucher and Pam Davies; former court reporter Tracy Nesdoly; Shannon Kari, the only person more often roused to rage than me; the members of the parliamentary press gallery in Ottawa who covered the Duffy trial, Vinay Menon of the *Star*, Barbara Brown, formerly of the *Hamilton Spectator*, and Mike Friscolanti of *Maclean's*) and terrific editors (Mary D. Shears at the *Star*; Lorrie Goldstein and Al Shanoff at the *Toronto Sun*; Colin MacKenzie at *The Globe and Mail*; Martin Newland and Jo-Anne MacDonald at the *National Post* and Rob Roberts, now with Canadian Press but an ex Postie too).

Among the fine young colleagues with whom I've had the pleasure of working are Sarah Boesveld of *Chatelaine*, Aileen Donnelly and Ashley Csanady of the *Post*, Adam Miller of Global Television and Rosemary Westwood of *Metro News*.

They give me hope for journalism, if not exactly for newspapers.

The best newspaper owners I was lucky enough to work for were the late Doug Creighton (founder and publisher of the *Sun*) and Conrad Black (founder and publisher of the *National Post*). Years later, I also covered much of the latter's trial, in Chicago.

Too many photographers have come and, sadly, gone to name, but the best of them—such as Laura Pedersen, Tyler Anderson and Peter Thompson of the *Post*—are also astute observers and reporters.

Now that video is a regular part of the job, and one I have come to love, I must also thank Rob Granatstein of the *Post* and his crew, and in particular Laura P. (again), who is my regular videographer.

A bow too to Mike Bendixen, John Moore, Robert Turner, Drew Garner and Ryan Doyle, all of Newstalk 1010 Radio, where I regularly get to talk about the trials I cover.

Then there are the lawyers, prosecutors and defence counsel both.

I loved watching and hope I learned something from Paul McDermott and Allison Dellandrea, Robin Flumerfelt, Milan Rupic, John Rosen, Earl Levy, the late Austin Cooper and Eddie Greenspan, Marie Henein and of course John Struthers, my go-to choice if, God forbid, I am ever in legal trouble.

Big thanks to Thomas Zuber, former judge of the Ontario Superior Court and the Ontario Court of Appeal, and retired Superior Court judge Eugene Ewaschuk for their frankness and fearlessness, on and off the bench.

And finally, thanks to my editor, Bond, and my collection of wonderful friends out of court.

I know where you all live.

SOURCES

CHAPTER I

Vaillancourt is "very patient, a good listener": Daniel LeBlanc and
Sean Fine, "'Bold' Toronto Judge to Preside over Mike Duffy's
Trial," *The Globe and Mail*, March 25, 2015.

A total of 3,369 lawyers have applied: Judicial Appointments Advisory
Committee, *Annual Report for the Period from 1 January 2013 to
31 December 2013* (Toronto, 2014), www.ontariocourts.ca/ocj/
files/open/JAAC-2013-Ann-Rep.pdf.

It makes for a "comfortable living": Justice Ian Binnie, "Judicial
Independence in Canada." Paper presented at the Second
Congress of the World Conference on Constitutional Justice,
Rio de Janeiro, Brazil, January 2011. See: www.venice.coe.
int/WCCJ/Rio/Papers/CAN_Binnie_E.pdf.

Broad and troubling transparency issues: Philip Slayton, *Mighty
Judgment: How the Supreme Court of Canada Runs Your Life*
(Toronto: Penguin Canada, 2011).

Why do we still start trials: Neal Hall, "Slow Justice: Trial Delays
Could Put BC Criminals Back on the Street," *Vancouver Sun*,
October 13, 2006.

That prompted then Supreme Court Chief: Ian Mulgrew, "Top Judge Angry at Oppal's Comments," *Vancouver Sun*, November 1, 2006, http://www.canada.com/story.html?id=c5d7c40b-e32a-45e2-8f9e-d774f66c852d.

It was sparked when John Ivison: John Ivison, "Tories Incensed with Supreme Court as Some Allege Chief Justice Lobbied against Marc Nadon Appointment," *National Post*, May 1, 2014, http://news.nationalpost.com/news/canada/canadian-politics/tories-incensed-with-supreme-court-as-some-allege-chief-justice-lobbied-against-marc-nadon-appointment/.

But Rees also told the CBC that: Leslie MacKinnon, "Beverley McLachlin, PMO Give Duelling Statements on Nadon Appointment Fight," *CBC News* (online), May 1, 2014, http://www.cbc.ca/news/politics/beverley-mclachlin-pmo-give-duelling-statements-on-nadon-appointment-fight-1.2628563/.

The Advocates' Society publicly released a letter: See: http://www.newswire.ca/news-releases/the-advocates-society-speaks-out-regarding-comments-from-the-prime-ministers-office-about-the-chief-justice-of-canada-514228121.html.

The ideology of a small and unrepresentative clique: Robert Martin, *The Most Dangerous Branch: How the Supreme Court of Canada Has Undermined Our Law and Our Democracy* (Montreal: McGill-Queen's University Press, 2003).

CHAPTER 2

He reported back: Frank Iacobucci, *First Nations Representation on Ontario Juries: Report of the Independent Review Conducted by The Honourable Frank Iacobucci* (Toronto: Office of the Attorney General, February 2013), http://www.attorneygeneral.jus.gov.on.ca/english/about/pubs/iacobucci/First_Nations_Representation_Ontario_Juries.html.

the Canadian Judicial Council's Model Jury Instructions: Canadian Judicial Council, *National Committee on Jury Instructions* (Ottawa:

National Judicial Institute, 2008), http://www.nji-inm.ca/index.cfm/publications/model-jury-instructions/.

Ralph Artigliere wrote in a 2010 paper: Ralph Artigliere, "Sequestering for the Twenty-First Century: Disconnecting Jurors from the Internet During Trial," *Drake Law Review* 59 (Spring 2011).

A Reuters Legal analysis done in 2010: Brian Gow, "As Jurors Go Online, U.S. Trials Go Off Track," *Reuters*, December 8, 2010, http://www.reuters.com/article/us-internet-jurors-idUSTRE6B74Z820101208/.

A retired Florida judge: Ralph Artigliere, Jim Barton and Bill Hahn, "Reining in Juror Misconduct: Practical Suggestions for Judges and Lawyers," *The Florida Bar Journal* 84, no. 1 (January 2010), http://www.floridabar.org/divcom/jn/jnjournal01.nsf/8c9f13012b96736985256aa900624829/d9a2f95a71f304778525769b006dd8d5/.

Robbie Manhas, then a law student: Robbie Manhas, "Responding to Independent Juror Research in the Internet Age: Positive Rules, Negative Rules, and Outside Mechanisms," *Michigan Law Review* 112, no. 5 (May 2011).

Judge David Watt: David Watt, *Watt's Manual of Criminal Jury Instructions* (Toronto: Carswell, 2008).

Consider what Georgia State: Caren Myers Morrison, "Can the Jury Survive Google?," *Criminal Justice* 4 (Winter 2011).

Morrison's paper: Caren Myers Morrison, "Jury 2.0," *Hastings Law Journal* 62 (July 2011).

As one juror wrote: John Schwartz, "As Jurors Turn to Web, Mistrials Are Popping Up," *The New York Times*, March 18, 2009, http://www.nytimes.com/2009/03/18/us/18juries.html?_r=1. See also: Deirdra Funcheon, "Jurors Gone Wild," *Miami New Times*, April 23, 2009, http://www.miaminewtimes.com/news/jurors-gone-wild-6332969/.

the revered 18th Century English jurist: William Blackstone, *Commentaries on the Laws of England* (1765).

a letter from Shelton's mother: Theresa Shelton, "Is This Justice?," *The Globe and Mail*, June 9, 2004, http://www.theglobeand-mail.com/opinion/letters/is-this-justice/article1000245/.

as Roger D Groot writes: J.S. Cockburn and Thomas A. Green, eds., *Twelve Good Men and True: The Criminal Trial Jury in England, 1200–1800* (Princeton: Princeton University Press, 1988).

a 1994 paper by: Albert Alschuler and Andrew G. Deiss, "A Brief History of the Criminal Jury in the United States,"*University of Chicago Law Review* 61, 867 (1994).

R. Blake Brown writes: R. Blake Brown, *A Trying Question: The Jury in Nineteenth-Century Canada* (Toronto: University of Toronto Press, 2009).

his Rationale of Judicial Evidence: Jeremy Bentham, *Rationale of Judicial Evidence, Specially Applied to English Practice* (London: 1827).

CHAPTER 3

Next day, the Ottawa Citizen *reported*: Jake Rupert, "Elliott's Guilty Plea Ends Long Legal Saga," *Ottawa Citizen*, December 17, 2005, http://www.canada.com/story.html?id=69541800-ed9e-4db7-af3d-a6570ac3db6a.

Quoting Professor Shimon Shetreet: Shimon Shetreet, *Judges on Trial: A Study of the Appointment and Accountability of the English Judiciary* (Amsterdam: North Holland Publishing Co., 1976).

When I stumbled upon: Jeremy Gans, "Charter of Frights," *Inside Story* (blog), November 10, 2008, http://insidestory.org.au/charter-of-frights/.

A delightful piece: Jim Rusk, "PM Pays Off Faithful: MacEachen, Mackasey Rewarded," *The Globe and Mail*, June 30, 1984.

The Globe's *Jeff Sallot*: Jeff Sallot, "Trudeau Failed to Consult Bar on Judge: CBA," *The Globe and Mail*, July 18, 1984.

The first study: Peter H. Russell and Jacob S. Ziegel, "Federal Judicial Appointments: Appraisal of the First Mulroney

Government's Appointments and the New Judicial Advisory Committees," *The University of Toronto Law Journal* 41, no. 1 (Winter 1991).

The second study: Lori Hausegger, Troy Riddell, Matthew Hennigar and Emmanuelle Richez, "Exploring the Links Between Party and Appointment: Canadian Federal Judicial Appointments from 1989 to 2003," *Canadian Journal of Political Science* 43, no. 3 (September 2010).

judicial affairs tells committee members: See: http://www.fja-cmf. gc.ca/appointments-nominations/committees-comites/ guidelines-lignes-eng.html.

in his book: James Allen, "Judicial Appointments in New Zealand: If It Were Done When 'Tis Done, Then 'Twere Well It Were Done Openly and Direcly," in *Appointing Judges in an Age of Judicial Power: Critical Perspectives from around the World*, eds. Kate Malleson and Peter H. Russell (Toronto: University of Toronto Press, 2006).

make laws in Canada: See Kirk Makin, "Two-Thirds Back Electing Judges," *The Globe and Mail*, April 9, 2007, http://www. theglobeandmail.com/news/national/two-thirds-back-electing-judges/article1073476/; Chris Cobb, "Canadians Want to Elect Court," *National Post*, February 4, 2002; Jeff Shallot, "Public against Judges Making Laws: Poll," *The Globe and Mail*, August 11, 2003, http://www.theglobeandmail. com/news/national/public-against-judges-making-laws-poll/article1165393/.

As Elizabeth Handsley wrote: Elizabeth Handsley, "The Judicial Whisper Goes Around: Appointment of Judicial Officers in Australia," in *Appointing Judges in an Age of Judicial Power: Critical Perspectives from around the World*, eds. Kate Malleson and Peter H. Russell (Toronto: University of Toronto Press, 2006).

As Jim Allan wrote: James Allen, "Judicial Appointments in New Zealand: If It Were Done When 'Tis Done, Then 'Twere Well

It Were Done Openly and Directly," in *Appointing Judges in an Age of Judicial Power: Critical Perspectives from around the World*, eds. Kate Malleson and Peter H. Russell (Toronto: University of Toronto Press, 2006).

Russell was then working: Peter H. Russell, *The Judiciary in Canada: The Third Branch of Government* (Toronto: McGraw-Hill Ryerson, 1987).

The JAAC even publishes: Judicial Appointments Advisory Committee of Ontario, *Where Do Judges Come From? The Process of Appointment of Ontario Provincial Judges* (Toronto: JAAC, 2003).

As Russell wrote: Peter H. Russell, conclusion to *Appointing Judges in an Age of Judicial Power: Critical Perspectives from around the World*, eds. Kate Malleson and Peter H. Russell (Toronto: University of Toronto Press, 2006).

CHAPTER 4

as quoted in their 1995 book: Scott Burnside and Alan Cairns, *Deadly Innocence* (New York: Warner Books, 1995).

As the author Stephen Williams dryly wrote: Stephen Williams, *Invisible Darkness* (Toronto: Little, Brown & Company, 1996).

wrote in a working paper: Law Reform Commission of Canada, *Criminal Procedure: Control of the Process*, Working Paper 15 (Information Canada, 1975).

the Commission now said: Law Reform Commission of Canada, *Plea discussions and agreements*, Working Paper 60 (Law Reform Commission of Canada, 1989).

Martin presented his 500-page report: Martin G. Arthur, *Report of the Attorney General's Advisory Committee on Charge Screening, Disclosure, and Resolution Discussions* (Toronto: The Committee, 1993).

The deal would be reviewed: Patrict T. Galligan, *Report of the Honourable Patrick T. Galligan Appointed to Inquire Into and*

Report on Certain Matters Relating to Two Decisions Respecting Karla Homolka Made by Officials in the Ministry of the Attorney-General (Toronto: Ministry of the Attorney-General, 1996).

As Stephen Williams wrote: Stephen Williams, *Karla: A Pact with the Devil* (Montreal: Cantos International, 2003).

As Kristen's dad . . . told Maclean's: Joe Chidley and Danylo Hawaleshka, "OPP Charge Former Bernardo Lawyers," *Maclean's*, February 3, 1997.

Adam Dodek wrote: Adam M. Dodek, "Canadian Legal Ethics: Ready for the Twenty-First Century at Last," *Osgoode Hall Law Journal* 46, no. 1 (Spring 2008).

As Tracey Tyler reported: Tracey Tyler, "The Dark Side of Justice," *Toronto Star*, March 3, 2007, http://www.thestar.com/news/2007/03/03/the_dark_side_of_justice.html.

MacKenzie's book: Gavin MacKenzie, *Lawyers & Ethics: Professional Responsibility and Discipline* (Toronto: Carswell, 1993).

appeared in the Toronto Star: David Young, "Why Should Lawyers Be Exempt from Law?," *Toronto Star*, May 23, 2002.

Kirk Makin wrote: Kirk Makin, "Deal Would Set Rules for Paralegals," *The Globe and Mail*, April 24, 2002, http://www.theglobeandmail.com/news/national/deal-would-set-rules-for-paralegals/article4134144/.

Her book, called Wally's World: Marsha Boulton, *Wally's World* (Toronto: McArthur & Co., 2006).

A recently published column which had suggested: Lynn Crosbie, "Lynn's Case: The Argument," *The Globe and Mail*, December 1, 1997.

On Jan. 6, 1998, Bird . . . wrote: Heather Bird, "Ban Broken on Bernardo/Homolka Tapes?," *Toronto Sun*, January 6, 1998.

By Jan. 11, Bird was reporting: Heather Bird, "So, Did He . . . or Didn't He?," *Toronto Sun*, January 11, 1998.

Bird wrote on Jan. 18: Heather Bird, "Families Seek Wider Probe," *Toronto Sun*, January 18, 1998.

In a separate news story: Heather Bird, "Probe Bernardo Book Pics: Families," *Toronto Sun*, January 18, 1998.

he told the Canadian Press: Canadian Press, "Homolka Book to Be Altered," *The Globe and Mail*, March 4, 2003, http://www.theglobeandmail.com/news/national/homolka-book-to-be-altered/article1158773/.

he told The Globe and Mail: Kirk Makin, "Author to Post Bernardo Case Archive on Web," *The Globe and Mail*, April 30, 2003, http://www.theglobeandmail.com/news/national/author-to-post-bernardo-case-archive-on-web/article1014246/.

Tim Danson told the paper: Kirk Makin, "Web Archive of Bernardo Case Sparks Legal Fight," *The Globe and Mail*, May 1, 2003, http://www.theglobeandmail.com/news/national/web-archive-of-bernardo-case-sparks-legal-fight/article1014247/.

The Canadian Journalists for Free Expression: Canadian Journalists for Free Expression, *The Case of Stephen Williams: Secret Publication Bans, Selective Prosecution and Prosecutorial Conflict of Interest* (December 2003).

Todd wrote an e-book: Paula Todd, Finding Karla: *How I Tracked Down an Elusive Child Killer and Discovered a Mother of Three* (Toronto: Canadian Writers Group/The Atavist, 2012).

CHAPTER 5

In a delightful story: Jack Batten, *Learned Friends: A Tribute to Fifty Remarkable Ontario Advocates, 1950–2000* (Toronto: Irvin Law, 2005).

a (now discredited) 9,000-word story: Sabrina Rubin Erdely, "A Rape on Campus," *Rolling Stone*, November 29, 2014.

Cooke wrote: Michael Cooke, "Why the *Star* Chose to Publish Jian Ghomeshi Allegations," *Toronto Star*, October 26, 2014, http://www.thestar.com/news/gta/2014/10/26/why_the_star_chose_to_publish_jian_ghomeshi_allegations.html.

Writing in the National Post: Reva Seth, "Why I Can't Remain

Silent about What Jian Did to Me," *The Huffington Post* (blog), October 30, 2016, http://www.huffingtonpost.ca/reva-seth/reva-seth-jian-ghomeshi_b_6077296.html.

Montgomery later told Chatelaine: Sue Montgomery, "I Was Raped and Never Reported It. Why I'm Talking About It Now," *Chatelaine*, December 3, 2014, http://www.chatelaine.com/living/i-was-raped-and-i-never-reported-it/.

an internal CBC memo: Alyshah Hasham, "CBC Fired Jian Ghomeshi after Seeing 'Graphic Evidence': Internal Memo," *Toronto Star*, October 31, 2014, http://www.thestar.com/news/gta/2014/10/31/cbc_fired_jian_ghomeshi_after_seeing_graphic_evidence_internal_memo.html.

identified herself in a column: Kathryn Borel, "Jian Ghomeshi Harassed Me on the Job. Why Did Our Radio Station Look the Other Way?," *The Guardian*, December 2, 2014, http://www.theguardian.com/commentisfree/2014/dec/02/-sp-jian-ghomeshi-sexual-harassment-cbc-ignored/.

a June 17, 2015 piece: Leah McLaren, "The Cult of Jian: His Life as an Outcast, Who's Standing by Him, and Why He's Sure He'll Walk," *Toronto Life*, July 2015, http://torontolife.com/city/crime/cult-of-jian-ghomeshi-leah-mclaren/.

who wrote in a Feb. 18, 2016 column: Antonia Zerbisias, "Memo to My Sob-Sister Fourth-Wave Feminists: Get over It," *NOW Magazine*, February 18, 2016, http://nowtoronto.com/news/memo-to-my-sob-sister-fourth-wave-feminists-get-over-it/.

Wrote a piece in The Guardian: Bernard Hogan-Howe, "Suspected Sex Offenders Have Rights the Police Must Respect," *The Guardian*, February 10, 2016, http://www.theguardian.com/commentisfree/2016/feb/10/accused-sex-crimes-anonymous-until-charged-reputations-police-complaint/.

He referred to a sweeping 2015 review: Elish Angiolini, *Report of the Independent Review into the Investigation and Prosecution of Rape in London* (April 2015).

That came from the November 2014 report: Thomas P Winsor, *State of Policing. The Annual Assessment of Policing in England and Wales 2013/2014* (November 2014).

He was furious that he'd been smeared: Patrick Sawer and Robert Mendick, "Lord Bramall Slams 'Heavy Handed' Police for 'Grotesque Witch Hunt' over Child Sex Claims," *The Daily Telegraph*, January 16, 2016, http://www.telegraph.co.uk/news/uknews/crime/12102888/Lord-Bramall-has-been-told-he-faces-no-further-action-after-being-interviewed-by-police-investigating-child-sex-abuse.html.

he wrote in The Boston Globe: Patrick Witt, "A Sexual Harassment Policy that Nearly Ruined My Life," *The Boston Globe*, November 3, 2014, http://www.bostonglobe.com/opinion/2014/11/03/sexual-harassment-policy-that-nearly-ruined-life/hY3XrZrOdXjvX2SSvuciPN/story.html.

The Times's *"public editor"*: Arthur S. Brisbane, "The Quarterback's Tangled Saga," *The New York Times*, February 4, 2012, http://www.nytimes.com/2012/02/05/opinion/sunday/the-quarterbacks-tangled-saga.html.

sports columnist Cam Cole wrote: Cam Cole, "John Furlong's Ordeal While Trapped in No-Win Situation," *Vancouver Sun*, November 23, 2015, http://www.vancouversun.com/sports/Cole+John+Furlong+ordeal+while+trapped+situation/11540791/story.html.

In a 1976 interview: Tom Nixon, "No Jock Talk from City's New Recreation Director," *Prince George Citizen*, July 9, 1976.

The Georgia Straight *published*: Laura Robinson, "John Furlong Biography Omits Secret Past in Burns Lake," *The Georgia Straight*, September 26, 2012, http://www.straight.com/news/john-furlong-biography-omits-secret-past-burns-lake/.

She presented a paper: Laura Robinson, "Truth, Lies and History: John Furlong and Canadian Sport's Moral Vacuum." Paper presented at Play the Game 2013, Aarhus, Denmark, October 30,

2013. See: playthegame.org/media/3285725/Laura_Robinson_
Truth_Lies_and_History_ed.pdf.

This from a January 2015 brief: Sex Information and Education
Council of Canada, *Sexual Health Education in the Schools:
Questions and Answers* (2015), sieccan.org/wp/wp-content/
uploads/2015/08/SIECCAN-QA-Sexual-health-education-
in-the-schools-2015-Ontario.pdf.

In a much-cited 2012 analysis: Holly Johnson, "Limits of a Criminal
Justice Response: Trends in Police and Court Processing of
Sexual Assault," *Sexual Assault in Canada: Law, Legal Practice
and Women's Activism*, ed. Elizabeth A. Sheehy (Ottawa: University of Ottawa Press, 2012).

Maclean's magazine decried: "A National Conversation about
Sexual Assault Has Begun. Finally," *Maclean's*, November 5,
2014, http://www.macleans.ca/news/canada/a-nationwide-
conversation-about-sexual-assault-has-begun-finally/.

Citing a review: Vivien Stern, *The Stern Review: A Report by
Baroness Vivien Stern CBE of an Independent Review into How
Rape Complaints Are Handled by Public Authorities in England
and Wales* (London: Government Equalities Office, 2010).

As the Vice *writer Drew Brown put it*: Drew Brown, "The Fog of
Avalon: Inside Canada's Most Bizarre Electoral Race," *Vice*,
September 14, 2015, http://www.vice.com/en_ca/read/the-
fog-of-avalon-inside-canadas-most-bizarre-electoral-race/.

John Ivison wrote: John Ivison, "Trudeau-Mulcair Distrust
Deepens Amid Sexual Harassment Scandal," *National Post*,
November 6, 2014, http://news.nationalpost.com/full-com-
ment/john-ivison-trudeau-mulcair-distrust-deepens-amid-
sexual-harassment-scandal/.

Moore told The Globe: Josh Wingrove, "NDP MP Details Abuse
Allegation, Calls for Probe," *The Globe and Mail*, November 25,
2014, http://www.theglobeandmail.com/news/politics/ndp-
mp-details-abuse-allegation-calls-for-probe/article21787508/.

An accompanying 35-page document: Government of Ontario, *It's Never Okay: An Action Plan to Stop Sexual Violence and Harassment* (Toronto: Queen's Printer for Ontario, March 2015), docs.files.ontario.ca/documents/4136/mi-2003-svhap-report-en-for-tagging-final-2-up-s.pdf.

Craig wrote: Elaine Craig, "The Ethical Obligations of Defence Counsel in Sexual Assault Cases," *Osgoode Hall Law Journal* 51, no. 2 (Winter, 2014).

Tanovich wrote: David M Tanovich, "'Whack' No More: Infusing Equality into the Ethics of Defence Lawyering in Sexual Assault Cases," *Ottawa Law Review* 45, no. 3 (2015).

Headlined "Whacking the complainant": David Tanovich and Elaine Craig, "Whacking the Complainant: A Real and Current Systemic Problem," *The Globe and Mail*, February 10, 2016, http://www.theglobeandmail.com/opinion/whacking-the-complainant-is-a-real-and-current-systemic-problem/article28695366/.

DeCoutere told Chatelaine's *Sarah Boesveld*: Sarah Boesveld, "Exclusive: Lucy DeCoutere on the Ghomeshi Disaster," *Chatelaine*, March 24, 2016, http://www.chatelaine.com/news/exclusive-lucy-decoutere-on-the-ghomeshi-disaster/.

INDEX